ADVANCE PRAISE

"This book is a timely and important contribution to scholarship on abolition, prisoners' rights and labour organizing. The urgent topic of prison labour unionization has rarely been articulated or proposed. The authors discuss the intricate links between capitalism and imprisonment, showing how unionization of prison labour can ameliorate some of the harms of incarceration, is compatible with larger projects of prison abolition and how prisoners' inclusion in workers struggles will be beneficial to broader struggles against capitalist exploitation."

— Jessica Evans, Toronto Metropolitan University

"From Amazon to COVID, from racial justice struggles to housing, workers have been the backbone of collective struggle. In this book, Rashid and House take us behind bars to explore the histories and contemporary struggles of incarcerated workers and the possibilities for organizing. A must read for all interested in abolition movements, workers' struggle and the urgent need to collectively organize for a better world."

— El Jones, author of *Abolitionist Intimacies*

"*Solidarity Behind Bars* should be read by social justice and labour scholars and activists. House and Rashid take the reader through the byzantine bureaucratic, labour and punitive structures that render prisoners' work invisible, denying them the same rights as free labourers. Well researched and engagingly written, *Solidarity Behind Bars* not only describes the current (and deplorable) state of prison labour but also explains how legal paradoxes and capitalist impulses brought Canada to this point and what the paths forward may be."

— Melissa Munn, co-author of *Disruptive Prisoners* and *On the Outside*

"A solid piece of scholarship exploring carceral customs in Western capitalist societies, grounded in a coherent political economy."

— Bob Gaucher, co-founder and previous editor of the *Journal of Prisoners on Prisons*

SOLIDARITY BEYOND BARS

SOLIDARITY BEYOND BARS

UNIONIZING PRISON LABOUR

JORDAN HOUSE AND ASAF RASHID

FERNWOOD PUBLISHING
HALIFAX & WINNIPEG

Development editing: Fazeela Jiwa
Copy editing: Lisa Frenette
Cover design: Jess Koroscil
Text design: Jess Herdman

Printed and bound in Canada

Published by Fernwood Publishing
2970 Oxford Street, Halifax, Nova Scotia B3L 2W4
and 748 Broadway Avenue, Winnipeg, Manitoba, R3G 0X3

www.fernwoodpublishing.ca

Fernwood Publishing Company Limited gratefully acknowledges the financial support of the Government of Canada through the Canada Book Fund and the Canada Council for the Arts. We acknowledge the Province of Manitoba for support through the Manitoba Publishers Marketing Assistance Program and the Book Publishing Tax Credit. We acknowledge the Province of Nova Scotia through the Publishers Assistance Fund.

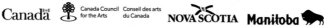

Library and Archives Canada Cataloguing in Publication

Title: Solidarity beyond bars : unionizing prison labour /
by Jordan House and Asaf Rashid.
Names: House, Jordan, author. | Rashid, Asaf, author.
Description: Includes bibliographical references and index.
Identifiers: Canadiana (print) 20220274673 | Canadiana (ebook)
2022027472X | ISBN 9781773635613 (softcover)
ISBN 9781773635811 (EPUB) | ISBN 9781773635828 (PDF)

Subjects: LCSH: Convict labor. | LCSH: Labor unions. | LCSH: Prison-ers—
Legal status, laws, etc. | LCSH: Labor movement.

Classification: LCC HV8888 .H68 2022 | DDC 365/.65—dc23

CONTENTS

Acknowledgements ix

Acronyms.. xi

Introduction: Prison Labour and Punishment........................... 1

1   Why Care About Prisoners' Labour Rights?...................... 13

2   All Work and (Almost) No Pay 43

3   Injury, Illness and Death 71

4   "Sweat the Evil Out": The Evolution of Canadian
    Prison Labour... 89

5   What Are the Alternatives?... 110

6   The Case for Prisoners' Labour Unions......................... 128

Conclusion: And Justice for All? 161

Notes 171

References.. 208

Index 234

About the Authors.. 244

To all the workers struggling to get free.

ACKNOWLEDGEMENTS

We've long been involved in activism around labour and prison justice — although mostly as two separate issues. Despite the historical tensions between the prison justice and labour movements, we've come to believe that the success and failures of the prison justice and labour movements are substantially bound up with one another. We hope this book serves as a contribution, even if only a small one, to the cause.

Like all good books that deal with politics, this one emerges from conversations, debates and exchanges with many brilliant thinkers and dedicated organizers to whom we owe an enormous debt. First we must thank Shane Martinez — who in many ways got the ball rolling on this project — for all his support and encouragement. We would also like to thank Sarah Ovens, El Jones, Rick Sauvé, Calvin Neufeld, Johanne Wendy Bariteau, Erin Moores, Ghassan Salah, John Chaif, Adelina Iftene, David Jolivet, Jarrod Shook, Chester Abbotsburry, Greg McMaster, Jessica Evans, Stephanie Ross, Dennis Pilon, Phil Goodman, Mark Thomas and Erin Hatton. This book was also informed and inspired by a number of activist organizations engaged in critical organizing and education efforts. Thank you to the Anti-Carceral Group, Barton Prisoner Solidarity Project, Beyond Prison Walls Canada, Criminalization and Punishment Education Project, Demand Prisons Change, East Coast Prison Justice Society, End the Prison Industrial Complex, Evolve Our Prison Farms, Inmates 4 Humane Conditions, the Incarcerated Workers Organizing Committee, Saskatchewan Manitoba Alberta Abolition Coalition and PASAN.

A special thank you to Austin Gooder for his invaluable newspaper research assistance, Andrew Tubb for bibliography work and Dawn Collins for French translation help. We would also like to acknowledge that this book immensely benefited from the source material made available by The Gaucher/Munn Penal Press Collection, the Information Transparency Project (a now-defunct working group of OPIRG Kingston) and Evolve Our Prison Farms. Sincere thanks to Fazeela Jiwa and everyone at Fernwood Publishing for their support and patience throughout this process. Finally, thank you to our families for their love and encouragement.

ACRONYMS

ACLRC	Alberta Civil Liberties Research Centre
CBI	Collins Bay Institution
CCC	Canada Car Company
CCRA	Corrections and Conditional Release Act
CCRR	Corrections and Conditional Release Regulations
CFAW	Canadian Food and Allied Workers Union
CIRB	Canadian Industrial Relations Board
CLU	Canadian Labour Union
CORCAN	Correctional Service of Canada's prison industry agency
CPP	Canada Pension Plan
CPLC	Canadian Prisoners' Labour Confederation
CSC	Correctional Service of Canada
EEP	Employment and Employability Program
FCA	Federal Court of Appeal
FSRS	Fonds de soutien à la réinsertion sociale / Social Reintegration Support Fund
GCC	Guelph Correctional Centre
ILO	International Labour Organization
ISO	International Organization for Standards
LCO	Law Commission of Ontario
MP	Member of Parliament
MPP	Member of Provincial Parliament
NDP	New Democratic Party
NELOF	Native Extraordinary Line of Furniture
NRCC	Nanaimo Regional Correctional Centre
OAI	Offender Accountability Initiative
OCI	Office of the Correctional Investigator
OLRB	Ontario Labour Relations Board
OMIP	Outside Managed Industrial Programs

PDFS	Post-Doctoral Fellows
PPE	personal protective equipment
PSLRA	Public Sector Labour Relations Act
PSLRAB	Public Service Labour Relations Board
PUC	Prisoners' Union Committee
RCMP	Royal Canadian Mounted Police
SAWP	Seasonal Agricultural Workers Program
SCC	Supreme Court of Canada
STG	Security Threat Group
TFW	temporary foreign worker

INTRODUCTION

PRISON LABOUR AND PUNISHMENT

Canadian prisons don't work. But Canadian prisoners, for the most part, do. This book follows many others in arguing that, not only are Canadian prisons ineffective in their stated goals of public safety, they are, in fact, a source of harm that makes our society worse off.[1] Common sense holds that prisoners work as part of their punishment. However, according to the law and correctional policy, prisoners don't work *as punishment*. The stated reasons that prisoners work are related to "rehabilitation."[2] However, as we will argue, there is not sufficient evidence that prison labour programs are very effective in their rehabilitative potential.

Prisoners work for two main reasons: first, because of the widely held ideological commitment to the idea that work is a moral virtue. Canada is a capitalist country and, as such, work and labour lie at its very heart. Modern prisons emerged alongside industrial capitalism. The Industrial Revolution dramatically reshaped society. It drastically changed the way people lived and worked. The growth of factories fuelled urbanization, encouraged immigration and also caused social dislocation, disorder and a rise in crime — or at the very least a perception in the rise of crime.[3] Prisons, in the form of the penitentiary system, were one of the responses to this. But, as historians have demonstrated, penitentiaries were as much about creating good, docile workers as they were about fighting crime.

The second, and perhaps most important reason why prisoners work is to offset the costs of their incarceration. In the earlier years of the penitentiary, some of their advocates believed that if properly managed, prison industries could do better than simply recoup some costs and generate profits.[4] Today there are some enterprising business owners that make money off of Canadian prison labour but, in the grand scheme of things, this isn't that significant of a factor. Only a handful of Canadian prisoners work in programs that involve private employers. For example, the contract between Correctional Service of Canada (CSC) and Wallace Beef, a private meatpacker that operates the abattoir at Joyceville Institution, states the company shall provide "training" for a minimum of ten prisoners at any given time. In fact, the company routinely employs fewer prisoners than that — and at times the company has operated without any prisoners working at all.[5] The vast majority of Canadian prison labour is institutional maintenance work — the cooking, cleaning, clerical and other work necessary for prisons to function. Similarly, most of the goods and services produced by prison industry programs are for "state use," meaning they are sold exclusively (or near exclusively) to government departments and agencies.

As such, the most significant reason Canadian prisoners work is because correctional systems rely on unpaid or poorly paid prison labour to subsidize their operations. Due to their status as "offenders," prisoners are coerced — sometimes explicitly, sometimes in roundabout ways — to work and they perform this work without any of the normal legal rights protections that we expect workers to have. This creates a situation where prisoners work in dangerous conditions, for little pay, all in the name of their own rehabilitation. As we'll also discuss in detail, there isn't much evidence that prisons effectively rehabilitate prisoners — and lots of evidence indicating the opposite.

The concept of rehabilitation should be problematic for anyone who takes the position that prisons need to be challenged and even abolished as part of contesting the conditions of capitalist society as a whole. The way this concept has been used by correctional administrators makes it a huge barrier to employee status and prisoner unionization, clouding the employment relationship between prisoners and their institutions. It should be inescapable to anyone who observes the cleaning, cooking, maintenance, manufacturing, as well as the production and vocational work in the Correctional Service of Canada's prison industry agency (CORCAN), that the work is, well, work! If free workers were brought in to do the work that prisoners do, suddenly the same activities, called "rehabilitation" for prisoners, would be transformed into employment. There is no clear distinction, or even any basis for why there should be one, between rehabilitative work programs and employment. How is cleaning a toilet or making furniture for use by government departments, manufacturing licence plates or personal protective equipment (PPE) part of rehabilitation or self-improvement? When the work of prisoners is called rehabilitation, minimum employment standards and rights required for employees are lost, including the prospect of unionization. Terrible pay and poor working conditions are excused because prisoners are told they are only doing programming and their pay is nothing more than a "privilege."[6] Indeed, the problems of rehabilitation have been acknowledged by the government itself. As the 1977 *MacGuigan Report* states:

> we do not recommend imprisonment for the *purpose* of rehabilitation. Even the concept is objectionable … It implies that penal institutions are capable of adjusting an individual as if he were an imperfectly-operating mechanism … We prefer to approach the problem with a new term — "personal reformation" — which emphasizes the personal responsibility of prisoners instead.[7]

While rehabilitation sounds positive, especially when contrasted with punishment, claims of rehabilitation serve as a powerful cudgel against prisoners' rights. We will elaborate on overcoming the barriers of the rehabilitative construct in Chapter 6.

The massive scale and racial disparities evident in the US prison system has made the question of mass incarceration a key issue of social justice in that country. As a part of the public debate over the nature and role of prisons in US society, prison labour has also received renewed public attention. Prison labour has been the topic of documentary films and has been featured in television shows based on prison life — for example, "The Farm: Life Inside Angola Prison" (1998), "13th" (2016), "American Jail" (2018), "Oz" (1997–2003) and "Orange Is the New Black." The links between slavery and modern prisons in America have been explored by academics, journalists and filmmakers, and activists — both inside and out of prison — and have drawn attention to the phrasing of the 13th amendment to the US Constitution, which abolished slavery "except as a punishment for crime whereof the party shall have been duly convicted."[8]

Canada's prison systems have many similar problems, but prison labour in Canada has not come under nearly the same scrutiny. While books on incarceration in Canada are published regularly, there has been no book dedicated to the subject of prison labour in contemporary Canada. This book is an attempt to fill what we see as an important gap in discussions of prisons in Canada.

In writing this book, we aim to shed light on incarcerated peoples' struggles for better conditions. We also suggest ways that the prison justice and labour movements can work together, because as we argue in this book, they are intricately related. Most importantly, this book is written in support of prisoners who want to improve their working conditions — and by extension, their lives. We argue that prisoners' exclusions from labour protections cannot be justified on the grounds that their work is rehabilitative. Prisoners' exclusion from legal protections can be understood as incompatible with our basic understanding of work in a society governed by liberal capitalist values. Prisoners are subject to forms of coercion that would be rightly understood as intolerable in other circumstances. Given that their employer is also their jailer, prisoners' rights as workers are of the utmost urgency. We believe that working prisoners should have all the same rights and responsibilities that workers have in the "free world" — they should be covered by employment standards and health and safety laws, and they should be able to join and form unions and engage in collective bargaining. We refer to this as the "normalization" of prison labour. Moreover, we argue that an immediate goal of both prison justice and labour movements should be supporting prisoners in unionization efforts.

In making this argument, we do not want to be misunderstood: again, we reject the idea that prison labour is "rehabilitative." We do not think the normalization of prison labour will necessarily make prisons more effective in their rehabilitative aims. We are not primarily (or even significantly) concerned with improving the rehabilitative outcomes of prison labour schemes. Instead, we see the normalization of prison labour as a strategic reform that can advance the goals of prison justice.

Second, we do not believe normalizing prison labour will change the fact that Indigenous people are massively overrepresented in the prison population. It also won't end torturous practices of solitary confinement or increase much needed access to health care. As such, assertion of prisoner labour rights must occur in concert with many other changes, including those that will result in decarceration, such as sentencing reform and expanded parole. Still, we think the assertion of prisoners' labour rights is particularly strategic from the point of view of the prison justice movement. Prisoners' work — and the potential to refuse that work — is a powerful tool to back prisoners' voice with real power. Despite how often unions have been hostile to prisoner workers out of concerns that prison labour might undermine the wages and conditions of "free" labour, there are also historical examples of solidarity between unions and prisoners. If prisoners were to be successful in winning formal unionization and collective bargaining rights, as some provincial prisoners in Ontario did in the past, they may be able to use the rights afforded to unionized workers to check the power of prison administrators. Collective bargaining over labour issues would be a clear opportunity to challenge the unilateral control of administrators over prison labour programs. But there are also broader implications. Despite the limits of what labour scholars refer to as the "industrial pluralist" model of labour relations in Canada, a certified union of prisoners could, for example, strategically assert the rights of prisoners to attend union meetings. This happened in the case of unionized prisoners at the Guelph Correctional Centre, who were able to receive temporary leave to attended union meetings in the community.[9] In the United States, prison union organizers fought critical battles around free communication and censorship on the basis of labour rights, albeit mostly unsuccessfully.[10] Finally, a prisoners' union could form the basis to link activists and organizations involved in labour, anti-racist and decolonial struggles, contributing to building a broad political coalition around these and other issues.

We are aware that some comrades within the prison justice movement may argue unionizing prison labour would further entrench prisons as an appropriate response to crime and social ills. While we understand this point, for the reasons we've laid out above, we argue the right of prisoners to unionize is an important structural reform that supports the goals of the abolitionist movement.

PRISON JUSTICE AND LABOUR ORGANIZING

Our goal is a more just world. Prisons are a particularly ugly form of injustice within Canadian society. However, for the most part, they are not the cause of injustice but rather a symptom of the inequalities produced by the systems of power — social, economic and cultural — that define this country. As such, we must have a clear grasp of the purpose of incarceration in Canadian society. In our view, this means a reckoning with the capitalist system and the particular ways it has developed in Canada. Prison is a capitalist institution — which, in the Canadian context, cannot be disentangled from colonialism. Prisons, along with the broader criminal justice system, play a key role in asserting the sovereign authority of the Canadian colonial state and maintaining the conditions necessary for the continued accumulation of capital. We say more about the relationship between prison and class in Chapter 1 and explore the historical development of the penitentiary alongside industrial capitalism in more detail in Chapter 4. For now, we would like to emphasize that absent something like prisons, it would be necessary to find some other means to allow for what Massimo Pavarini has termed the "inclusion of the outcasts in the labor market."[11] While it is possible to imagine a society that could accomplish this task without institutions of state coercion, we do not believe it is likely to be possible within a capitalist economy — even one that exists alongside a robust welfare state. Capitalism is inseparable from the coercion of market forces and the state institutions that maintain those markets. For these reasons prison (and police) abolitionism is impossible within the bounds of capitalism.

Many of our abolitionist friends may agree with this statement and, as such, our disagreement with some in the prison justice movement may merely come down to differences of opinion over rhetoric.[12] The prison justice movement cannot be divorced from broader movements for egalitarian social change; to quote pioneering Canadian prison justice activist, Claire Culhane, "We can't change prisons without changing society."[13]

This book is about prison labour. To keep our focus, we do not explore grand debates about reform and revolution too deeply. Rather, we want to emphasize the necessity and urgency of including prisoners in the labour movement, winning labour rights and successful unionization. These demands are winnable. All too often, radical rhetoric (for example, "fire to the prisons," or "free them all") substitutes for strategic, winnable demands that can be supported by a (broad) political coalition powerful enough to win them. It is exactly because prisons are so oppressive and abhorrent that political rhetoric and strategy matter so much.

Indeed, many of the activities taken up by prison abolitionist groups — books to prisoners projects, pen pal programs, noise demonstrations — could be criticized through an abolitionist lens as merely reformist (or performative) and actually functional to the existence of prison by providing outlets and coping mechanisms for prisoners who could otherwise be revolting. Such activities are, in themselves, unlikely to lead to meaningful change. But we see all of these activities as potentially useful and often necessary to negate the worst forms of harm and isolation that is inflicted upon prisoners.

Those doing abolitionist work are engaged in important agitational and education work, and even activities as modest as pen pal programs are incredibly valuable to those who directly benefit from them. Still, we argue it is beneficial to the prison justice movment to: 1) win reforms that immediately improve the lives of prisoners; and 2) win what some have referred to as "structural," "revolutionary" or "non-reformist" reforms."[14] These are strategic reforms that not only win improvements in the lives of prisoners but have the potential to shift power within the prison system and broader society.

Broad political coalitions are necessary to accomplish these goals. Given the centrality of wage labour, the inequality between bosses and workers in capitalism, and the labour movement's history as a force for progressive change, we see the labour movement as a potential key component of a more muscular movement for prison justice. Prisoners, of course, must be central to such a movement.

We understand that some abolitionists might object to the need for prisoners' labour unions on the grounds that a basic aim of any trade union is to protect the jobs of its members and, as such, a prisoners' union might serve to deepen prisoners' dependency on the prison system and act as an impediment to decarceration. But this has not been a concern for the many incarcerated workers who have fought for unionization over the past five decades; the history of existing prisoner unionism demonstrates that prisoners' unions, even in their most conservative "bread and butter" form, have resulted in the creation of a countervailing force to the power of guards and administrators and expanded rights and freedoms for prisoners. It is for this reason that we argue prisoners' unions should be characterized as a kind of "non-reformist" reform in the struggle for prison justice.

Unions are "sectional" organizations, representing specific groups of workers.[15] As such, the interests of particular unions are not always in alignment with the interests of the working class as a whole or the public more broadly. Recent debates about the role of prison guard and police unions in the labour movement is a good example of this potential tension between union interest and the public good.[16] There is a well-developed debate about what might constitute a "just transition" for workers in industries harmful to society, such as fossil fuels or the arms manufacturing industry. If the labour movement can conceive of a plan for these workers, we do not think it is unreasonable to say that a prisoners' union could have a similar conception of "just transition." Moreover, we believe labour movement support for prisoner unionization could serve as an opportunity for unions to stem and reverse the decline they've been experiencing for the last five decades. This book is also a challenge to those in the labour movement to rethink what role unions should play in society — and what would be required to rebuild a labour movement with teeth.

PRISON RESEARCH AND CENSORSHIP

Researching and writing about Canadian prisons is difficult. Bureaucratic opacity is reinforced by safety and security protocols and policies that mean communication with the experts — those inside the prisons — is difficult and expensive. In Ontario, for example, before 2019, provincial prisoners could only make collect calls to landlines and were limited to twenty minutes a call. They had to pay a connection fee and rates that could amount to almost $30 for a long-distance call. In 2019 a new telephone service provider, Synergy Inmate Phone Solutions Inc., was awarded a contract to handle prison jail phone systems. The government announced that Synergy would "permit inmates to call cellphones and international numbers at lower rates."[17] Calls are monitored and mail is read, meaning criticisms can potentially result in repercussions for prisoners when they do speak to researchers, journalists and activists. To give one recent example, Jonathan Henry, a federal prisoner who spoke to the media about the federal CSC's lack of preparedness for COVID-19 in March 2020, had his phone privileges revoked for forty-five days.[18] It is obviously exceptionally risky for prisoners to communicate about collective organizing and unionization. The prison administration sees the efforts of prisoners to collectively raise issues as threats needing to be stopped, often leading to lockdowns and segregation for organizers or the prison population as a whole. For example, in 2013 when prisoners in institutions across the country refused work and programming to protest cuts to their wages, authorities responded with lockdowns. In some cases, lockdowns occur in anticipation of prison protest.[19] These punitive responses to organizing occur even in instances where protests are peacefully and orderly.[20]

Even information that's nominally public can be needlessly difficult to obtain. At the time of writing, the most recent annual reports for a variety of government agencies and departments such as the Canadian Nuclear Safety Commission, the National Film Board and the Canadian Dairy Commission were easily accessible via their websites or the website of the federal government. In contrast, the website for the CSC's prison industry agency, CORCAN, states, "CORCAN is committed to not only reporting on our results as they relate to our mandate and organization, but also ensuring that we highlight our results for Canadians and our contribution to enhanced public safety. Please contact us if you would like a copy of one of our Annual Reports." As forthcoming as that may sound, when one of us requested copies of annual reports listed on the CORCAN website several years ago, it took half a dozen emails and a month of waiting to get them.

This means members of the public with an interest in prison issues must rely on Access to Information processes, which have been widely criticized as slow and often expensive.[21] Moreover, once access has been granted, released documents are often heavily redacted.

Given this situation, *Solidarity Beyond Bars* is based on a wide variety of sources, including government reports and documents, journalistic and scholarly work, testimony from currently and formerly incarcerated people, documents obtained through Access to Information and more. While we hope to shed as clear a light as possible on the topic of prison labour in Canada, it remains the case that further investigation and analysis of prison labour — and Canadian prisons in general — is needed.

THE BOOK'S STRUCTURE

This book attempts to look at both the history and the current status of prison labour and prisoners' rights in Canada. The first part of this book, Chapters 1–4, cover the problems faced by incarcerated workers and the history of Canadian prison labour. In the second part, Chapters 5–6, we make our case for the normalization of prison labour and the need for a union for Canadian prisoners.

In Chapter 1, we zoom out and give a broad overview of the Canadian prison system. We explain why people should care about prisoners rights and specifically prisoners' labour rights. We consider the case for prisoners' rights from the perspectives of human rights, public safety and social inequity. While we think there are good reasons to support prisoners' labour rights from a moral perspective, supporting prisoners' unions does not require this. Those who claim to believe in notions of human rights should support prisoner labour rights because holes in human rights protections can be pitfalls for other vulnerable workers. Similarly, we argue against the idea that public safety is undermined when prisoners are given more rights and dignity. If anything, the opposite is true. Finally, we argue that people who are concerned with issues of social inequity should support unions for prisoners. Incarcerated workers are disproportionately Black and Indigenous. They are poor, have high rates of mental illness and have overwhelmingly suffered abuse and mistreatment.[22] A prisoners' union could meaningfully empower a population that represents the most oppressed and marginalized people in Canadian society.

In Chapter 2, we map out prison labour in Canada. We cover institutional labour — all the cooking, cleaning, administrative and other work done to make prisons function every day — and prison industry programs. We also look at the prison industries that produce a diverse range of goods and services, most of which are consumed by the prison system itself. We also cover some of the main issues related to prison labour in the federal system and provincial systems, including low wages, lack of work and meaningful work and unemployment, as well as a number of issues specific to racialized prisoners and women, trans and gender nonconforming people. We conclude Chapter 2 with three recent controversies that put prison labour in the spotlight, even if only briefly. These three cases — the 2013 federal prison strike, the debates over Canada's prison farms and prison labour during the COVID-19 pandemic — allow for considerable insight into how prisons manage prisoner labour.

Chapter 3 covers the subject of health and safety in Canadian prisons as it relates to general prison conditions and work. We consider the ways prisoners are excluded from health and safety laws and policies, some of the hazards that prisoners face and a number of cases of illness, injuries and deaths that shed light on the conditions and consequences of prison labour. We also demonstrate the ways in which, despite their vulnerabilities, prisoners resist their precarious positions.

Chapter 4 places the contemporary situation in historical perspective. Here we consider the role of prison labour in the founding of the Canadian prison system and how prisoner's work has evolved over time. We argue that prison labour has been and continues to be fundamental to Canadian incarceration both for ideological as well as very practical financial reasons. The exact justifications for prison labour have changed, as have the expectations around revenue potential. Despite this — and all the ways prisoners' work has changed — the history of prison labour demonstrates the continuous organizational, humanitarian and criminological failures of prison labour schemes premised on exploiting prisoners who aren't even given the dignity to be considered "real workers."

In Chapter 5 we discuss alternatives to the existing form of prison labour in Canada, considering proposals ranging from abolition and privatization to prisoners' co-ops and sole proprietorships. We look at existing and historical examples of alternative forms, where they have been present, and consider the possibility of expanding on them. We also discuss critiques of unionizing prisoners from both the prison justice and labour movements. While historically unions have opposed prison labour on the basis of fearing competition with incarcerated workers, we assert the labour movement must develop a class analysis if it is going to reverse its decline and once again become a meaningful vehicle to advance the causes of working people. Such an approach would mean understanding prisoners not as "criminal others" or harmful competitors in the labour market but rather as fellow members of the working class with particular needs and capacities. We end this chapter with a discussion of why we believe the unionization of prisoners would be productive to struggles for not only prison justice, but social justice in our society more broadly.

Chapter 6 takes up the question of prisoners' unions in more detail — past experiments in unionization, their successes and failures and the organizational, political, and legal constraints that they faced. We consider the Canadian Food and Allied Workers (CFAW) Union Local 240, which successfully unionized prisoner meatpackers in the Guelph Correctional Centre in Ontario in the late 1970s. This is the clearest case of a successful effort by prisoners to unionize. While the formation of CFAW Union Local 240 came about under very particular circumstances, it remains an important example of how a prisoners' union can practically exist. We also look at an attempt by prisoners to assert themselves as employees and to unionize during the 2010s. This case reveals the terrain of struggle prisoners face in present and future attempts to unionize. We also examine how the prison system has attempted to conceal prisoner labour under the veil of rehabilitation, how the courts have avoided recognition of prisoner workers under all federal labour boards and the reasons behind this avoidance. Based on these past experiments and struggles, we offer some thoughts about what a prisoners' union could look like, how it could form and some of the potential barriers such a union would have to overcome.

I

WHY CARE ABOUT PRISONERS' LABOUR RIGHTS?

Discussions about prisoners' rights can be controversial; it is a popular opinion that imprisonment should mean rights are revoked.[1] We will begin with basic facts of imprisonment in Canada that provide the scaffolding for our more specific analysis and calls to action around prison labour.

The arguments presented in this chapter are not original. Many good books have been written on the failures of prison systems, including Canada's. These include Ruth Morris' *Penal Abolition: The Practical Choice*, Michael Jackson's *Justice Behind the Walls: Human Rights in Canadian Prisons*, Paula Mallea's *Beyond Incarceration: Safety and True Criminal Justice*, and Chris Clarkson and Melissa Munn's *Disruptive Prisoners: Resistance, Reform, and the New Deal*.[2] There is also a plethora of media reporting, academic research and government reports, commissions and inquiries. The reasons to support prisoners' rights — and therefore prisoners' labour rights — can be grouped into to three categories, which we will discuss in turn: human rights, public safety and social inequity.

HUMAN RIGHTS

On April 17, 2017, in a statement issued on the 35th anniversary of the *Canadian Charter of Rights and Freedoms*, Prime Minister Justin Trudeau proclaimed: "Today, I remind Canadians that we have no task greater than to stand on guard for one another's liberties. The words enshrined in the *Charter* are our rights, freedoms, and — above all — our collective responsibility."[3] While Trudeau's record of protecting the rights of Canadians can be called into question, we think it is fair to say, at least when posed abstractly, a significant majority of Canadians would support the prime minister's statement.

The *Charter* outlines Canadians' fundamental freedoms and their democratic, legal and other rights. The *Charter* sets out rights that are supposed to be inalienable, unless the state can justify a public safety, public health or administration of justice objective that overrides them. And even then, the limitation on any right is supposed to be minimally restrictive.[4] According to Charter rights, everyone has the right to be free from arbitrary detentions and searches, and everyone has the right to liberty. But as soon as criminal and penal law enters into the picture, those rights end up being severely curtailed. Obviously, the right to liberty is denied for those in prison. However, imprisonment is supposed to be a last resort, with most sentences not involving imprisonment.

THE LEGAL BASIS FOR PRISONERS' RIGHTS

A pre-Charter Supreme Court of Canada (SCC) case, *Solosky v. The Queen* held that, "a person confined to prison retains all of his civil rights, other than those expressly or impliedly taken from him by law."[5] In other words, even prior to the *Charter*, a prisoner was not supposed to be arbitrarily denied any civil rights. However, the reality is that prisoners have been denied their rights in a blanket fashion and have had to fight vigorously for them over the years. For example, it was only in 2002 that federal prisoners finally won the right to vote in federal elections.[6] All Canadian citizens have the right to vote in federal and provincial elections according to section 3 of the *Charter*, yet, somehow it had been justified for years that prisoners serving federal sentences lost their right to vote on account of the "bad behaviour" that landed them in prison. This never had anything to do with public safety and had everything to do with zeal for punishment and the dehumanization of prisoners. There is simply no logic to denying the right to vote somehow being useful for rehabilitation or reintegration, supposedly the objectives of the prison system. Participation in voting is lauded as being a civic responsibility — if not a moral good.

Another example of a denial of civil rights of prisoners is the right to be free from cruel and unusual punishment under section 12 of the *Charter*. Canada's international obligations under the Convention

Against Torture and Other Cruel, Inhuman or Degrading Treatment or Punishment reinforce this right.[7] As can be seen by the persistent use of solitary confinement, this right has been utterly ignored in Canadian prisons. Throughout Canadian history, prisoners have been placed into abhorrent conditions of solitary confinement for months or even years. In a recent notorious example, Indigenous prisoner Adam Capay spent 1,647 days in a plexiglass cell with the lights on twenty-four hours a day. His charge of murder was stayed in 2019 when an Ontario judge recognized that there was a "complete and utter failure" of Ontario's correctional system to allow such extended, severe deprivation.[8] It was only in 2019, finally, that Canadian courts recognized solitary confinement past fifteen days as torture.[9] The international *Mandela Rules* (United Nations Standard Minimum Rules for the Treatment of Prisoners), updated in 2015, had already recognized solitary confinement (at least twenty-two hours in a day in isolation) of more than fifteen days as torture.[10] There is no rational basis whatsoever that solitary confinement is a necessary and minimal intrusion on liberty that complies with the right against torture.

It is hypocritical to argue that Canada is a rights-based society governed by the rule of law but that people convicted of crimes should be exempt from the rights and freedoms prescribed by law. But when the nature of civil rights is examined, it should be no surprise that the most vulnerable in society, prisoners being among those, are devoid of most rights from the outset. This is because of the individualistic nature of Canada's human rights system, which parallels other liberal capitalist countries. The way rights actually function in the Canadian system is they have to be asserted. They are more of a sword than a shield. If the government intrudes on a person's rights, they have to actively wage a fight to have those rights vindicated. For example, if someone is charged with narcotics possession after a warrantless search of their house by police, they would have to raise Charter arguments in their defence to have the evidence excluded — and have a better shot of being found not guilty of illegal drug possession. A defendant — even an innocent one — will have to spend time and money on their fight. If they are poor or working poor and do not qualify for legal aid and cannot find a pro bono lawyer, they will be severely disadvantaged in that fight. Some may not fight at all because they do not have the resources. And in the end, the police may get away with stepping all over a person's rights. In a money-based legal and justice system, individual rights are more of a privilege.

The rich, by virtue of their wealth, are simply better able to defend themselves in legal matters and actively assert their rights.

There is something fundamentally different about collective or social rights. Collective rights are those people have as a group or as a society. The Universal Declaration of Human Rights, adopted on December 10, 1948, closely followed the end of the Second World War. Through this declaration, countries around the world and in both the capitalist and communist blocs vowed to offer protections to their people against state abuses. The declaration was the easy part, as it is non-binding. But when it came to creating enforceable international law, there was intense division. The Soviet Union and other countries that espoused communism favoured human rights centred around state obligations to house, feed and educate people, among other requirements. However, Canada, the United States and other countries firmly in the capitalist camp favoured individualistic rights consistent with capitalist, liberal democracy. There was so much contention that two separate international agreements were created: the International Covenant on Civil and Political Rights (primarily individualistic) and the International Covenant on Social, Cultural and Economic Rights (based on state obligations). Not surprisingly, the latter is only aspirational in Canada. There is currently no enforceable right to housing, food or any standard of living in Canada because Canada has refused to accept any obligations that compel the government to spend money on people within its jurisdiction.[11]

There are exceptions to the individualistic nature of fundamental rights in Canada. Perhaps the most important of these is the right to freedom of association in the *Charter,* through which the scc recognized the right of workers to unionize.[12] This is an inherently collective right, as no one can unionize alone. It should be obvious why this right to unionize has been such a late addition to the basket of rights that people in Canada have: it runs contrary to the ideological persuasion of the individualistic rights-based system in Canada. The right to unionize had to be fought for vigorously.[13] Just five years after the *Charter* came into effect in 1982, the issue of Canadians' constitutional right to unionize was already at the scc in 1987. At that time, workers did not achieve victory.[14] It took years and substantial pressure to finally win recognition of a constitutional right to unionize. Most significantly, it required organized workers who had collective resources to wage the fight against powerful government adversaries. No individual worker would have been able to wage this fight.

In saying this, we want to be careful not to overvalue the usefulness of courts for workers. The branding of labour rights as human rights is not without its detractors in the labour movement. At times much of the labour movement considered the courts to be conservative, elitist and unfriendly — if not outright hostile — to labour. Over the past several decades the labour movement has become more interested in pursuing its interests through legal strategies that rely on the judicial system. Nevertheless, critics of this approach remain. These critics note that the legalistic framings of labour rights as human rights have the potential to demobilize workers who defer their struggles to small cabals of lawyers, arbitrators and judges. There are also questions about the material impacts of legal victories. For example, it is not totally clear that the recognition of a constitutional right to strike by Canadian courts has resulted in increased workers' power. Furthermore, critics of a labour-rights-as-human-rights approach have voiced concerns about the willingness of the labour movement to favour legal wrangling over the exercise of political and economic power. If the courts grant rights, they can also take them away.[15]

Rights, however, are not simply a matter for the courts. Rights discourses are powerful components of political movements. They allow people to assert their humanity in moral terms regardless of the position of judges or politicians. Labour rights are fundamental to prisoners because labour rights are human rights. They are also collective rights. Through them, prisoners — who have next to no resources — can mobilize broader political coalitions to win better working and living conditions and to make gains that go beyond conditions of confinement. The fight for the human rights of prisoners can be advanced through winning labour rights, notably the right to unionize. After all, in a capitalist society, the only sure way to defend and advance interests is organized workers exercising their will as workers through collective action against their bosses.

The obstacles for prisoners' rights goes beyond the issue of the individualistic nature of human rights and prisoners' lack of resources to mount legal challenges. Historically, there has also been a de facto policy to let prisons run themselves free from oversight and interference from the courts. The "hands-off" doctrine is a US-based term in prison law history, which essentially kicked the courts out of prisons.[16] Prisons were supposed to be an exceptional space, where laws applying in the ordinary world were left at the gates. This approach to prison oversight would not be overturned until the 1960s, when legal challenges and prisoner organizing aimed at asserting prisoners' basic constitutional rights made important breakthroughs.[17] Despite these breakthroughs, prisons continue to lack oversight and there are serious barriers to public and media scrutiny.

A similar idea to the "hands-off" doctrine has existed in Canadian prisons, which were given substantial latitude in deciding how prisoners should be treated for much of their history.[18] It was only in 1979 when the SCC finally allowed prisoners the right to have institutional decisions reviewed by the federal court.[19] However, a formal barrier to oversight by the courts continues to exist in Canada through the requirement that prisoners must first utilize internal grievance systems before trying a case in court. In the case of *Lauzon v. Canada* prisoners at Joyceville Institution, who designed and produced t-shirts with inverted Canadian flags for Prisoners Justice Day, had their shirts confiscated by CSC on the grounds that the design "dishonoured police and soldiers."[20] The prisoners responded with a class action lawsuit, arguing their rights to freedom of expression under the *Charter* were violated. When the case came to the Ontario Superior Court, the court dismissed the class action due to the existence of an "alternative" procedure, namely the inmate grievance procedure under section 90 of the Corrections and Conditional Release Act.[21] Years later, the SCC held that the grievance procedure ought to be used as the primary means to challenge CSC decisions or actions, unless in exceptional circumstances.[22]

The problem with using this so-called alternative is that the federal inmate grievance process has been widely criticized for years as slow and ineffective.[23] The Office of the Correctional Investigator (the federal prison watchdog) routinely notes issues with the inmate grievance system in its annual reports.[24] Critically, the process lacks a third-party adjudicator, meaning the process lacks any semblance of impartiality.[25] Yet, despite widespread knowledge that the grievance process is dysfunctional, prisoners are still expected to go through with it before they can gain access to the courts. The federal prison grievance procedure would also be the expected course of action for addressing issues on the job for prisoner workers, but it certainly does not function like grievance arbitration for unionized workers, where decisions are published and open to public scrutiny. Scholar Amanda Bell Hughett has described prison grievance systems as "safe outlets" — from the point of view of the prison system — for prisoner discontent, tracing how they emerged as an explicit means to undermine prisoner organizing and protest efforts in the 1970s. While Hughett focuses on the United States, the analysis could equally apply to Canada.[26]

International law also has rules in place regarding prisoner labour. While prison labour is allowed, there are conditions. Under Article 2(c), the International Labour Organization's Forced Labour Convention states that forced labour does not include

> any work or service exacted from any person as a consequence of a conviction in a court of law, provided that the work or service is carried out under the supervision and control of a public authority and that the said person is not hired to or placed at the disposal of private individuals, companies or association.[27]

In simple terms, prisoner labour is not automatically forced labour but only takes on this character if used to make profits for the private sector.

Similarly, the *Mandela Rules* has very detailed rules on prisoner labour, including:

- prisoners have the opportunity to work (Rule 96);

- So far as is possible, the work must maintain or increase the prisoners' ability to earn an honest living after release (Rule 98);

- The organization and methods of work in prisons shall resemble as closely as possible those of similar work outside of prisons, so as to prepare prisoners for the conditions of normal occupational life (Rule 99);

- The interests of the prisoners and of their vocational training, however, must not be subordinated to the purpose of making a financial profit from an industry in the prison (Rule 99);

- Unless the work is for other departments of the government, the full normal wages for such work shall be paid to the prison administration by the persons to whom the labour is supplied, account being taken of the output of the prisoners (Rule 100);

- The precautions laid down to protect the safety and health of free workers shall be equally observed in prisons (Rule 101);

- There shall be a system of equitable remuneration of the work of prisoners (Rule 103).[28]

While Canadian correctional officials pay lip service to some of these points, none of the above-noted *Mandela Rules* are being followed in a substantive way. In the conclusion, we will revisit these rules with examples from the book that demonstrate this unequivocally.

THE PROBLEMS OF LEGAL EXCEPTIONS

The extraordinary status of prisoners should trouble anyone who purports to hold a belief in the notion of inalienable human rights. As we will continue to demonstrate, the privations experienced by prisoners go far beyond what is justified — even on the law's own terms. The justification for curtailing prisoners' basic rights relies on an assumption that those in prison deserve to be there. Such an assumption fails to consider the reasons why people end up in prison in the first place, as well as the legally innocent and wrongfully convicted people that languish in this country's jails and prisons.

This prisoners' rights exceptionalism allows the blame to be shifted away from the structural reasons crimes are committed and the class and racial disparities apparent in policing, prosecutions and sentencing. Policing and criminal prosecutions are a not natural response to crime but rather the result of policy decisions that set certain priorities.[29] Decisions to prioritize responding to street crime over white-collar crime, for example, means a conscious choice has been made to target some groups of people over others. Such decisions are entirely related to issues of class and race. The result is the over-policing, over prosecuting and over sentencing of poor, working class and racialized people. We will discuss the class and racial dynamics of the Canadian prison system in more detail later in this chapter.

Curtailing prisoners' rights also forgets that some are wrongfully convicted or legally innocent but incarcerated. The number of wrongful convictions in Canada is unknown.[30] The list includes high-profile cases of Donald Marshall Junior, David Milgard, Guy Paul Morin, Stephen Truscott, Tammy Marquardt and many others. These cases involved people spending many years in prison for crimes they did not commit. Those who are wrongfully convicted are often the victims of systemic injustice, including racial bias, which was the case for Donald Marshall Junior who faced systemic bias as an Indigenous person.[31] Furthermore, Canada's jails are full of people who haven't been convicted of a crime. In fact, there are more legally innocent people in prison in Canada than there are people who have been duly convicted of a crime. According to Statistics Canada, "Since 2004/2005, the average number of adults in the remand population (awaiting trial or sentencing) in provincial/territorial correctional services has been greater than the adult sentenced inmate population."[32] While many of these people will ultimately be convicted or agree to plea deals, some will have charges dropped or will be found not guilty of the crimes for which they have been accused. Pre-trail detention flies in the face of the basic legal principle that a person is innocent until proven guilty. Many commentators, including the Canadian Civil Liberties Association, have criticized the excessive use of pre-trial detention, arguing current practices are "contrary to the spirit — and, at times, the letter — of the law."[33] The practices of cash bail, requirement for sureties and the identification of factors such as unemployment, homelessness and substance use as "risks" of releasing a person, mean that poor, marginalized and vulnerable people are more likely to face pre-trial detention. Ironically, people who are detained but not convicted of crimes often face hasher conditions and less access to services and programming — including employment programming and opportunities — than those who have been convicted.[34]

To allow diminished human rights — including diminished labour rights — for prisoners means accepting the denial of humanity of the wrongfully convicted and the further denial of humanity for those who have suffered dehumanization before entering prison. Short of eliminating prisons as a whole, the goal of those who support human rights should be to reduce the deprivations experienced by prisoners to the greatest degree possible.

DO PRISONERS HAVE MORE RIGHTS THAN OTHERS?

There is a myth that prisoners enjoy economic security, the fabled "three hots and a cot" (or three meals and a bed) and services many "free" citizens do not. The media seems to love to highlight stories of people who prefer prison to the "free world" for reasons of laziness, irrationality or their extreme level of deprivation outside of jail. It only takes a quick Google search to find reporting on individuals who commit crimes to go "to jail on purpose."[35] Such stories rarely, if ever, meaningfully interrogate the systemic failures that would have to occur for a person to prefer prison to freedom — at best they are presented as tragic one-off cases. The realities of prison conditions and the "pains of imprisonment" are likewise downplayed or ignored.[36]

Politicians are also responsible for perpetuating the false notion that prisoners have it easier than Canadians who "work hard, pay their taxes and play by the rules."[37] Federal prisons have been particularly targeted as "Club Feds." By opportunistically suggesting that prison life is easy, politicians from across the political spectrum are able to justify the harshening of prison conditions in the name of doing something about crime — regardless of the efficacy of such measures.[38] The simple fact is that for the incarcerated, prisons are places of insecurity. Prisoners, like many Canadians, must contend with low pay and high costs of living. They must shoulder the economic burden of purchasing food to supplement cafeteria meals, personal hygiene items, phone calls and more. Prisoners, of course, do all of this while deprived of basic liberties and living in hyper-authoritarian environments. We'll tackle the misconception that prisoners are economically secure in additional detail in Chapters 2 and 4. For now, we would like to dispel the myth that prison conditions are humane, let alone desirable.

Prison conditions do, to some degree, vary from institution to institution. However, to put it succinctly, prison conditions are bad. We'll touch on many of the issues facing Canadian prisoners — infectious disease and substandard medical care, lack of access to services and programming, violence and solitary confinement — at different points throughout the book. These problems are not just allegations made by disgruntled prisoners. All of these issues — and many more — are routinely acknowledged in government reports, inquiries and commissions.[39] For now, we think it will suffice to address the idea that because prison offers "three hots and a cot," and because people outside of prison do not have a right to food and shelter, prisoners are actually some kind of privileged group within society. We'll start with the cot (basic living conditions), and then discuss the hots (food).

Many Canadian prisons are dirty, pest infested and filled with mould and asbestos.[40] Even when they aren't, prison conditions routinely fall below what reasonable people would consider humane. The issue is not simply aging infrastructure. Conditions are also terrible in modern faculties. This is best exemplified by the case of the Toronto South Detention Centre, a "state of the art" provincial jail built in 2014. "The South" promised to be an efficient and modern alternative to Toronto's notorious and ancient Don Jail and other aging provincial facilities. Instead, the $1.1 billion institution immediately became known as a "hellhole," plagued by technical malfunctions and staff shortages resulting in near-constant lockdowns.[41] These lockdowns mean prisoners are confined to their seven-by-sixteen-foot cells, with two prisoners to a cell, often for twenty-four hours a day.[42] When locked down, access to phone calls, showers and exercise is extremely limited or non-existent. Stephen Tello, a former prisoner at the South, recounted his experiences of lockdowns to *Toronto Life*:

> We're two grown men … We're not showering. And the cell gets hot, there's no airflow. You're dripping sweat … You sleep your day away. Your sense of time is gone. You're in a tiny room, and your living space is maybe six square feet of that. You'll punch each other, get into shoving matches. Tensions boil. You're in each other's space 24 hours a day.[43]

Tello reported that, during his time at the South, he spent forty-five consecutive days in full or partial lockdown, including a seventeen-day stretch where he didn't leave his cell at all. His case is not unique.

The South is a remand facility, meaning most of the people incarcerated there are awaiting trial — and assumed to be legally innocent (others have been sentenced but are serving very short sentences — 60 days or less).[44] As mentioned previously, some of these people will have their charges withdrawn. Others will be found not guilty of their charges. Of course, some are guilty and will be sentenced to time in the federal or provincial prison system. Others will be found guilty but not given a custodial sentence. Perhaps most disturbingly, the South has a reputation as a "plea factory."[45] Some remand detainees will plead guilty to crimes they didn't commit or otherwise waive their rights to due process to expedite their cases and get out of the South — even if that means doing prison time somewhere else. Ontario judges have called the South "absolutely unacceptable," "oppressive" and "harsh and unconscionable" and have routinely reduced the length of prison sentences imposed by the court in acknowledgement of the inhumane conditions in the jail.[46]

The South is not a unique case. Issues of persistent lockdowns, violence, mould and pests, and lack of health services and programming plague federal and provincial systems.[47] Despite recent court orders to reduce the use of solitary confinement, a practice that researchers have labelled "torture by another name," and that violates Canadian and international law, forms of enforced isolation continue to be used frequently in both federal and provincial prisons.[48] Suffice it to say, very few people would voluntarily opt for a cot in Canada's prisons. The hots leave much to be desired as well.

In the recently released *Report on The Human Rights of Federally-Sentenced Persons,* the Standing Senate Committee on Human Rights explained some of the problems that have resulted from CSC's move to "cook-chill" food preparation process in many federal institutions:

> Senators were informed that the food is of poor quality and is often served cold or overcooked. The committee heard that portion sizes are inadequate and do not meet the needs of fully-grown adults. The timing of food delivery is also questionable. Their last meal of the day is served at 4:00 P.M. before the guards' shift rotation, and lights out is at 10:00 P.M. Though federally-sentenced persons were sometimes provided a banana to hold them over, the committee was told about, and witnessed, bananas so green they could not be eaten for several days. In addition to much food wastage because many consider the food inedible, the committee is concerned that this cost-saving measure is having the opposite effect on federally-sentenced persons' already meager salaries. To supplement their diet, federally-sentenced persons told the committee that they relied on overpriced canteen food which generally consisted of processed snacks like chips, chocolates and ramen noodles.[49]

Poor quality prison food can have serious consequences. Bad food and small portions were identified as significant factors that triggered the 2016 Saskatchewan Penitentiary riot. In one email to his staff, the federal

Correctional Investigator Ivan Zinger succinctly described the state of food in Canadian prisons: "Yuck."[50] It's not only the federal system that uses "cook-chill" systems. Some provinces, such as Ontario, do as well.

Corrections Canada and its provincial and territorial counterparts are very aware of these issues. They are consistently raised through inmate grievances, media reporting, scholarly studies and annual reports made by the Office of the Correctional Investigator (the federal prison watchdog) and provincial ombuds. But poor prison conditions are not simply the result of mismanagement. Deprivations are intentional, exemplified by the Harper government cuts in 2013, when new room-and-board fees effectively reduced federal prison wages by 30%. We will expand on this in Chapter 2.

Since their inception, penitentiaries have been subject to the principle of "less eligibility." The concept, which has its origins in the English Poor Laws, holds that "no relief recipient should receive aid that placed them above the material station of the least well remunerated of the population actually working."[51] The concept continues to be the "guiding principle" of modern social welfare schemes, ensuring that government supports provide only "the least attractive alternative possible to the worst jobs on offer."[52] When applied to the context of prison, less eligibility means that "the standard of living within prison must be below the minimum standard of living for those who live outside the prison."[53] Even if not official dictum, the idea of less eligibility dominates popular understandings of corrections.

Less eligibility means prison systems are designed to make certain that sentences of incarceration have a deterrent effect — at least in theory. It bears repeating that empirical studies prove incarceration does not effectively deter criminal behaviour.[54] Despite this, an ideological commitment to less eligibility persists. Prisons are neither comfortable, nor do prisoners have it easy. The tension that exists between the rights and privileges of prisoners and basic rights and entitlements of everyone else cannot be easily dismissed. However, the way this tension is typically articulated is unproductive. The issue shouldn't be that prisoners have access to (limited) recreational activities, or dental care or jobs. The problem is that *not everyone* has access to these things because of the way our society is structured — but it doesn't have to be that way. The correct response to a gap between the social and economic rights of prisoners and "free" citizens should be demands for expanded social and economic rights for all. This is both necessary to uphold principles of human rights and to advance public safety and social justice. This is also true of labour rights. The exclusion of prisoners from labour protections serves to undermine the rights of all workers. With rising precarity and "gigification" of work, struggles over employee status and access to basic labour protections are rapidly becoming a central battle for the labour movement.[55]

PUBLIC SAFETY

Prisons, as we understand them, are a relatively new phenomenon. As we discuss in more detail in Chapter 5, they are not universal or transhistorical. Modern prisons, in the form of the penitentiary, only emerged during the Industrial Revolution. At the time, their proponents argued they were more humane and effective ways to respond to criminal behaviour than the forms of punishment (such as capital and corporal punishment, public humiliation, exile, etc.) that preceded them. These "houses of correction," and "reformatories," it was argued, would be able to do exactly what their names implied — correct and reform criminals into law-abiding and productive citizens. This did not happen, and prisons were recognized as failing in their stated goals almost as soon as they began to receive their first occupants.[56] Rather than deter criminal behaviour, prisons served as "schools of crime" in two ways. They offered a place for criminal entrepreneurs to build social networks and share skills. But they also inflicted harm, immiseration and stigma that made it more difficult, not easier, for prisoners to reintegrate into society at the end of their sentences.[57] They continue to do this. Most people in Canada's prisons will, sooner or later, be released. The question is, will people re-enter communities *worse off* than when they began their sentences, and what are the consequences of that to public safety?

HOW PRISONS UNDERMINE PUBLIC SAFETY

Critics have pointed out the ways in which imprisonment tends to damage existing relationships and exacerbate mental health issues.[58] In some cases, individuals can undergo processes of "institutionalization" and "prisonization" where their capacities to navigate life on the outside atrophy to the point that they have trouble with simple tasks, such as handling their own finances, shopping for themselves or navigating government services.

Many issues could be explored to show how the punishment and indignities prisoners endure makes them less able to successfully integrate into society — for example, solitary confinement, lack of harm reduction services, insufficient training for work outside, meagre (or non-existent) prison pay and insufficient funds to survive once released. We'll be discussing prison pay in greater detail in the next chapter but given its close relationship to prison labour schemes, we'll take a moment to discuss the impact of low or no prison pay on public safety. We'll look at two particular issues in focus: the maintenance of family relationships and community connections and the need for savings upon release.

In 2013, the federal government, led by Conservative Prime Minister Stephen Harper, instituted cuts to prisoner pay. Federal prisoners' pay was reduced by 30% and pay incentives for prisoners working in CORCAN prison industries were eliminated entirely. One federal prisoner responded to the pay cuts in the pages of *Cellcount*, a prisoner newsletter, by stressing how wages were a necessity for maintaining community relationships:

> Many of the families of people doing time are from low income circumstances and do not have enough money to pay large phone bills so we use what extra money we can to pay our way while being incarcerated. We also use our pay to help get our families up here to visit us.... Without a decent pay it is very hard to keep these close [community supports]. We send money home to help out with bills, payments, gifts for our children, for our aging parents.[59]

Reduced savings before release also increases the likelihood that people will return to criminal activities to make ends meet. The Office of the Correctional Investigator summarizes the situation this way: "Releasing an offender from prison to the community with little in the way of savings, limited means or capacity to secure and retain employment, apply for a record suspension, pay rent, obtain a health card or buy a bus pass undercuts chances for long-term success."[60]

It should be noted that the cost savings involved in the Offender Accountability Initiative, which included pay cuts for prisoners, were extremely modest in comparison to the cost of corrections in Canada, which reached a historic high of $2.7 billion in 2013.[61] The government claimed the changes would save taxpayers nearly $10 million per year — hardly a drop in the bucket in the scheme of correctional spending. To put this into perspective, $10 million could have been trimmed off the correctional budget by paroling about one hundred federal prisoners (around 0.7% of the federal prison population).[62] The upsurge of the "defund" movement in the aftermath of the murder of George Floyd by Minneapolis police in the summer of 2020 has forced new public debates about the costs of policing and prisons relative to community and social services — however, thus far significant reforms have failed to materialize.[63]

Despite federal and provincial prisons systems' emphasis on vocational training and employment programming, employment is a common struggle for recently released prisoners. This fact demonstrates how little jobs on the inside do to develop marketable skills for prisoners. Structural issues such as gaps in employment on resumés and lack of familiarity with new technologies are issues. The stigma of a criminal record and a prison sentence also creates serious barriers securing employment upon release.[64] Here's how one life-sentenced prisoner who is currently on parole described his post-release job hunt:

> In the first six months that I spent living at a halfway house I submitted over 500 resumés. I spent time at employment resource centers, registered on every local job-hunt website that I could find, subscribed to every possible employment opportunity notification, and even paid to have my resumés professionally revised. I felt that I had done everything possible a person could do to acquire some form of employment. Despite all of these efforts, I think I was invited to a total of three job interviews. The frustration left me screaming into a black hole with only silence as my answer.[65]

Deprivation and mistreatment are not conducive to "rehabilitation." Those who are serious about public safety should demand that prisoners maintain their dignity and rights, even if only for practical rather than humanitarian reasons.

PRISONERS' RIGHTS VS. VICTIMS' RIGHTS

Often, objections to prisoners' rights are contrasted with victims' rights and public safety in zero-sum terms. Gains for prisoners are understood to be losses for victims and the public. We reject this assertion outright. Such thinking misunderstands (or intentionally mischaracterizes) the categories of "victims" and "offenders" — something that we'll explore further below. It also flies in the face of the widely accepted findings of social scientific studies disproving that "tough-on-crime" approaches improve public safety.[66]

The notion that punishment equates to justice for victims can be challenged on several grounds. First is the issue of "victimless crimes" — it's simply not the case that every person in prison has victimized people. In fact, administrative offences such as failing to appear in court or notifying parole officers of a change of address account for a substantial amount of the charges working through the court system. There is also the problem of conflating "forward-looking" and "backward-looking" policy aims in correctional policy. Forward-looking positions consider future events, scenarios and affairs. Prison sentences can be aimed at influencing future events by "incapacitating" or "deterring" a person from committing a similar offence or targeting a past victim in the future, although criminologists and critics have challenged the degree to which prisons are effective in both these regards.[67] Prison sentences do little to deal with "backward-looking" aims. They do not undo harm to victims or make restitution. It is for this reason that "alternative sentencing" practices such as sentencing circles or restorative justice processes have been taken up to some degree by the criminal justice system. While not always the case, overall victims and victim's rights organizations are some of the strongest voices in support of these measures and other alternatives to incarceration.[68]

In the most absurd cases, people face criminalization *in the name of protecting them from victimization.* As sex workers and their advocates have consistently demonstrated, laws aimed at safeguarding sex workers from exploitation are routinely used to criminalize the very people that they purport to protect. As a recent report on the impact of Canadian anti-trafficking policies notes, these "laws have led to extraordinary surveillance and unjustified criminal charges, particularly within migrant sex work communities."[69] Such cases should, at the very least, trouble conventional delineations between "offenders" and "victims."

If people are serious about protecting public safety and think forward-looking policy is necessary, it is critical to consider what kinds of support and services are needed by people who get caught up in the criminal justice system. The idea that better services and opportunities for prisoners and ex-prisoners could actually reduce victimization has long been advanced by prisoners themselves. This was a core belief of prisoners involved in the Canadian Prisoners' Labour Confederation (CPLC), whose constitution asserted: "Reduced recidivism means fewer new victims of released offenders."[70]

SOCIAL INEQUITY

One of the most remarkable things about criminal justice systems in liberal democratic societies is the way criminal law has the appearance of universal application, even while it is deeply unequal in practice.[71] In recent years, the assumption that the law is colourblind has been challenged in critical ways; it is widely accepted that the criminal justice system — which includes prison systems — perpetuates racial injustice and oppression. In the United States, presidents, professional sports teams, rappers, faith leaders, and many others — both liberal and conservative — have all made statements to such an effect, albeit not always for the same reasons.[72] The Canadian prison system does not occupy as large a space in the popular imagination. Still, scholars, journalists and activists have repeatedly pointed out the ways prisons exacerbate and produce social, racial and economic disparities.[73] Journalist Justin Ling has written a number of pieces about the deprivations faced by prisoners in recent years. In his February 2021 article for *Maclean's,* "Houses of Hate," he stated, "Black and Indigenous inmates are both twice as likely to be subject to use of force, more likely to be classified for maximum security, more likely to be involuntarily put into solitary confinement, and less likely to be paroled."[74] Mount St. Vincent University professor and prison abolitionist El Jones was interviewed by *The Nova Scotia Advocate* about the 2018 Burnside jail protest of prison conditions and in solidarity with striking prisoners across the US and Canada. She pointed out severe deprivations:

> First, this is about extremes. I don't know if people understand the depth of not having access to healthcare we are dealing with

here. We are talking about women in high risk pregnancies, who could lose their babies, who are denied prenatal appointments. We are talking about people being cut off medications, after having been on them for years, and going into a psychotic state as a result, having hallucinations and harming themselves. People breaking a bone and having to wait weeks to even get a scan."[75]

The prison system creates and amplifies the racial, gender and class inequalities in our society and it is worth considering each in some detail.

RACE

The racial character of Canadian prisons is significant, leading some commentators to declare Canada's prisons "the new residential schools."[76] While making up only 5% of the general population, Indigenous people make up 30% of the federal prison population. The situation is even worse in federal institutions for women, where Indigenous people make up 42% of the population. The overrepresentation of Indigenous people in many provincial and youth systems is even more grim.[77] It is not simply the sheer number of Indigenous people in Canadian prisons that make the comparison to residential schools apt; despite efforts to prioritize "culturally appropriate" programming, prisons operate on a logic strikingly similar to residential schools. For both residential schools and prisons, labour discipline — one's ability to be a "productive citizen" by finding and maintaining employment within the framework of capitalist economic relations — was (and is) key.[78]

The act that established Kingston Penitentiary in the Province of Upper Canada in 1834 proclaimed, "if many offenders convicted of crimes were ordered to solitary imprisonment, accompanied by well-regulated labour and religious instruction, it might be the means under Providence, not only of deterring others from the commission of like crimes, but also of reforming the individuals, and inuring them to habits of industry."[79] The statement is remarkably similar to the logic motivating the establishment of residential schools. In 1879, John A. MacDonald argued to Parliament:

It has been strongly impressed upon myself, as head of the Department, that Indian children should be withdrawn as much as possible from the parental influence, and the only way to do that would be to *put them in central training industrial schools where they will acquire the habits and modes of thought of white men.*[80]

While the latter statement is clearly racialized in a way the former is not, the idea of assimilation into society through industrial activity (i.e. work) is clear.

Prison labour is sometimes explicitly racialized, as in the case of CORCAN's fur and shearling program. The program hires Indigenous prisoners who produce Native handicrafts, such as dream catchers, drums and moccasins. The finished products, which are sold directly to the public, are marketed as "handcrafted by Canada's First Nations, Inuit and Métis people," although they are not explicitly identified as prison made.[81] The program developed in response to the need for culturally specific correctional programming for Indigenous prisoners, but has come under fire as culturally exploitative.[82]

Black over-incarceration is not an issue unique to the United States. In Canada, Black people make up around 3.5% of the general popula-tion, but 8% of those in federal custody.[83] Black prisoners, along with Indigenous prisoners, are disproportionately involved in use of force in-cidents.[84] They are also more likely to be given higher security classifica-tions. These instances of discrimination are not the result of increased criminality amongst Black and Indigenous "offenders." Rather, it is clear that they are the outcome of correctional policy. For example, in 2018, the SCC ruled that CSC failed to take "all reasonable steps" to ensure its risk assessment tools were not culturally biased.[85] It is also likely that explicit racial discrimination and prejudice by individual actors in the criminal justice system plays a significant role in these disparities.

Black over-incarceration is also an issue in provincial systems. In a recent study of race and incarceration in Ontario, researchers found:

> Black men were five times more likely to be incarcerated than White men and Black women were almost three times more likely to be incarcerated than White women in 2010. We also found that at least one in 14 Black men aged 18–34 experi-enced incarceration in provincial correctional facilities in 2010. Furthermore, Black men spent longer in provincial cor-rectional facilities and were more likely to be transferred to

federal prison compared with other men. Finally, Black men and women incarcerated in Ontario's provincial correctional facilities in 2010 were more likely to come from socially disadvantaged neighbourhoods.[86]

Other troubling racial disparities in Canada are reproduced in the prison environment, including those related to labour and employment. In 2013, the Office of the Correctional Investigator found "The prison unemployment rate in 2012–13 in federal correctional facilities was 1.5%; however, for Black inmates this rate was much higher at 7%."[87] In 2016, the unemployment rate for both Black men and women was 10.2%, while the general unemployment rate was 7%.[88] While Black unemployment is lower in federal prison than in the general population (as most would expect), the gap between Black and non-Black unemployment in federal prisons is actually *larger* than in the general population. This is no accident. Job placements are institutional decisions, with better jobs generally going to those at lower security levels and who are considered closer to release. Prisoners' Correctional Plans will suggest employment programs accordingly. Prisoners can request jobs but will be denied the better ones if they are too many steps away from release.

Former federal prisoner, Rick Sauvé, who was at the centre of prisoners winning the right to vote in federal elections in 2002, has spent much of his time since his parole release in the 1990s assisting prisoners in parole hearings and programming to assist in their release. He has seen and heard about many problems and barriers to employment in prisons and the racialized nature of these barriers. One of Sauvé's key observations is many Black and Indigenous prisoners are classified as part of Security Threat Groups (STG), which translates into plain English as gangs. They are rated at higher security levels and considered higher risks of violence and other anti-social behaviour. The profiling has a lot to do with the neighbourhoods Black and Indigenous people are from, which are classified as high crime neighbourhoods by police, resulting in the residents profiled as being gang members. Once the label sticks, it is very hard to shake it off.[89]

As a result of being labelled members of STG, Black and Indigenous prisoners are generally unable to obtain jobs that prove they are ready for release. These include jobs with perimeter clearance, which are crucial for improving risk assessment ratings showing a prisoner is able to be in the community again. Jobs that are part of work releases, which are at the pinnacle of jobs demonstrating "release readiness," are impossible to obtain for those labelled as connected to a STG. Those with the STG label end up languishing with jobs such as cleaning, if any job at all, and not progressing toward release. This dynamic feeds into the higher unemployment and underemployment in terms of job levels of Black and Indigenous prisoners.[90] Obtaining jobs that demonstrate release readiness is crucial for cascading down from medium to minimum-security institutions, which is a necessary step toward early release and greater access to programming, recreation and entertainment activities. Overall, due to Black and Indigenous prisoners overrepresentation in the STG category, their releases are often delayed beyond their white counterparts.

A further challenge Black and Indigenous prisoners face is upon release itself. Having been denied the better jobs and higher pay scales in prison, they have less, if any, savings upon release. And still having the label of STG upon release, which will be available to employers for a prisoner released on parole, will result in much higher rates of rejection from job opportunities, especially for any decently paying jobs. All this leads to higher rates of recidivism for Black and Indigenous prisoners.

GENDER

The number of women in Canada's federal prisons has dramatically increased over the last decade and "Aboriginal women represent the fastest growing offender category under federal jurisdiction."[91] Despite a flurry of changes to federal corrections aimed at addressing the issues of women prisoners in the aftermath of the 1994 Women for Prison riot, many critical issues persist.[92] Women generally have fewer programming opportunities than their male counterparts. Women, as a population, are also "overclassified" in maximum-security facilities, which compounds the issue of access to services and programming.[93] Women in provincial and federal prisons contend with lack of access to reproductive health services and mother-child programming, among other issues.[94] They are also particularly vulnerable to sexual violence while incarcerated.[95]

Research on women prisoners further troubles the clear demarcation between "offenders" and "victims" articulated by correctional staff and administrators, politicians, journalists and many criminologists. Women prisoners have, overwhelmingly, been the victims of crime and abuse. A 2010 study of federally incarcerated women by CSC found that 85.7% had a history of physical abuse and 68.2% a had history of sexual abuse. More than half experienced abuse as children.[96] While research on abuse and victimization of male prisoners is lacking, studies have found that childhood abuse is extremely common regardless of gender. One recent study determined that 35.5% of male prisoners have experienced childhood abuse (21.9% of whom experienced childhood sexual abuse).[97]

Women have other particular issues related to prison labour. While levels of unemployment prior to their incarceration for men is high, it is even higher for women.[98] The Office of the Correctional Investigator summarizes the gendered character of federal prison employment programming:

> It was particularly disappointing to see that CORCAN work options offered at women's sites were grounded in gendered roles and expectations, including jobs and training in areas such as sewing, floral and jewellery design and wool shearing. In 2017–18 for example, for women offenders, most CORCAN employment opportunities were within the Textiles Business Line (83.5% (197)). Assignments in the construction business line and in the manufacturing business line represented 15.3% (36) and 1.3% (3) of CORCAN assignments for female offenders. We heard from women who reported wanting more options that were not "so feminized," opportunities other than construction such as accounting, office administration, computer training and residential/business painting.[99]

CSC has reported that it will address these issues; however, change is yet to be seen. Research has consistently shown that women "are less likely than men to secure employment prior to the end of their federal correctional sentence."[100] Indigenous women and women of colour are even less likely than their white counterparts to secure employment upon their release.[101]

This discussion of gender and prison work has largely focused on the general issue of inadequate programming for women and the more specific issue of the gendered nature of work programming that is available. Trans and gender nonconforming people face their own unique issues in prison, which include heightened risks of violence and denial of gender-affirming therapies and health services. Trans prisoners regularly struggle to have their gender identity officially recognized and to be housed in appropriate prisons. While these issues are well known, much about trans and gender nonconforming prisoners is not — data and statistics on trans and gender nonconforming prisoners is extremely limited.[102] More analysis of the experiences of trans prisoners as workers is needed; however, a couple points can be stated here. It is clear transgender people face significant discrimination in the job market, regardless of their criminal records.[103] This discrimination in terms of employment is likely to be more substantial for trans people who have served prison sentences. For trans women in federal prison, the challenges are potentially further exacerbated by the structural gender inequities in corrections. If trans women are successful in being correctly gendered and appropriately housed, this virtually guarantees they, along with other federally sentenced women, will have inferior access to employment programming.

CLASS

The Canadian criminal justice system and Canadian prisons cannot be accurately understood unless they are properly situated within this country's political economy. In other words, we must understand Canada's criminal justice and prison systems to be inseparable from capitalism and class society.

The criminal justice system is a social response to crime (although, again, we would emphasize it is largely ineffective in this goal). However, it is also a system that maintains and reproduces ruling-class power. Anatole France, the French journalist and novelist, perfectly captured the failures of liberal universalism as they manifest in the criminal justice system: "The law, in its majestic equality, forbids rich and poor alike to sleep under bridges, to beg in the streets, and to steal their bread."[104] While France was observing the French criminal justice system a century ago, structural inequalities continued to be baked into the system itself.

The private nature of legal defence is an obvious example — the rich can afford private lawyers while legal aid offices are severely under-resourced. Those without adequate legal representation are more likely to represent themselves, take unfavourable plea deals or plead guilty to crimes they didn't commit.[105] Indeed, the very notion of "high powered attorneys" should offend those who believe in the principle of equal access to justice.[106] For these reasons — as well as others such as the "over-policing" of working class and racialized neighbourhoods, disparities in charging and sentencing, and the identification of needs as criminogenic "risks" — "the rich get richer and the poor get prison."[107]

It is obviously the case that Canadians prisoners are overwhelmingly poor and working class, yet data on prisoners' class backgrounds is sparse. As such, to understand the class position of prisoners, it is necessary to use a number of metrics as stand-ins for class. Most often these metrics include unemployment rates, homelessness, level of education achieved and experiences of addiction. While imperfect measures of class, these metrics are obviously correlated to class in key ways.

The logic of class — even if unacknowledged — plays out in a vicious cycle within the Canadian criminal justice system. The same factors that make people more likely to come into contact with the criminal justice system — things like homelessness and unemployment — are used as measures of "risk" that ensure the poor are incarcerated more often and for longer periods of time.[108] A 2010 study by the John Howard Society of provincial prisoners in the Greater Toronto Area found one in five were homeless at the time of their incarceration.[109] By 2020, despite efforts to reduce the provincial prison population in response to the COVID-19 pandemic, this number had climbed to one in four.[110] Over 60% of the federal inmate population has a formal education of grade eight or less.[111] Unemployment is such a significant issue that it has been deemed a "criminogenic" (crime causing) factor. Of those admitted to federal prisons or held in pre-trial custody, 40% are unemployed.[112] Other studies have found up to three-quarters of federal prisoners were "assessed as having some or considerable difficulty in the area of employment."[113] As the Standing Senate Committee on Human Rights has recently reported:

> Defining characteristics among this population [federally sentenced people] include: poverty, homelessness, trauma, abuse, mental health issues, substance addiction as well as low education. Those from marginalized and vulnerable populations, whose challenges are amplified by systemic racism and discrimination, such as Indigenous Peoples and Black persons, are disproportionately incarcerated. For many federally-sentenced persons, imprisonment exacerbates those challenges.[114]

Because class cannot be disentangled from race, Black and Indigenous over-incarceration also represents the class nature of imprisonment in Canada. As such, Canadian incarceration is also very much about "locking up the lower class."[115] For all of these reasons, those who say that they care about issues of gender, racial or economic justice should be urgently concerned with the situation in Canadian prisons.

Part of the reason there is not good data on imprisonment and socioeconomic status or class position has to do with how class is not deeply interrogated in Canadian society. At best, all the major Canadian political parties position themselves as parties of the "middle class and those working hard to join it," to quote Prime Minister Justin Trudeau.[116] The poor and working people do not have parties to represent them. Even the nominally social democratic New Democratic Party (NDP) has been all too ready to slash social spending, curb collective bargaining rights for workers and pander to the interests of "small business" when it has had the opportunity to form government at the provincial level.[117] The rich, of course, are well represented in the halls of power.

In our view Canada is a class-based society, and despite the diversity and complexities of this society, it is one that is largely made up of two classes of people: those who own productive capital — factories, businesses, apartment complexes, etc. — and those who don't. Those who don't own productive capital must sell their ability to work (their "labour power" in Marxist terminology), or else try to scrape by on meagre social supports and private charity. For our purposes in this book, we understand the working class to exist in this broad sense. There are of course disparities within the working class — a low-paid migrant farm worker on a temporary work visa clearly has very different experiences in work and in life than a highly paid unionized autoworker. However, they do have much in common — critically, both produce value for capitalists. It is for this reason that — despite their differences — workers have more in common with each other than they do with their bosses.[118]

While we draw much from Marx and Marxism in our understanding of class, we do differ with some Marxist orthodoxy regarding what has been called the "lumpenproletariat." The term is typically used to describe an underclass of people largely shut out from the formal labour market. While crime is one response to this social and economic exclusion, there has been an unhelpful and problematic conflation of the lumpenproletariat and a so-called "criminal class." Crime exists among people of all social classes — although society's response to criminality through things like priorities for law enforcement or level of moral outrage differs significantly. A number of commentators have noted the ways in which "crimes of the powerful" are understood and responded to in very different ways than other forms of crime, in particular street crime. Critically, all too often "the state is either powerless to act, or complicit" in cases of crimes of the powerful.[119]

To try to simplify a somewhat theoretical discussion, we believe prisoners should be considered "workers" and as part of the "working class." Most prisoners have worked jobs — even if they have had difficulties with employment — throughout their lives. Except for a few historical cases, prison labour is not legally considered employment. Even in the case where prisoners are primarily warehoused rather than exploited as cheap labour, incarceration has an impact on labour markets — and vice versa. For example, incarcerated people are not included in standard unemployment figures.[120] As Greg McElligott has noted, prisoners tend to come from the communities hardest hit by deindustrialization and the rollback of public services, including welfare, education and retraining. As such, McElligott suggests, "Although criminalization is inseparable from a number of factors, such as abuse and addiction, it is not much of a stretch to say that the degradation of work pioneered by McDonald's and Wal-Mart has been a crucial contributor to current crime rates."[121] Research also shows formerly incarcerated people are more pliant workers for structural reasons — for example, discrimination based on criminal records limits employment opportunities, and time inside creates barriers to maintaining marketable skills. Some interesting research from the United States has even suggested former prisoners are less likely to join and form unions than their counterparts who have not experienced periods of incarceration.[122] This is not necessarily because former prisoners more likely harbour anti-union views; rather, their vulnerable position in employment makes unionizing a riskier endeavour. This makes successful union organizing in prison even more important.

IS PRISON LABOUR COERCED?

We think prison labour ought to be understood as a particular manifestation of "unfree" or "coerced" labour within Canadian society. It is important to acknowledge it is only one of the many forms of coerced labour that have existed historically. These include corvée labour (a form of labour tax placed on feudal tenants by landlords or residents by governments), indenturement, chattel slavery, civilian internment and conscription and other forms of forced military service. Furthermore, it is critical to acknowledge that coerced labour continues to persist in Canada and around the world. Some of this coerced labour falls under the category of "human trafficking" and is decried and denounced by the Canadian government and everyday Canadians. However, other forms, such as prison labour and temporary foreign worker programs like the Seasonal Agricultural Worker Program and the Live-in Caregiver Program where workers are on closed work permits, enjoy the full support of the government and are largely unremarked upon by the public.[123]

All of these different forms of coerced labour have defining characteristics that differentiate them. For example, some involve temporary periods of coerced labour, such as corvée labour or internment. Others, such as chattel slavery, are permanent conditions. Some might be paid wages, in the case of conscripts or some prisoners; others would not. All work is under threat of punishment, although the severity and form of punishments also vary. These categories of coerced labour can also take different forms. For example, prisoners working on a southern chain-gang would typically work under threat of severe punishment (including corporal punishment) for no pay on public works projects such as roads or ditches. This differs considerably from a prisoner working in a contemporary prison industry. A prison industry worker might face punishment for not working or poor work performance, but this punishment might be more subtle — for example, an unfavourable report that might negatively influence the decision of a parole board. They might also be paid, even if only poorly. In the federal system, "good conduct" (a lack of institutional offences) can result in "statutory release" after two-thirds of a sentence is complete.[124] In the provincial systems, a prisoner can earn fifteen days of credit for each month of good conduct.[125] As we will address in Chapter 2, performance of work reflects on conduct.

The reasons why prisoners would describe prison labour as slavery is understandable — it draws attention to the links between contemporary imprisonment and chattel slavery and emphasizes the racism (and especially anti-Black racism) evident in prison systems, especially in the United States. (Canada does have a history of racial chattel slavery, although the linkages between slavery and prisons is less direct). The 2018 national prison strike in the US included national demands covering a wide range of issues. Prominent among them was the issue of "prison slavery" — one of the national demands was "An immediate end to prison slavery. All persons imprisoned in places of detention under United States jurisdiction must be paid the prevailing wage in their state or territory for their labor."[126] Such a position seems to imply paid labour is "free" and unpaid labour is "slavery," a dichotomy that obscures how coerced labour can be compensated and paid workers can and do face unjust and unjustifiable exclusions from full labour protections.

We think there is also another critical issue to be discussed in questions of "free" and "unfree" labour: economic compulsion. Workers who do not have significant income beyond the wages they receive in exchange for their labour, which is to say most workers, need to work to keep a roof over their heads and food on their table. Even if they aren't obliged to work for a particular employer, they are beholden to employers *as a class*. This is hardly an original observation; as Karl Marx puts it:

> The worker leaves the capitalist to whom he hires himself whenever he likes, and the capitalist discharges him whenever he thinks fit, as soon as he no longer gets any profit out of him, or not the anticipated profit. But the worker, whose sole source of livelihood is the sale of his labour-power, cannot leave the whole class of purchasers, that is, the capitalist class, without renouncing his whole existence. He belongs not to this or that capitalist but to the capitalist class, and, moreover, it is his business to dispose himself, that is to find a purchaser within this capitalist class.[127]

This dependency is why people do difficult, dirty and dangerous work they might otherwise try to avoid. Moreover, for the most part, workplaces in capitalist societies look much more like dictatorships than democracies. Ideas of free speech and autonomy, including various degrees of bodily autonomy, stop at the entrances of the factories, warehouses, stores and offices in which we work. The conditions at Amazon, where workers routinely urinate in bottles out of desperation for a bathroom break, is a bleak but obvious example — and there are plenty more.[128]

This is not to say there is no difference between prison labour and conventional work. Rather, it's to say a sharp division of work into categories of "free" and "unfree" does not stand up to scrutiny. As Todd Gordon succinctly puts it, "There is no free-unfree labour binary in this sense, just a continuum of unfreedom and different forms of compulsion."[129] Such an analysis allows us to better understand how workers are compelled to work in different ways. While we think the power that bosses have over workers by virtue of their ownership of the means of production is unjust and should be countered, we also believe it is critically important to root out and oppose forms of coercion that go beyond economic compulsion. This "extra-economic" coercion can take many different forms, but it is clearly experienced by prisoners who face severe penalties for failure to work or poor work performance. Many prisoners are not free of this "extra-economic" coercion even after they are released — community supervision requirements can mean that a loss of a job could result in parole being revoked.[130] Formerly incarcerated people continue to contend with extra levels of control over their work even in the "free" labour market.

———

We have elaborated on the necessity of recognizing that the human rights of prisoners must be inalienable just as they should for others; that public safety is not improved by prisons but made worse; and that social justice requires addressing the inequities within prison, which mirror those outside its walls. These details are important to provide the context in which prison labour takes place. We have also drawn comparisons between prisoner labour and other forms of coerced labour outside of prison to show how prisoners who work are connected to workers outside, both historically and contemporarily. With all that in mind, we will now discuss what prisoner labour looks like in Canada in more detail.

2

ALL WORK AND (ALMOST) NO PAY

Most people in Canada, wherever they are, have either had or seen an Ontario licence plate, but most are probably not aware that Ontario licence plates are made in the Central East Correctional Centre in Lindsay, Ontario.[1] This makes them the most easily recognizable prison-produced good in Canada. But there is no label on the plates informing any bearer of this fact. It, like many other aspects of prison labour, remains hidden.

Here, we provide a picture of what prison labour looks like in Canada and explanations for its existence. We cover institutional labour done to make prisons function every day and the prison industry programs that produce goods and services, most of which are consumed by the prison system itself. We also address the conditions of prisoner labour, including low wages, lack of work and meaningful work and issues specific to racialized prisoners and gendered work. We conclude the chapter with recent controversies that put prison labour in the spotlight, including COVID-19.

To reveal prison labour, we think it is helpful to uncover who is incarcerated in Canada and who among the incarcerated performs labour. According to Statistics Canada, in 2018–19, there were approximately 38,000 adults in provincial/territorial and federal custody per day, with nearly 24,000 adults in provincial/territorial custody and just over 14,000 in federal custody. Those in federal custody are serving sentences of greater than two years, while those in provincial institutions are either denied release while awaiting trials ("on remand") or are sentenced to less than two years in prison. Over 60% of the prisoners in provincial jails are on remand and therefore legally innocent, or awaiting sentences — which may or may not involve prison time in the end. As we will elaborate, prisoners in both provincial and federal institutions work, as do a number of people imprisoned in other carceral institutions.

In addition to those charged with, or convicted of, criminal offences, an unknown number of people are also in prison for defaulting on payment of fines relating to motor vehicle offences. "Time in default" had been available for many other offences not relating to motor vehicles, but the possibility of imprisonment for failing to pay non-motor vehicle fines has now been phased out. Another option for those who could not pay their fines is something called the "fine option program," which allows a person to work off their fine debts by providing service for approved organizations. This has also largely been phased out, but there are still some examples of this practice in Canada.[2]

People incarcerated in psychiatric institutions also sometimes work. These institutions hold individuals who are found "not criminally responsible" due to mental health struggles for offences for which they were convicted. They also house those who are initially in other prisons, but have mental health issues deemed to require ongoing residential treatment. Interestingly, the case that lays out the legal test for whether workers in a rehabilitation program can be employees is from a British Columbia psychiatric institution rather than a federal or provincial jail.[3]

Canadian provinces and territories are responsible for youth justice services, including youth correctional facilities. Youth corrections emerged out of the industrial school system, which saw "industrial training," a dressed up term for forced work, as the best response to youth crime and delinquency. Industrial schools also provided schooling and religious instruction, but as the name of the institution implies, work was the central activity.[4] While the focus of this book is on adult corrections, it is noteworthy that some contemporary youth facilities have employment programming. For example, until 2018, Manitoba's Agassiz Youth Centre ran carpentry, gardening and animal husbandry and butchering programs.[5]

Finally, there are prisoners, albeit very rarely, serving sentences for violation of the National Defence Act in Canada's military prison located in Edmonton, Alberta. As reported by *Global News* in 2018, the Canadian Forces Service Prison and Detention Barracks, the Canadian military prison, is mostly empty. When it does house military prisoners, "Inmates spend their waking hours in training, drill, exercise and cleaning and polishing everything around them to a terrifying standard."[6]

In addition to the above elements that make up the Canadian carceral state, Canada also holds immigration detainees in provincial correctional institutions and immigration holding centres. Immigrant detainees often spend months or even years in indefinite detention for mere regulatory offences. Canada shares the distinction of practising indefinite detention with other countries known for particularly terrible treatment of prisoners, such as the United States and Australia.[7] There has been pressure on Canada to end immigration detention, but Canada continues to detain thousands annually, with 8,825 people detained in just 2019–20.[8] Immigration detainees are not supposed to perform "rehabilitative" work because they are not serving criminal sentences.

INSTITUTIONAL MAINTENANCE AND PRISON INDUSTRY

Prisoners, though their work, effectively reproduce the conditions of imprisonment. They do not really have a choice in this. Across federal and provincial prisons, prisoners perform work of two different kinds, both as necessary for prisons to exist as the walls and bars.

First, prisoners perform "institutional maintenance" — all the work that keeps institutions operating and "livable." This includes clerical work, cooking, cleaning, maintenance and other upkeep of the prisons. It is essential for this work to be done for the institutions to operate day to day and to not physically fall apart. This work offsets the costs of incarceration, which is their most significant function, regardless of what spin is placed on the rehabilitative character of cleaning floors or toilets. The federal and provincial governments that run prisons can avoid the higher labour costs of non-incarcerated workers by having prisoners work for pennies, meagre canteen credits or simply nothing at all except the opportunity to "do something."

Second, prisoners work in prison industries, which produce a variety of goods and services. Prison industries, such as CORCAN at the federal level or Trilcor in Ontario, are presented by CSC and provincial corrections departments as critical revenue — or even profit — generating programming. Even if prison industries are unprofitable, the revenues they generate represent a subsidy for employment programming.

Prisoners' work is also critical for ideological reasons and, as such, prisoners could also be said to do the work of justifying the existence of prisons to society. "Rehabilitative" and "reintegrative" work assignments theoretically prepare prisoners for a life outside of prison and, regardless of their efficacy, are used as key examples of how prisons are supposed to make society safe. Despite some research indicating that involvement in educational, vocational and employment programming is associated with lower likelihood of reoffending (by some measures), there are significant hurdles to understanding rates of reoffending and recidivism in Canada. For example, calculations of recidivism rates for federal "offenders" generally do not take into account post-release convictions that result in sentences to provincial/territorial custody. As the 2017–18 annual report of the Office of the Correctional Investigator States, "The current national base recidivism rate is simply not known. After decades of experience with research and performance measurement in the field of corrections and criminal justice, Canada still lacks a robust, regularly maintained, national recidivism database."[9] The fact that prisoners are kept busy through jobs and other programming is taken as evidence that rehabilitation is occurring.

FEDERAL PRISON WORK

According to the available data, as of 2018, on a given day approximately 8,000 federal prisoners, or about 56% of the federal prison population, work. The vast majority — around 6,775 — work in institutional maintenance while around 1,400 work in CORCAN prison industries. The CORCAN website also claims, "Over the course of a year, more than 3,700 offenders benefit from CORCAN's on-the-job skills training."[10] While CORCAN's ability to effectively provide meaningful skills training has been questioned, it is clear that CORCAN participants are workers on the job.[11] All federal prisoners are subject to disciplinary offences for failing to report to or refusing work.[12]

Not all jobs in prison are valued equally. From a certain perspective, institutional work is the lowest rung on the job ladder because it indicates being further from release, while prison industry jobs, such those with CORCAN, are theoretically geared toward preparing prisoners to re-enter society. Still, prisoners' individual preferences also play a role. As federal prisoner and prisoner rights activist Gregory McMaster explains:

Some guys want to sweep a floor because they don't want to get involved in anything. Other guys want the challenge of having a position of trust and there's probably three or four offices within the institution that inmates are responsible for, like the Inmate Committee or the Lifer's Group office. And so it depends. It depends on what level of responsibility you want. If you want you can go work in the factory if you want to do something productive. If you want to work with food you go directly towards the kitchen. Some guys want to go work in a library and some guys work in what we call the Works Department, which would be the plumbing and the carpentry — the basics that keep the penitentiary running.[13]

Before considering work in provincial institutions, it is useful to discuss CORCAN, the federal prison industry program, in more detail.

CORCAN

CORCAN was first established in 1980 as part of a significant reorganization and restructuring of federal prison industries. CORCAN operates under the authority of Correctional Service Canada and the Treasury Board of Canada and is described by CSC as:

a key rehabilitation program of the Correctional Service of Canada (CSC). It contributes to safe communities by providing offenders with employment and employability skills training while incarcerated in federal penitentiaries, and for brief periods of time, after they are released into the community. This is done through on-the-job and third-party certified vocational training that focuses on our four business lines: Manufacturing, Textiles, Construction, and Services. CORCAN's work supports the social policy of the Government of Canada to safely reintegrate offenders into society in a way that promotes their success as Canadian citizens.[14]

In 1992, CORCAN was given "Special Operating Agency" status, allowing it to "operate in a business-like manner while respecting government policies and regulations."[15] CORCAN is expected to operate as a self-sustaining enterprise, although throughout its existence it has struggled to accomplish this and remains heavily dependent on an annual "correctional training fees" paid by CSC to CORCAN. The amount varies year to year but is significant; in 2019, CORCAN was paid over $31 million in such fees.[16]

While CORCAN has some partnerships with private employers who hire prison labour, this represents only a small portion of CORCAN participants. Most prisoners working for CORCAN do so in CORCAN facilities and under the supervision of CORCAN shop "instructors." While some goods are sold directly to the public, the bulk of CORCAN's sales are to government departments.

PROVINCIAL PRISON WORK

In provincial institutions, data on how many prisoners actually work is sorely lacking. Behind the walls and under scrutiny of prison guards, it is likely that most sentenced prisoners work. Every province and territory has legislation governing prison work.[17] Many provinces and territories' corrections acts explicitly state prisoners must work while incarcerated. The provinces and territories of British Columbia, Alberta, Nova Scotia, Newfoundland, Prince Edward Island, Yukon, Northwest Territories and Nunavut all have language in acts or regulations mandating prisoners to work if work is assigned. Alberta's and Nova Scotia's laws may be the most explicit in the mandatory language for prisoner work. Alberta's Corrections Act states, "The director of a correctional institution shall cause every sentenced inmate in the correctional institution to be engaged or employed in an employment program to the extent that the institution can accommodate the program, if the inmate is medically fit to engage in the program."[18] Nova Scotia's Act states, "Except where exempted by a health-services professional, a superintendent shall ensure that every offender works or participates in programs at a correctional facility."[19]

The provinces of Saskatchewan, Manitoba, Ontario and New Brunswick all have less clear language about mandatory work. However, prisoners can still be punished for refusing assigned work, an action that could constitute an institutional offence. For example, the New Brunswick Corrections Regulation states that a prisoner can be disciplined if failing to be "prompt and conscientious in the performance of regular duties of work which may be assigned."[20] Among other possible punishments, failure to be a good worker can result in "performance of additional work," or segregation for an indefinite period of time, not to exceed five days"[21] Additional work duties may be imposed as punishment for breach of institutional rules.

PROVINCIAL PRISON INDUSTRIES

While CORCAN is the largest prison industry operation in Canada, there are also prison industries and public works programs at the provincial level. Historically, many provinces ran lumber operations as part of their provincial correctional systems, although these have largely been phased out.[22] In addition to licence plates, prisoners in Ontario prepare food for Ontario prisons, clean up graffiti, do roadside waste removal, maintain cemeteries and other government properties, work in laundry and engraving services and manufacture bedding and uniforms through Trilcor, the province's prison industry program.[23]

In British Columbia, prisoners clean up provincial parks and do small construction jobs for non-profit organizations. They also support wildfire crews by managing equipment, maintaining tools and setting up and dismantling firefighting base camps.[24] In the past, prisoners in BC have also dug out invasive shrubs and sandbagged during floods.[25] In Alberta, prisoners split firewood, manufacture toys for non-profits, do snow removal for seniors and refurbish bicycles.[26]

Quebec has extensive prison industries that produce a wide variety of goods and services. These include textile and sign manufacturing, as well as snow removal, landscaping, gardening, printing, welding, cleaning, laundry and food services.[27] In 2019, there were 533 jobs in Quebec prison industries (289 of which were unpaid positions). Prisoners' wages are capped at 35% of the provincial minimum wage, although in 2019 the average wage was only $3.85 per day. Of prisoners' pay, 10% goes to an institutional Fonds de soutien à la réinsertion sociale, or "Social reintegration support fund" (FSRS). FSRSs, which also generate revenues from fees on canteen sales, are used to offset the cost of vocational, educational and recreational programming.[28] While most goods and services are purchased by government departments, prison labour is also increasingly being marketed to private employers. A website, solution-maindoeuvre.ca, gives a breakdown of services available at each correctional centre in Quebec and suggests employers consider contracting with correctional services if they are facing labour shortages; however, the fine print also notes that prison labour services are not intended to replace existing workforces.[29] For a time, Quebec utilized prison labour to supplement its seasonal agricultural workforce, although this appears to have been phased out by increasing temporary foreign workers through the 1990s.[30]

Through its provincial industry program, PRISM, provincial prisoners in Saskatchewan produce, among other things, textiles, welded goods, woodcrafts and laundry services. In 2003, Saskatchewan scaled back its prison industries and closed workshops in three provincial institutions. In justifying the cuts, the NDP provincial government stated the operations that were slashed were underutilized — some involving only two or three prisoners a day. The closures, which resulted in layoffs for eight jail staff, were stated to save $422,000. The shuttering of PRISM workshops and job losses was protested by the guards' union, the Saskatchewan Government and General Employees Union, who stated, "inmates with time on their hands can cause problems and make jails more dangerous for everyone."[31] In 2016, the Government of Saskatchewan entered into a partnership with private food service business Compass to train prisoners in food service work. In discussing the program with the media, Drew Wilby, spokesman for the Saskatchewan Ministry of Justice, gleefully stated, "What our plan is, is to turn what we term tax-seizers into taxpayers."[32]

In 2018, Manitoba shut down its provincial industry program, ManCor, ending carpentry, graphic design, gardening, animal husbandry, butchering, upholstery and tailoring operations.[33] Industrial operations in Manitoba, a province with the highest rates of adult incarceration in Canada, had previously also included a call centre at the Portage Correctional Institute, a women's facility.[34] The government claimed that the relatively short fifty-two day average length of stay in Manitoba jails meant industries were underutilized. The program employed around seventy-five adult and youth prisoners at a given time. Furthermore, the cuts would save over $900,000 a year and free up eleven staff members for redeployment. The government claimed employment programming could be more effectively administered by an expanded temporary absence system for low-risk "offenders." The move was criticized by the opposition NDP and Manitoba Government and General Employees' Union.[35]

Manitoba is not the first province to favour temporary absences that allow for community employment over prison industries. The territories and many smaller provinces, such as those in the Maritimes, do not have significant prison industry programs, and many struggle to offer sufficient employment programming — and programming in general. For instance, a 2008 review of corrections in Newfoundland noted:

> [The need for more] work programs, and for programs to teach basic skills, along with those which focus on creative and artistic endeavors is clear. While the limited programming offered was valued by the inmates, the common complaint was that there are not enough programs and other activities to constructively occupy their time.[36]

Statements such as this reveal the pressing need for employment programming of some kind in correctional systems. This is for practical reasons related to cost savings, but also ideological reasons — work is broadly understood to be rehabilitative in itself. Prison industries may not be viable if prison populations are too small or transient. Meanwhile institutional maintenance programs, which offer a direct subsidy to correctional systems by utilizing free or cheap prisoner labour for jobs that would otherwise go to non-incarcerated workers at prevailing wages, are basic features of every provincial and territorial system. The problem with institutional maintenance programs tends to be that there are too many prisoners for too little work. As such, smaller provincial systems often emphasize the ability for prisoners to pursue employment through temporary absence programs, although the extent to which this actually occurs is unclear.[37] While the use of temporary absences may seem reasonable, such schemes are not without their problems. Temporary absences are only available to prisoners deemed "low risk" and applications must be approved on a case-by-case basis, limiting the pool of prisoners who could be eligible. But the existence of temporary absences programs, which tend to have very few issues of prisoner escapes or rule violations, raises an important question.[38] If prisoners are low risk enough to be released to go to work every day, should those people even be incarcerated?

As fires, floods and other extreme weather events increase in frequency due to climate change, it is likely governments will be tempted to rely more heavily on prisoner labour as a cheap means to respond to ecological crises. Prisoners already work on public works projects in several provinces. For example, Saskatchewan has established urban "work camps" to allow provincial prisoners to engage in lawn mowing, snow shovelling and cleanup work.[39] The editorial board of the *Winnipeg Free Press* has recently called for increased use of provincial prisoners for storm cleanup and other public works projects.[40] Some jurisdictions, such as California, are heavily reliant on prison labour to combat wildfires.[41] While there is clearly some inherent danger involved in firefighting, this work does not have to be poorly compensated and outside of the standard health and safety regulatory regime. Whether or not public works jobs are degrading and super-exploitive depends on workers' ability to organize and assert their labour rights.

Prisoners with jobs have more potential leverage than others because they can withdraw their labour to apply pressure on their employers, who are typically prison authorities. Since fewer prisoners in provincial and territorial facilities work, they have less opportunity to leverage this form of power. Of course, labour action and economic power is not the only way for prisoners to advance their interests; there is a rich history of creative prison organizing and protest strategies — for example hunger strikes, canteen boycotts and strategic legal action.[42] These kinds of strategies can complement labour action. The wave of hunger strikes in provincial facilities during the COVID-19 pandemic demonstrates how prisoners deploy protest tactics that respond to "the specific contours of penal managerialism in a given time and place."[43]

While there may be less employment programming in provincial and territorial correctional facilities, some of the work done is of critical importance. Large kitchen operations serving multiple facilities, or industries such as the stamping plants that produce Ontario licence plates, represent potential chokepoints even if relatively few prisoners work these jobs. As such, even small numbers of incarcerated workers have the potential to leverage considerable power. Provincial authorities have long recognized this. In the mid-1970s, one Ontario Ministry of Correctional Services official noted, "Inmates are well aware of the fact that licence plates must be produced and on occasion have utilized sit-downs etcetera to enforce demands or grievances."[44]

HIRING PRACTICES AND PAY

Prisoner pay ranges from nothing to terrible. In the federal system, prisoners are paid a paltry daily rate, which has not increased since 1981. Pay in provincial systems varies considerably. In some provinces, all prisoners are afforded a small daily stipend regardless of whether or not they participate in employment programming. Other provinces offer incentive pay or canteen vouchers for work in prison industries.

Prison hiring practices vary considerably from system to system and even from institution to institution. In some instances, prisoners will be assigned work with little input. In other cases, such as in the federal system, prisoners may be able to, or required to, apply for work assignments. One federal prisoner describes his experience this way:

> [I would apply to] specific job locations. Like, if I were to apply for a cleaning job, and I didn't put a specific area, they would look at it but they would just shred it. I need to specify that I want to be a cleaner at the school, or I want to be a cleaner at the health care, or cleaner of the whole unit ... I see it in job posters.... I applied for the job when someone said that they were hiring at CORCAN metal shop.[45]

Prison industries, especially those where more emphasis is put on "businesslike" productivity, must contend with tension between their dual mandates to train prisoners and efficiently generate revenue. Often this tension plays out in recruiting biases that favour the most adept candidates and filter out candidates who are more in need of skills training. While this is reasonable in the business world, in the case of employment programming, it can mean employment opportunities are more likely to go those who enter the prison with employment skills, rather than those most in need of the "skills training" prison labour programs allege to offer. When prisoners are later released, the program can be deemed successful because its participants have work skills, while those who were initially left behind remain so. This issue was evident in the privately run abattoir operation at the Guelph Correctional Centre, discussed in more detail in Chapter 6.[46]

FEDERAL PRISONER PAY

A standardized system of prisoner pay was first introduced to the federal penitentiary system in the aftermath of the 1934 British Columbia Penitentiary strike and riot, during which chants of "wages, wages, wages," could be heard over the penitentiary walls. Beginning on January 1, 1935, less than a month after the protest, working prisoners began earning a daily stipend of five cents a day.[47] John Kidman has summarized the confluence of interests that backed pay for prisoners:

> The outcry for remuneration for convict labour is a three-direction one: (1) from the warden's side, who sees that his men work more willingly and turn out better goods when they have a positive stimulus, rather than the negative one of loss of privileges; (2) from the welfare agencies on whom falls the problem of looking after prisoner's dependents; and (3) from the general public and even the government, who realize that it is inhuman to turn a man out from an institution without something in his pocket to regain a footing in the world.[48]

Prisoners' wages remained frozen at five cents a day until after the Second World War, when significant reforms to Canadian corrections occurred. Based on recommendations from two government reports on federal corrections, the 1938 *Archambault Report* and the 1947 *Gibson Report,* a new pay system was implemented in 1951. The base rate of pay was raised to ten cents, and prisoners who demonstrated good behaviour and industriousness could earn up to twenty cents per day. A canteen system allowed prisoners to purchase some small amenities.[49]

The potential advantages of higher pay to incentivize participation in employment programs and productivity in prison labour had been highlighted by the 1977 *MacGuigan Report*, as it had been in a number of earlier government investigations. Taking up the recommendations of the *MacGuigan Report*, the government introduced a new system of pay for federal prisoners in 1981. As put in the *1981–82 Solicitor General Annual Report*:

> The new inmate pay plan has two major objectives. The first, to provide a nationally standardized basis for the compensation of inmates; the second, to provide a system of remuneration for in-

mates based on the principles of pay for work and training, pay rate differentials reflecting the knowledge, skills, and abilities required to perform various jobs and increments within each rate of pay to compensate for the length of time in a position. Inmates can now earn from $3.15 to $7.55 per day, depending on the security level of the institution and the nature of the job.[50]

This pay scale was based on a calculation of minimum wage minus room and board. Shortly after the scale was introduced, the highest pay grade was reduced to $6.90. Despite the fact that the new pay scale increased wages generally, bonus and overtime schemes related to institutional maintenance work were removed. This meant, for some prisoners in some institutions, the new pay scale actually resulted in decreases in pay. Indeed, displeasure at the new pay scheme was cited by some as "the straw that broke the camel's back," triggering the Matsqui prison riot in 1981.[51]

While changes to incentive pay only affected some workers, wages were also clawed back for all prisoners through hikes in prices and new fees for services. For example, the 1981–82 annual report of the Solicitor General notes that "inmates are now required to rent, purchase or pay a deposit on certain types of recreational equipment which had previously been issued free."[52] The new wage scale had no cost of living adjustment mechanism, meaning that inflation soon ate into prisoners' purchasing power. While wages remained frozen, the cost of canteen goods increased at the same time prisoners were made to bear more costs.[53]

This loss of purchasing power was palpable by the end of the 1980s. In January 1989, prisoners at four federal institutions in Ontario — Collins Bay, Joyceville, Millhaven, and Warkworth — engaged in sporadic work refusals to protest their wages. Hundreds of prisoners also filed formal grievances challenging their low pay and increasing cost of living.[54] The *Toronto Star* reported that due to work refusals at Collins Bay, which included prisoner kitchen workers, correctional officials were forced to purchase 500 prisoners McDonald's hamburgers, chicken nuggets and french fries, at a cost of at least $1,500. A CSC spokesperson justified the expense to the media, saying that the price tag of the fast food meal was less than what it would have cost in overtime pay to bring in staff to prepare meals.[55] After several months of agitation around the wage issue, CSC told the media that the wage scale was under a "formal review."[56] If this review occurred, nothing came of it because wages would remain untouched until 2013, when new room and board fees effectively reduced federal prison wages by 30%.

Prisoners pay is categorized under correctional law as "stipends" — encouragement for participation in programming rather than remuneration for work. Wages are transformed into pats on the back and insufficient honoraria for prisoners who must save up for release. This is just another way to suggest prisoners do not earn money for their labour, but are in fact the beneficiaries of "rehabilitation" for their toil. The pay of prisoners is and has been a very contentious issue that brought prisoner labour across the country to a standstill in 2013 during the nationwide prison strike against wage cuts, which we explore in more depth below.

Since 1989, frozen wages and rising costs have only worsened the economic position of federal prisoners. Prisoners obtain supplemental food, hygiene and other personal products at the prison canteens, but the costs of items at the canteen have increased astronomically over the years. A 2018 CBC investigation revealed prisoners regularly pay twice as much as what the public pays for the same products. This situation has led to prisoners labelling canteen prices as "outrageous."[57]

In the federal system, prisoners face significant difficulties in achieving top pay levels for their work. In its 2015–16 annual report, the Office of the Correctional Investigator found less than 9% of the federal prison population received the maximum pay level. The largest share of prisoners (37%) received C level pay — mere $5.80 per day, minus mandatory deductions.[58] For many, it's a challenge to get a job at all. Pay levels and jobs are based on participation in programming, good behaviour and being closer to release. As noted in the introduction, the unemployment rate for prisoners is disproportionately high for Black and Indigenous prisoners versus their white counterparts. The Senate Standing Committee on Human Rights, which recently heard from federal prisoners about their experiences, revealed substantial concerns for Black prisoners:

> lack of access to culturally specific programs and interventions, overrepresentation in segregation, and severe underemployment relative to the general population.[59]

As we have previously stated, racism in prison is a reflection of racism outside of prison. Exacerbating underemployment in prison for Black people should completely undermine the argument that CSC is making a sincere effort to assist in rehabilitation and reintegration.

PROVINCIAL PRISONER PAY

As bad as the pay is for Black prisoners and prisoners as a whole in the federal system, it is worse in provincial jails. Prisoners are generally not paid for work in the provincial and territorial systems. As such, they cannot rely on an income to supplement their diet or other needs through provincial canteens. Provincial prisoners must rely on savings or family members and friends to send them money for canteen use. As an example, in Ontario, prisoners have trust accounts where money for canteen spending is deposited, but the system is very restrictive:

> You may use money from your trust account … to buy canteen items. You will have the opportunity to buy canteen items once a week. You are allowed to spend up to $60 each week. You need the Superintendent's permission to spend more than this. Products offered through the Canteen Program include other choices to basic products that are provided by Correctional Services at no cost. Canteen items have fees and applicable taxes.[60]

Often, the incentives to participate in provincial prison industries are fairly minor — sometimes not much more than the opportunity to "do something." Prisoners might also agree to prison industry work with the idea of demonstrating industriousness to a parole board. In some provinces, prisoners are incentivized to participate in prison industries with canteen credits. Others, such as Quebec, offer modest incentive pay.[61]

In 2017 prisoners at the Regina Correctional Centre in Saskatchewan struck against reduction of jail stipends being reduced from $3 to $1 a day and the high costs of phone calls. The new stipend rates meant prisoners would have to save up more than a day's pay just to send a letter ($1.25), more than two day's pay to make a phone call ($2.50), and nearly a week's pay for a stick of deodorant ($4.95).[62] The strike was unsuccessful at reversing the cuts, but the sense of discontent remains. Cory Charles Cardinal, a Cree poet, spoken word artist and prisoner justice advocate, who tragically died of a drug overdose in June 2021, reflected on the dual injustice of exploitative prison labour and forced idleness in Saskatchewan jails:

Very few inmates have paid jobs. Those who do are paid as little as $1 a day. Further cuts to these jobs, which were a small but important "privilege," collapsed the small inmate economy used to support the inmate committee, our collective representative body. As workers, we are exploited, propping up the system that turns us into products for colonial gain.[63]

Cardinal lays out the superexploitation of provincial prisoners succinctly and emphatically. Lack of pay for provincial prisoners results in a double deprivation — impoverishment and the silencing of prisoners voices by undermining the ability of inmate committees to function.

RECENT DEVELOPMENTS AND CONTROVERSIES

Most Canadians don't give prison labour much thought. Unlike the United States, prison labour only tends to become a topic of public debate when a major controversy erupts — and these are generally few and far between. Still, in recent years there have been three such controversies — one over prisoners wages, one over prison farms and one over prisoner labour during the COVID-19 pandemic. We believe these instances of public debate over prison labour are very instructive for understanding the dynamics at play in and around Canadian prison labour, including superexploitation, the incredible resilience of prisoners and the disfunction and corruption evident in prison labour schemes.

THE 2013 NATIONAL PRISON STRIKE

In May 2012, Stephen Harper's Conservative government announced an "Offender Accountability Initiative" (OAI) aiming to fulfil election promises to get tougher on crime and reduce public spending. The OAI sought to harshen prisoners' time and save the public money by offloading additional costs, such as the operation of phone systems, onto prisoners and reducing prisoner pay. All prisoners would be subject to a 30% "room and board" fee, which allowed the government to reduce pay without having to change the federal prison pay scale. While instituting pay cuts in this way was unnecessarily convoluted, it was smart (albeit dishonest) politics. In discussing the OAI, the government failed to explain that the existing pay scale, which was introduced in 1981, already accounted for room and board. Moreover, the fact that prisoner pay hadn't increased in over thirty years meant inflation had significantly reduced prisoners' purchasing power. Over this thirty year period, prisoners became increasingly responsible for purchasing their own educational materials, medicine and hygiene items. While prisoners were responsible for buying more of their own everyday necessities, the cost of those items skyrocketed. Howard Sapers, the federal correctional investigator, noted the cost of canteen goods had increased by over 700% over the same period.[64]

The devastating effects of these cuts were immediately understood by prisoners, prisoner rights activists and a number of academics. The cuts would do more than reduce prisoners' abilities to buy a bag of chips or save up for a video game console. Less pay meant less money for supplemental food, extra underwear or even basic hygiene items. Even worse, prisoners, activists and many experts in the criminal justice system argued the cuts would likely cause newly released prisoners to have a significantly more difficult time reintegrating. It also meant prisoners would be less able to contribute to family expenses and have more difficulty affording phone calls or stamps, which would create barriers to maintaining strong community connections — something critical in parole evaluations. Once they got out, people would have less money to get them set up with things like housing or transportation. Some commentators noted this set up well-intentioned people to fail and made it much more likely that released prisoners would return to crime out of financial need. In the lead up to the implementation of the cuts, the Inmate Committee at the Bath Institution in Ontario argued in a press statement,

> We are concerned that the removal of incentive pay will make skills training programs collapse in federal prisons. We want the public to know that these policy changes only diminish prisoners' ability to turn their lives around and return to the community as law abiding citizens.[65]

Indeed, the effects seemed to be so significant, prisoners would later sue the government on the grounds that the policy violated the Corrections and Conditional Release Act by creating unnecessary barriers to community reintegration.

Prisoners and their allies were not alone in their criticism of the cuts — although reasoning for why the cuts were a bad idea varied considerably. In a relatively rare instance of guard support for prisoner demands, the president of the BC section of the Union of Canadian Correctional Officers, warned the reduction in pay had increased the danger of "an already volatile situation."[66] The elimination of incentive pay was also a major concern for the CORCAN Advisory Board, although all evidence indicates their objections went unheeded.[67] Others from within the world of corrections were also critical. For example, Mary Campbell, the recently retired director general of the Corrections and Criminal Justice Directorate at Public Safety Canada, commented on how the Harper government's criminal justice reforms represented a "deep, visceral nastiness" that "do nothing to reduce or address crime."[68] Despite all this, on October 1, 2013, the wage cuts came into effect as planned.

Prisoners immediately responded with the largest strike action in a generation. On October 1, prisoner work stoppages began in Ontario at the Bath, Collins Bay, Fenbrook and Warkworth Institutions. As media reported on these work stoppages, more and more prisons joined the effort. By the end of the first week, prisoners in New Brunswick, Quebec, Saskatchewan and Alberta had joined the strike. By October 10, the strike became truly national when prisoners in Manitoba and BC joined. When all was said and done, eighteen institutions in all five of CSC's regions participated in the strike against pay cuts. It's difficult to gauge the level of participation in each institution, but by most accounts participation levels were high. For example, the media reported, "it appears to be the majority of the population" was on strike in Drumheller Institution in Alberta.[69] In some institutions, work stoppages triggered lockdowns, meaning most prisoners could not attend work even if they wanted to. Despite some reported incidents of scabbing, there were no reports of violence related to the strike.

For the most part, CSC downplayed the extent and significance of the prisoner work stoppage. However, both prisoners and journalists noted work stoppages did have a significant impact on operations at many prisons. The CBC reported:

> a lot of these jobs that the inmates do keep the institution running — food preparation, clean up, garbage collection, administration tasks. So that means the staff have to pick up all of this.

It means a lot of overtime and these sort of things are very very costly to the system. I heard yesterday that teachers in one institution were actually cooking the meals so it really is quite disruptive to the system.[70]

Despite this impact, prisoners were unable to leverage sufficient power to force the government to the table and prisoners ended their strike actions and trickled back to work, institution by institution. For the most part, the strike was over by the end of October 2013, although prisoners at some institutions refused to work for months after that. Without incentive pay, CORCAN predictably struggled to recruit workers. Many strikers simply never returned to their CORCAN jobs and opted to find institutional maintenance jobs that paid just as well. As one participant of the 2013 strike put it, rather than work for CORCAN, "I'll take an easy job in the prison taking garbage out, thank you."[71]

The 2013 national prison strike failed in its aim to reverse the 30% wage cuts imposed on prisoners by the Harper government. Does this mean that prisoners don't have enough economic power to win demands through labour actions? We don't think so. Instead, we think the failure of the 2013 strike was largely a failure of organization. Despite their best efforts, strike organizers struggled to open up effective lines of communication between institutions. They likewise lacked the organizational infrastructure to do things like set up strike funds or seek public support in an organized and concerted way. These are exactly the kinds of capacities that a prisoners' union could build.

PRISON FARMS

Prison farms have been a feature of incarceration in Canada since before Confederation. In 2009, the Harper Conservatives announced that prison farms at federal correctional institutions would be closed. Kelly Struthers Montford succinctly summarizes the situation of the prison farms at the time of the announcement:

Prior to their closure, the penitentiary farms employed approximately 716 federal prisoners (less than 1 percent of the prison population) in six institutions whose work included animal-based farming activities such as dairying, egg-production, and the rearing, slaughtering, and butchering of farmed animals.

The government stated that less than one percent of prisoners working in agribusiness found work in this field upon release. Furthermore, at the time of closure, the farms were operating at a loss of $4 million per year — costing $11 million to operate, the farms generated $7 million in revenue. The government positioned the farms as both financially unviable and as having little return on "investment" in that prisoners were not trained in marketable skills. The government had announced that this program would be replaced by updated and relevant employment training initiatives.[72]

The announcement sparked a significant public outcry and brought together a coalition of individuals and groups opposed to the closures. While both sides of the prison farm debate made a number of claims about the best interests of prisoners, prisoners themselves were largely absent from the public conversation.[73] Despite the protests, prison farm operations were shuttered in 2010. This would not, however, be the end of prison farms in Canada. In 2018, the Liberal federal government announced that farm operations would be restored at two federal prisons, Collins Bay and Joyceville, both located near Kingston, Ontario. These new farming operations would centre goat dairy operations; however, they would look very different from the prison farms of the past.

In the previous era of prison farming in Canada, milk at prison farms was sold by CORCAN to CSC for internal use. This was the case until the prison farm program ended in 2009. On December 16, 2016, CORCAN wrote a briefing note to the commissioner of corrections about reopening prison farms at Collins Bay Institution. Since CSC "modernized" their food service operations by lowering food quality to save money, prisoners were getting powdered rather than fresh milk. So, redeveloping the prison dairy farming industry for internal use would require the milk to be either powdered for use, or the institution would have to revert to fresh milk, which would increase costs, undoing a key aim of the so-called food modernization initiative.[74] As of 2021, it appears that CSC and CORCAN are undertaking a fundamental shift in direction, with indications that milk will be sold as part of a for-profit prison farming industry.

In early 2018, the federal government committed $4.3 million to a five-year plan for the resumption of prison farming in Canada, with planned operations in Joyceville and Collins Bay institutions in the Kingston area. By the summer of 2019, beef and dairy cows had already been moved to Joyceville and Collins Bay institutions for preliminary work, and by 2020, new information showed that plans were in place for something far more substantial. The animal rights advocacy group Evolve Our Prison Farms (Evolve) learned that CORCAN was planning a large industrial goat milking operation in the Kingston, Ontario area. Evolve obtained information that the operation was slated to begin by the end of 2020, and would produce as much as nine thousand litres of milk per day, through approximately three thousand milking goats.[75] In other words, this would be a substantial industrial agricultural enterprise. Paul Manly, Green Party of Canada critic for Agriculture and International Trade and MP for Nanaimo-Ladysmith in British Columbia, took the opportunity to criticize the Liberal government for the prison farm operation by sponsoring a petition. In part, he said:

> The current government decided to reinstate prison farms, but instead of returning to the old farming model, they are starting a for-profit prison agribusiness …
>
> An industrial-scale goat farming operation at these facilities will reportedly supply milk to an infant formula factory in Kingston, Ontario, which is owned by the Chinese corporation Feihe International. *People who work at these farms will be paid less than a dollar an hour, putting cheap prison labour in competition with farmers in the open market.* In addition, intensive animal agriculture is associated with higher carbon emissions and environmental pollution.[76]

In addition to the political and moral implications of the plan, these concerns raised potentially serious legal issues for the goat milk operation.

Evolve, with the support of the Queen's University Business Law Clinic, posted a legal opinion about whether use of prison labour to produce infant formula for private international export for was legally allowable under International Labour Organization (ILO) regulations:

> Another argument that can be put forward is the poor work environment. *The benefits and wages should be comparable to free workers.* Countless amounts of data, articles and research

papers demonstrate the dismal conditions enforced onto prisoners. Using this data, it is possible to bring an argument stating
that *the conditions imposed on prison labourers are not comparable to free workers and as such the prison labour constitutes
forced labour which is a criminal offence....* [This] *new model of
selling prison labour goods to private companies is uncharted territory.* There seems to be no legal rules around the produce from
prison farms, nor are there rules regarding prison-produced ex-
ports from Canada. As such, this memo relied on international
organizations to determine if a valid argument is possible. If
enough evidence can be procured, the ILO would work the best.
If it can be proved that the labour is forced, *the ILO would deem
it criminal and would have to improve conditions for prisoners
and re-think the new prison farm model.*[77]

To summarize, prison labour for private export can be legally problematic if the working conditions of prisoners are not comparable to free
workers. Still, the case would have to be made to the ILO.

CSC has been very evasive about having any established contrac-
tual relationship with Feihe International and its Canadian subsidiary,
Canada Royal Milk. Documents obtained by Evolve through Access to
Information requests show on August 6, 2019, CSC Communications
Advisor, Marie Pier Lecuyer received an email from a redacted source
who asked, "Are there any deals or MOUs [memorandums of under-
standing] or agreements of any kind to sell products to Feihe or Canada
Royal Milk? Are any being negotiated now as of August 2019?" Lecuyer
avoided a direct answer: "Any commodity produced in the farming operations will be first reviewed for internal use and then other markets
may be considered."[78] CSC continued to remain tight-lipped about any
deal. On March 24, 2021, CSC published an opinion in the *Kingston
Whig-Standard,* where it claimed that a large-scale goat farming operation was not confirmed:

Contrary to the statements that prison farms at Joyceville and
Collins Bay institutions are being turned into intensive livestock
operations for the mass production of goat milk for export, CSC
has in fact not yet procured any dairy goats, nor has it entered
into any negotiations or contracts with any potential buyers of

goat milk. Speculation as to the direction of the program in the future is just that: speculation.[79]

Contrary to this statement, Liberal Member of Parliament, Mark Gerretsen (Kingston and the Islands) was reported to have said the expected buyer of the goat milk was Feihe International.[80]

From the point of view of incarcerated workers, whether prison-made goods are sold for state use or on the open market might not have much impact on their everyday lives. Working conditions and compensation would not necessarily change. However, a shift away from a policy of state use to one of increasing production of prison-made goods for sale on the private market has a number of political and economic implications. Private companies making increased profits from subsidized prison labour means prisoners are even more exploited. Such a move could challenge the notion that prison labour is primarily for rehabilitative purposes and does not interfere with, or undermine, free enterprise or "free" jobs. CORCAN's partnership with the private, for-profit meatpacker, Wallace Beef, which operates an abattoir at the Joyceville Institution, provides a useful basis for discussion.

Documents obtained by Evolve concerning the Wallace Beef operation shows the extent to which CORCAN subsidizes labour costs of private partners; it also shows the "rate of exploitation" of incarcerated workers. CORCAN and Wallace Beef have operated as a public-private partnership since 1995. Wallace operates the Joyceville abattoir in exchange for an annual leasing fee ($61,245.00) and utilities and property taxes ($70,962.00) and a per-animal processing fee ($8 per animal).[81] As part of the agreement, Wallace hires around ten federal prisoners to work in its operation. In 2019, Wallace Beef paid CORCAN $12.88 per "offender hour" worked, minus an hourly "training fee" of $4.52. Prisoners working in the abattoir received $3.00 per hour. These figures warrant scrutiny.

First, it should be noted that at $3.00 per *hour*, prisoners working in the Wallace operation make significantly more than the maximum federal pay level, which is $6.90 per *day*. While incentive bonuses for CORCAN workers were eliminated in 2013, it appears the Wallace operation received an exemption.[82] After paying $3.00 per hour to prisoners, CORCAN takes in $5.36 per hour worked in the Wallace operation. This appears to be pure profit, as the cost of facilities and training — a key aspect of CORCAN's mandate — are accounted for by other fees.

Second, $12.88 per hour for meatpacking work is substantially below the industry's prevailing wages. According to Statistics Canada, the average hourly wage in meatpacking in 2019 was $21.51.[83] Moreover, despite a provision in the contract between CORCAN and Wallace Beef stating the "rate of pay for offenders shall be based on community norms for equivalent work performed, and shall not be less than the Ontario provincial minimum wage," $12.88 per hour is also less than $14.00 per hour, the Ontario minimum wage in 2019.[84]

Training costs are typically borne by employers. Without knowing the ins and outs of the meatpacking industry it seems unlikely that training costs would amount to 35% of the value of wages. It is also not likely that training costs continue as a significant expense indefinitely. The contract between CORCAN and Wallace Beef indicates there is a cap in payment for training hours; however, that figure is redacted from the documents obtained by Evolve. A breakdown of "offender" training hours covering the period of March 22, 2018–March 31, 2019, suggests training fees were applied to each hour worked during that period.[85]

Given that CORCAN is responsible for selecting candidates for positions at Wallace, it also seems fair to assume recruitment costs are lower than is typical. Together, this seems to imply that Wallace receives a subsidy, possibly a quite significant one, by virtue of its CORCAN partnership. It is unclear how much Wallace Beef profited from subsidized prisoner labour, but what is clear is they are a for-profit company selling prisoner-produced beef to Kingston-area restaurants and grocery stores.[86] For example, the website for Glenburnie Grocery, located in Glenburnie, Ontario, lists Wallace Beef as one of the stores' "selected, top-quality brands."[87]

Overall, the plan to reintroduce prison farming through the proposed abattoir and milk production operations introduces a spectre of private profit-seeking through depressed wages and possible violations of the ILO Forced Labour Convention. Though many details are not confirmed, those made available by the time of this writing only underscore the importance of keeping a watchful eye on government plans for prison labour. This is especially important considering the vulnerability position of prisoners as a potential workforce that can be easily exploited. The experiences of prisoners during the COVID-19 pandemic emphasizes this point further.

COVID-19 AND ESSENTIAL PRISONER WORK

COVID-19 created a crisis in Canadian prisons just as it did in the rest of society. As of February 27, 2022, Criminalization and Punishment Education Project reported 22,428 positive cases and eleven deaths among prisoners across Canada.[88] The majority of the deaths were after December 2020, during the "third wave" of the pandemic — a fact that shows a lack of improvement in protections despite warnings. Staff shortages and COVID-19 measures resulted in prolonged lockdowns and suspended programming, services and visitations at institutions across the country. Not long after emergency measures were put in place in March 2020, Senator Kim Pate, formerly the head of the Elizabeth Fry Society of Canada, called for release of inmates to avoid a "disaster."[89] On April 9, alongside many other commentators, the Criminal Lawyers Association, which has a membership of criminal lawyers across Canada, called for a reduction in prison populations to save lives from the virus:

> Experience with cruise ships, hospitals and long-term care facilities show us that it is extremely difficult, near impossible, to limit a coronavirus outbreak in congregate living settings, especially those with close quarters, shared toileting and eating facilities, or service personnel moving between people confined to their rooms.[90]

While the federal system did not take up calls for decarceration in response to COVID-19, provincial and territorial facilities were made to respond to the crisis, largely due to strong pressure from advocates and publicization of the risk of disaster.[91] In Nova Scotia, for example, there was a 41% depopulation in provincial facilities. Despite this, prison justice activists in Nova Scotia have continued to press for greater decarceration as outbreaks continue.[92] As we've argued elsewhere, the response of prison authorities to COVID-19 endangers "those to whom they owe a 'duty of care' and threatens to undermine public safety by exacerbating the pandemic."[93]

In the midst of these oppressive conditions, many prisoners were made to do the essential work of keeping institutions safe. Most significantly, prisoners in the federal system were tasked with the production of personal protective equipment (PPE) for themselves, the prison administration and other government departments through CORCAN.

This work was necessary to help safeguard prisoners, guards and other federal government workers. On December 20, 2020, *Huffpost Canada* reported PPE made by prisoners were being provided to clients, "including federal government departments." Under the direction of CORCAN, prisoners made over 800,000 masks and over 32,000 disposable gowns and "installed portable and fixed barriers to modify clients' workstations as offices adapted layouts in response to the pandemic as of December 19, 2020."[94] Temporary pay increases were implemented to incentivize CORCAN workers. As reported by the Office of the Correctional Investigator (OCI):

> Inmate pay has also been restored to pre-COVID levels, in line with interventions I have made to the Commissioner and Minister of Public Safety. It is a sign of the times that some prison industries are retooling to fabricate protective facial coverings. These measures recognize the extraordinary circumstances, but also the resiliency and adaptability of staff and inmates alike living or working under the constant threat of contracting a potentially deadly disease.[95]

The OCI's comments are very important for contextualizing the nature of prisoner work as a whole. It benefits the institution and government departments, and it could also provide socially valuable production for the benefit of the public. However, to truly benefit *everyone,* socially valuable prison production is not enough — prisoners would also need to have a considerable say in their work and full access to labour rights.

Prisoners were also responsible for cleaning tasks without appropriate supplies to protect them from the spread of COVID-19. Despite their essential work, prisoners were forced to complain, beg and engage in work refusals to ensure basic safety on the job.[96] The federal correctional investigator reported prisoners continued to be denied hand sanitizer due to an unreasonable allegation that they would consume the substance due to its high alcohol content.[97] This is a clear demonstration of differential treatment, where guards and workers outside of jail did have access to hand sanitizer to protect their safety. As the pandemic worsened, journalist Justin Ling reported that, without proper protection, inmates were tasked to clean up areas where other inmates were sick.[98] In July 2020, prisoners in Joyceville Institution engaged in a labour strike

— demanding, among other things, PPE and "appropriate social distancing practices" for prisoner kitchen workers.[99]

The situation of provincial and territorial prisoner workers is even more opaque when it comes to COVID-19. Drawing on reports by the East Coast Prison Justice Society, legal scholar Adelina Iftene states provincial prisoners in Nova Scotia were concerned about access to masks and protections:

> While they reported receiving some cleaning supplies, they noted that no brushes or rags were made available to them, so they had to use their personal towels to clean surfaces, including toilets. Apparently, Correctional Services pays a prisoner to clean the common surfaces, but he receives only $10 bi-weekly. This is not much of a motivator to do a thorough job.[100]

Provincial prisoners doing essential work should have received "pandemic pay" bonuses like other essential workers, which included Trilcor supervisors and other correctional staff. The dearth of public information about provincial and territorial employment programs and compensation allows for greater abuse of incarcerated workers and impunity for administrators.

Finally, many working prisoners were also impacted by COVID-19 in much the same way as those outside of prison, suffering layoffs. The situation of some prisoners, such as those at the Whitespruce Provincial Training Centre in Yorkton, Saskatchewan, was clearly exacerbated by their incarceration. Despite being a "reduced custody facility" designed to facilitate community employment, in the fall of 2020 COVID-19 restrictions prevented prisoners from leaving the prison, resulting in missed shifts at jobs in the community.[101]

———

We have attempted to show what prison labour in Canada looks like, in both the federal and provincial systems, and shed some light on some of the issues such as meagre pay, poor conditions and unequal and discriminatory distribution of jobs that characterize prison labour schemes in this country. By examining some recent controversies related to prison labour, we emphasize that prisoners face severe exploitation and their vulnerable position has allowed correctional institutions and the private sector to take advantage of the labour of incarcerated people. These cases also critically demonstrate the ways in which prisoners organize to resist this exploitation — something we will take up in more detail in later chapters. The COVID-19 pandemic has severely impacted Canadian prisons and exacerbated problems related to prison labour. However, COVID-19 is not the only issue of workplace health and safety when it comes to prison labour programs. There are also enormous gaps in the protection of prisoners while working, which obviously saves costs for the governments responsible, but also indicates a devaluing of the lives of prisoners. This warrants its own discussion.

3

INJURY, ILLNESS AND DEATH

Prisons are universally recognized as dangerous places and considerable attention has been paid by scholars, journalists and activists to issues such as prison violence, drug overdoses and infectious diseases.[1] When understood as a workplace, issues facing correctional staff, such as high rates of post-traumatic stress disorder, are also relatively well known.[2] However, prisons are not only workplaces for guards and staff. While excluded from labour protections, prisoners nevertheless produce goods and services through prison industry programs and perform vital labour necessary to the day-to-day functioning of prisons. Working prisoners in Canadian prisons face a myriad of issues related to health and safety, and they do so as particularly vulnerable workers. These issues have only been exacerbated by the COVID-19 pandemic. Ultimately, we argue workplace health and safety issues can only be meaningfully addressed through the normalization of prison labour and the integration of prisoners' struggles into a more inclusive class-based labour movement. Prisoners' unions offer a strategic approach to resolving issues of workplace health and safety in prisons by backing prisoners' voices with power.

It goes without saying: the divisions between work and life are blurred in the prison context. Most prisoners live and work in the same facilities, and there is typically no clear distinction between their bosses in the workplace and the staff and administrators who control most other aspects of their lives — much of the time they are the very same people. This has implications for issues of occupational health and safety for prisoners.

However, it is important to note that many other workers face similar blurred lines between work and life, and some of the features that characterize prison labour are not unique to prisoner workers. The working and living situations of some migrant farm workers, live-in caregivers, extractive workers and seafarers make for obvious comparisons. While not literally incarcerated, it is not a coincidence that under some circumstances these workforces are sometimes referred to as "captive workers."[3] If the entire staff of a business sleeps in mouldy dorms provided by the employer, those dorm conditions are clearly a workplace health and safety issue — and there should be mechanisms for workers to address them as such. This point raises important differences between prisoners and most "captive" workers. While many workers face legal and regulatory exclusions, the degree to which prisoners work outside of any normal framework is significant. Beyond existing outside of the legal employment framework, the discourse of "rehabilitation" robs prisoners of the recognition that they preform productive labour. Captive workers, with prisoners being the epitome, are at the mercy of their employers when it comes to their health, both for their living and working conditions. They cannot "go home" for any reprieve.

Many of the health issues facing prisoners in Canada are well known. As a population, prisoners are deeply impacted by what scholars and policymakers call the "social determinants of health." Social determinants of health are non-medical factors, such as socio-economic status or housing conditions, that impact health outcomes. As we've discussed, prisoners in Canada have disproportionately experienced poverty, homelessness and unemployment. They have much higher rates of mental health and substance use issues than the general population. Scholars have also noted prisoners have much higher rates of traumatic head injuries and fetal alcohol syndrome than the general population.[4]

The prison environment also contributes to negative health outcomes for prisoners, and to some considerable degree, staff. Violence, both prisoner-on-prisoner and guard-on-prisoner, is one clear issue. Another is communicable disease. Tuberculosis, something of little concern to the vast majority of Canadians, is "relatively common" in Canadian prisons.[5] Hepatitis C and HIV are also found at much higher rates within Canadian prisons than they are in the general population. The issue is not simply that people with these diseases become incarcerated. According to health scholars, there "is evidence that people contract blood-borne infections while in custody."[6]

Even prison walls themselves have the potential to negatively impact the health of those they contain. Many Canadian correctional institutions contain asbestos and correctional systems have not always been transparent about the extent to which prisoners, staff and visitors may have been exposed to the potentially dangerous material. The CSC maintains a public accessible online inventory of buildings that contain asbestos.[7] This database shows the presence of asbestos in many CSC buildings, including in living units, visiting rooms, libraries, chapels and vocational and CORCAN facilities.[8] CSC maintains that it is "confident that our controls and assessments are efficient and allow us to ensure the health, safety and security of building occupants."[9]

Despite this assurance, disclosure of asbestos in federal prisons has been a problem in the past. In 2009 a contractor, Don Garrett, hired to replace toilets and sinks in the Kent Institution in BC, accused Public Works Canada of exposing himself and his employees to asbestos without proper warning. A later report by WorkSafeBC would confirm Garrett and his team were exposed to "asbestos containing material in the plumbing hardware." Garrett noted when the "asbestos finally got cleaned up there was an inmate who swept it up with a push broom."[10]

Asbestos is also an issue in provincial correctional facilities. In 2008, guards at the Cape Breton Correctional Facility engaged in a health and safety work refusal after becoming aware of the presence of asbestos in the jail. The Nova Scotia Government and General Employees Union, which represents the guards, would later demand charges be laid against government officials who had known of the presence of asbestos for nearly two decades without publicly disclosing the information.[11] Likewise, Ontario's Thunder Bay District Jail — which came under national scrutiny after the case of Adam Capay came to the attention of the public in 2016 — has been described by one commentator as a "neo-Gothic house of horrors, riddled with mould and asbestos."[12]

There is also the risk of injury on prison grounds, as well as in transportation to and from courts, medical facilities and worksites off prison property. In recent years there have been several road accidents involving prison transport vehicles.[13] The risk of injury in these vehicles is heightened by the fact that many lack seatbelts and some even lack proper seats. In his 2019–20 annual report, Ivan Zinger, the federal correctional investigator noted this ongoing risk and recommended that "CSC escort vehicles be equipped with appropriate safety equipment for inmate passengers, including hand holds and seatbelts."[14] In response to this recommendation, CSC stated options for "seat belts and hand holds" were under review and that "our suppliers must ensure the vehicles they provide meet the National Safety Standards established by Transport Canada."[15] However, it is not simply an issue of infrastructure, vehicle design or even correctional policy that renders prisoners particularly vulnerable to injury, illness, and death. Exclusions from laws designed to protect the health and safety of Canadians serves to render prisoners particularly vulnerable.

REGULATORY EXCLUSIONS AND ISSUES OF DATA AND TRANSPARENCY

Prisoners face key exclusions from health and safety laws and regulations. These exclusions are sometimes found expressly in the law — for example, "inmates" are excluded from the definition of "workers" in Ontario's Occupational Health and Safety Act and Saskatchewan's Employment Act. Federal prisoners are likewise excluded from the Canada Health Act.[16] Exclusion from the Canada Health Act "means federal inmates receive health care at standards far below what other Canadians can access," according to prisoner rights advocates.[17] Despite this, correctional systems do have a broad legal "duty of care" and a specific duty to provide medical care to prisoners.[18] At both the federal and, in many cases, the provincial level, health services are administered directly by correctional rather than health administrations. This means prisoners are subjected to different standards than those outside prison when it comes to their health, with healthcare providers facing potential constraints on the "freedom to exercise, without undue influence, professional judgment in the care and treatment of patients."[19] Even when they are not expressly excluded, prisoners are generally understood to fall outside of a wide range of regulations due to their incarcerated status.

While prisoners in the federal system have access to an inmate grievance system (which is substantially flawed), "matters relating to compensation for work injuries" are exempt from the process.[20] Instead, federal prisoners must make injury-related claims (only if the injury occurred during approved programming) through a Federal Offender Accident Compensation program, administered by Human Resources Development Canada. If successful in their claims, prisoners "receive benefits similar to workers' compensation."[21]

Together, these exclusions render prisoners — both at work and outside of it — particularly vulnerable. Despite this vulnerability, prisoners do sometimes resist what they deem to be unsafe work. Before discussing this resistance, we will consider why it's so difficult to know the extent to which prisoners suffer workplace injuries and overview some of the legal cases that provide insight into instances of prisoners injured on the job.

It is extremely difficult to know how significant the issue of deaths and injuries related to prison labour are in Canada, especially compared to the United States.[22] It is clear that injuries, including fatal ones, occur during work programming. Some incidents can be gleaned from media reporting: in 1914, a prisoner in Saint-Vincent-de-Paul Penitentiary in Quebec died after falling off a lumber pile.[23] In 1932, James Fitzgerald, a twenty-six-year-old prisoner serving a two- to twenty-four-month sentence in the Guelph Reformatory (which would later be known as the Guelph Correctional Centre), died in hospital an hour after being struck by a rail car while working at a construction site on the prison grounds.[24] In 1933, a *Globe and Mail* article on prison labour in Kingston Penitentiary mentioned a prisoner who had lost an eye in the prison blacksmith shop.[25] That same year, prisoners in Ontario's Burwash Industrial Farm (later known as the Burwash Correctional Centre) spoke out about incidents of mistreatment. Among their accusations, prisoners charged that one prisoner, Frank Smith, had been worked to death.[26] In 1934, two prisoners fell to their deaths, and another was seriously injured when scaffolding they were using to replace windows collapsed at the BC Penitentiary.[27] In 1949, a nineteen-year-old prisoner at the Ontario Reformatory (later known as the Guelph Correctional Centre) was killed while operating an elevator hoist.[28]

The above incidents obviously only represent a fraction of injuries and accidents at Canadian prisons. Official data on injuries resulting from prison work and vocational programming is extremely difficult to obtain. In its 2000–01 annual report, the OCI noted CSC "does not have a national policy on the recording, reporting and review of inmate injuries" and "the Service has no clear picture of how many offenders were injured during the past year as a result of work or program activities, assaults, drug overdoses, use of force incidents, attempted suicides, or institutional disturbances."[29] A national injury reporting system would not be implemented until 2004.[30]

Despite this, issues of reporting, even in the most serious cases that involve death, persist. As recently as 2016 the OCI has noted, "Despite the statutory requirement to investigate all fatalities, there is no legal obligation requiring CSC to openly or proactively share the findings of these investigations publicly or even with next of kin or designated family members of the deceased."[31] A 2017 review of provincial corrections in Ontario found similar issues with data collection and reporting in relation to deaths in custody.[32] If this is the state of reporting on *deaths* in custody, one can imagine the difficulties of attempting to get a clear picture of injuries. Still, some limited information does exist. A CORCAN report for 1988–89 is worth quoting at length:

> Safety is an important element of all Occupational Development Programs operations. The adoption of safe work habits is vital to an offender employee's personal success. Efficiency in this area is measured by the industrial or farm accident rate against an objective of operating accident-free. The industry standard for measuring industrial safety is days lost due to accidents. It is difficult to record this accurately for Occupational Development Programs. Industrial accidents are tracked, although it is difficult due to Correctional Service of Canada's definition of what constitutes an accident, to distinguish between minor incidents (i.e., splinters, minor cuts) and major industrial accidents which would involve loss of productive time for either an inmate or an Occupational Development Programs staff member. The statistics are not available for the agribusiness operation. In the industrial operation, there were 35 accidents (a rate of .004 per $1000 of production) in 1988/89.[33]

While this report tells us that there were thirty-five accidents in the 1988–89 year, without information about loss of time it is difficult to compare this with other workplaces — also, we are not given the breakdown of injuries among prisoners and CORCAN staff. Moreover, the fact that accidents in the agricultural operation were not tracked is significant, as accidents — including serious ones — have occurred on federal prison farms.

Nevertheless, this little morsel of data is so significant because it is some of the most detailed on workplace accidents made available by

CORCAN. While CORCAN annual reports often note the safety training provided to program participants, such as first aid and Workplace Hazardous Materials Information System, they do not generally include accident statistics. Once again, data is not any more forthcoming in provincial systems. Through unionization and collective bargaining, prisoners could demand disclosure of this data, as it relates to workplace health and safety. More data on accident statistics and the circumstances of those accidents would certainly help identify where problems lie and what needs to be improved. If prison labour programs were treated like any other "normal" workplace, and if prisoners were covered by employment standards, health and safety, and labour laws, incarcerated workers would be entitled to basic rights — such as the right to participate in joint health and safety committees and the right to refuse unsafe work — which, despite their limitations, are critical to preventing workplace injuries, illnesses and deaths.

THE LEGAL CASES

Some of the best information on workplace accidents involving prisoners is in legal filings and court decisions, although these are also limited. They only represent a select few cases that were serious enough to pursue — and were pursued by prisoners with the means to engage in litigation. As Canadian legal scholars have noted, there are "troubling obstacles to tort law claims against prisons."[34] In other words, prisoners who try to sue for injuries or other mistreatment have a difficult path to even have the chance of success. The reasons include difficulty in establishing fault by prisons, unavailability of lawyers, costs and legal barriers created by the supposed availability of internal mechanisms to address the problems. Still, it is worth detailing some of the major lawsuits resulting from injuries sustained in Canadian prison work programs.

THE MACLEAN, PRIDY, MCGUIRE AND SARVANIS CASES

In 1966 Thomas Francis MacLean was serving a two-year prison sentence in Stony Mountain prison in Manitoba. [35] MacLean requested a transfer from working in the machine shop to the prison farm. Shortly thereafter he was assigned work moving hay into a hayloft. While working, he fell fifteen feet from the loft onto the concrete floor, suffering serious injuries. In the words of the Supreme Court, the injury resulted in MacLean becoming "permanently crippled for life." The case eventually made its way to the SCC, who awarded a judgment of $75,000 in 1972 ($484,908 in 2021 dollars).[36]

In 1988, Milton Holmes Pridy was sentenced to fifteen days in the Nanaimo Regional Correctional Centre in BC after being convicted of driving with a suspended licence — his first and seemingly only jail sentence.[37] For work duty, he was assigned to a construction crew building a recycling plant on the jail property. While working one day, a tractor known to have a faulty hand break began moving with no one operating it. Pridy saw another prisoner in danger, standing directly in front of the moving tractor. In attempting to knock the tractor out of gear, Pridy's foot caught on a tire, resulting in the tractor running over both his feet. He suffered a severe fracture to his right ankle. Pridy later sued the correctional centre for $185,000 in damages, alleging negligence and arguing the tractor was "an accident waiting to happen."[38] In March 1994, the British Columbia Supreme Court sided with Pridy and found "the damages suffered by the plaintiff were caused by the negligence of the defendant [the Government of British Columbia]."[39]

The same year Pridy was injured in BC, prisoner Patrick McGuire was working in a barn at the Pittsburgh Institution, a federal prison located near Kingston, ON. On June 16, 1988, McGuire was struck in the head by 450-kilogram bale of hay. This resulted in injuries to McGuire's neck, shoulder and spine. In 1997, a federal court awarded him $75,000 compensation for pain and suffering and lost wages.[40]

It is unclear what changes, if any, were made at the Pittsburgh prison farm after Patrick McGuire's injury. It would only be a few years before another significant injury occurred in the same institution. On June 2, 1992, prisoner Ioannis Sarvanis was working in a hay barn at the Pittsburgh prison farm when he fell from the second floor through a trapdoor that had been covered in hay.[41] Sarvanis incurred significant injuries "including a broken wrist, a fractured cheek bone, damage to his teeth, nerve damage, contusions and abrasions to his face, a sprain and strain of his neck and right shoulder."[42] He also subsequently developed anxiety and depression. As a result, Sarvanis applied for disability benefits through the Canada Pension Plan (CPP), which were approved. Sarvanis also sued the federal government alleging negligence. The case, which hinged on whether Sarvanis could move forward with the lawsuit having already claimed disability benefits, would work its way up to the SCC. In 2002, the SCC ruled that disability benefits provided by the CPP were a "significantly different animal" than forms of federal compensation that would shield the Crown of liability.[43]

The cases of McLean, Pridy, McGuire and Sarvanis offer some important insights into injury compensation for prisoners. First, these cases demonstrate that injury claims due to the negligence of prison bosses can be successful. There are likely more cases where there would have been liability found, but most cases are likely settled out of court.[44] However, it must be reiterated that these cases beat the odds. As we have noted, there are substantial obstacles to bringing a negligence claim for prisoner injuries. Indeed, before the establishment of contemporary workers' compensation schemes, even non-incarcerated workers had a very difficult time winning compensation for injuries from employers. As Bob Barnetson argues,

> For the most part, the cost of legal counsel, the time involved, and the slim prospects of success meant that injured workers either did not bother or were unable to pursue claims. Consequently, employers were able to transfer production costs onto injured workers, their families, charities, and in rare cases, government.[45]

The normalization of prison labour would necessarily mean workers' compensation coverage would be extended to all working prisoners. While far from perfect, access to "predictable, immediate, and stable"[46] workers' compensation schemes would be a considerable improvement for incarcerated workers. Critically, claimants to workers' compensation do not have to prove their employer was negligent and failed to exercise "due care."[47] The case of Phillip Roasting demonstrates the difficulties of meeting this burden. That case also demonstrates that prisoners' access to workers' compensation in the absence of other labour rights is insufficient.

ROASTING V. BLOOD BAND, 1999 ABQB

In June 1993, Phillip Roasting was serving a sentence in the Kainai Community Correctional Centre, a minimum-security institution for aboriginal offenders in Standoff, Alberta.[48] The Kainai Community

Correctional Centre was managed by the Kainai Community Correctional Society, "an entity of the Blood Tribe and is operated under a Board Of Directors on a contract with the Alberta Justice Department."[49]

During his incarceration, Roasting was assigned to work on rodeo grounds owned and operated by the Blood (Káínawa) Tribe. The work primarily involved cleaning the rodeo grounds and moving corral barriers. While this work was being done, the rodeo ground's bleachers were also under construction — a canopy was being added and the bleacher's railings were being replaced. The bleacher construction work was not being performed by prisoners.

On June 28, 1993, shortly after the crew began work, Clarence Blackwater, the manager of the Kainai Memorial Complex who had contracted the work on the rodeo grounds, left to repair a flat tire on a truck needed to transport corral barriers. Sometime thereafter Laurie Tailfeathers, the correctional officer assigned to the work crew, drove to town with an employee of Blackwater, leaving the prisoners working on the grounds unsupervised. At some point after this, Phillip Roasting and one or more of the other prisoners on the work crew climbed the bleachers. Roasting fell off, suffering catastrophic injuries that resulted in him becoming a ventilated quadriplegic. Roasting was able to successfully claim workers' compensation through Alberta's Workers' Compensation Board. Given the fact that Roasting was working on a work gang contracted to perform labour for the Blood Tribe, a suit was filed to claim damages from the Band. The Alberta Court of Queen's Bench would rule against Roasting, finding that he was not an employee of the Band, and that the Blood Tribe did not have a duty to supervise Roasting. Moreover, the court ruled that the Blood Tribe was not responsible for Roasting's injuries under Alberta's Occupiers' Liability Act, saying "The danger posed by the bleachers was clear and should have been obvious to Mr. Roasting."[50]

Roasting is important for two reasons. First, the case represents another denial of employee status to working prisoners. The reasoning in *Roasting* continues to pervade the analysis of prisoners' labour rights by courts and labour boards. Second, the assignment of blame to Roasting speaks to a generalized tendency for governments and employers to blame workers for the injuries they suffer at work. In doing this, governments and employers obscure the basic power dynamic that lies at the heart of the employment relationship. Bob Barnetson elaborates:

It may seem unkind or unfair to blame employers for worker injuries. There are certainly other factors at play. For example, workers may make mistakes. They may even act recklessly. But these causes make a relatively small contribution to overall injury rates. Further, they are secondary causes: workers are only in a position to be injured by their error or stupidity because the employer has structured work to create this opportunity. This is, in fact, implicitly recognized in law. Employers are granted vast power over the workplace and workers and thus have a corresponding duty to ensure the workplace is safe — a duty that reflects their power to make workplaces unsafe.[51]

If, as Barnetson argues, employers are "granted vast power over the workplace," this is doubly true in the case of prisoner workers who must contend not only with economic compulsion but outright coercion. The case of Anton Foulds further illustrates these issues.

FOULDS V. BRITISH COLUMBIA, 2012 BCSC 941

In 1997 Anton Foulds was assigned to a farm gang at Nanaimo Regional Correctional Centre (NRCC), a provincial prison in BC.[52] On May 14, Foulds was working to clean brush and to pile wood. At some point Foulds and a fellow prisoner, Michael Cameron, decided to cut down a tree — although this was not a task that had been assigned to them. In attempting to cut down the tree, Foulds sustained an axe injury. The Supreme Court of BC would later describe the incident in the following terms: "Somehow, in a manner which was not explained, while either the plaintiff or Cameron was chopping the tree the plaintiff was struck on his left knee with an axe. No evidence was given about how this occurred." The plaintiff testified that he did not know how he had been struck, saying, "We were talking and I woke up on the ground."[53] Foulds sued Cameron (who would die before the case was settled) and the Province, claiming negligence and breach of duty to care, respectively. The Supreme Court of BC would reject the claim that Cameron was negligent, arguing that injuries "can happen without actionable negligence. The fact of injury alone does not lead to an inference of negligent causation."[54] Furthermore the court rejected the claim that a duty of care had been breached: "The standard of care imposed on the Province in managing the NRCC farm inmates cannot be one of continuous supervision of every inmate at all times."[55] Most interestingly, the court determined the prison farm at the NRCC, and the labour associated with it, allowed prisoners working in the program a greater degree of independence than most others. In the words of the court:

> That independence would be meaningless if there was continuous supervision. Nevertheless if there was not constant supervision the risk of injury associated with the use of tools of various kinds was increased. That risk had to be tolerated if independence to any degree was to be achieved. The standard of care imposed on the Province must be viewed in that light. I cannot find the Province was negligent.[56]

The court seems to assert that part of the utility of prison work programs in general — or at least the prison farm at the NRCC specifically — was to grant a greater than normal degree independence. In granting this independence, the court found the burden of the prison to ensure its duty of care was reduced. In short, this seems to imply that responsibility for injuries sustained in prison work programming is placed on prisoner workers to a greater degree than injuries sustained in some other aspect of incarceration.

Litigation has been an important means for prisoners to win reforms, including some significant ones. Much of this litigation has been taken up by public interest lawyers; however, self-taught "jailhouse lawyers" have also played a key role. Despite important wins, legal strategies for change are severely limited in the absence of complimentary political pressure. The case of Muri Peace Chilton demonstrates this fact and points once again to the need for an organization of prisoners capable of building broad political coalitions and backing demands with power.

CHILTON V. CANADA, 2008 FC 1047

On February 16, 2000, Muri Peace Chilton, who was incarcerated at Warkworth Institution, a federal prison in Ontario, injured his left thumb while operating machinery known to be faulty in the prison's CORCAN furniture shop.[57] On the day of the injury, shop instructor Kelly Nelles requested Chilton's help to operate an overhead router. Chilton's assistance with this task was necessary because the router was broken. As a federal court decision would later explain, "The overhead router control lacked a bolt that coupled an upper steel plate together with a lower plate rendering the hydraulic foot control inoperable."[58] In attempting to use the machine, Chilton's thumb became pinned between the two steel plates resulting in "a two-inch laceration on the underside of his left thumb and a three-quarters inch laceration below the thumbnail nail. His thumbnail was partially torn free."[59] Chilton was sent to the prison hospital and Nelles attempted to utilize the machine again with the assistance of shop supervisor Hubert Brown. In the words of the court, "Mr. Brown suffered a similar mishap" and the machine was shut down for repair. In 2008, a federal court awarded Chilton $2,500 in damages.

Chilton is significant for a few reasons. It represents a rare example of a case where correctional officials admitted liability for a workplace injury.[60] The minimal award is also noteworthy. Chilton failed to convince the judge he suffered psychological injuries, which could have resulted in greater damages. However, the case is also important in another way. Beyond monetary compensation, Chilton sought "declarations from the Court concerning inmate work, health, and safety conditions."[61] These declarations included a recognition of the right to refuse unsafe work under the Corrections and Conditional Release Act, that "First Aid Kits be placed in such a manner that they are readily accessible to inmate workers," that Institutional Health and Safety Committees require prisoner members, and more.[62] The court declined to make the declarations sought by Chilton, arguing "An inmate grievance procedure is available for these issues."[63] While these reforms may not be won through litigation, they could be achieved through collective bargaining.

The above cases offer important glimpses into the day-to-day workings of prison labour programs usually far away from the public view. They also demonstrate a few important things. First, workplace accidents, including serious ones, do occur with some regularity. While prisoners are sometimes able to receive compensation, as the cases of Patrick McGuire and Ioannis Sarvanis demonstrate, even when the courts find wrongdoing by prison officials sufficient remedial action to prevent future accidents is not necessarily taken. Workers in Canada are generally understood to have three key rights in relation to workplace health and safety: the right to know about health and safety hazards, the right to participate in decisions related to health and safety in the workplace and the right to refuse unsafe work.[64] There is no reasonable justification to exclude incarcerated workers from these rights.

That said, it is also widely understood that even workers covered by health and safety legislation struggle to enforce their rights.[65] This is yet another demonstration of the need for a prisoners' union. Unions play important roles in ensuring safe workplaces and research demonstrates the existence of a "union safety effect." To give just one example of this effect, researchers have demonstrated that unionization is associated with lower rates of lost-time injuries.[66]

While we have thus far emphasized the need to normalize prison *labour,* discussions of injury, illness and disability demonstrate the need for a normalization of legal protections and greater access by prisoners to advocacy and other support services. Since labour has been central to penitentiaries since their inception, the issue of disability has also loomed large.[67] In recent years, CSC has been criticized for failing to meet the needs of disabled prisoners, including by ensuring equal access to employment programs.[68] As the Alberta Civil Liberties Research Centre (ACLRC) has noted, this issue is compounded by a "general greying of the prison population."[69] Older prisoners are more likely to have physical disabilities or ailments that impact their ability to carry out certain tasks or work certain jobs. At times the situation has been acknowledged by CSC, although it has resulted in little action. The situation is likely similar, if not worse, in provincial correctional systems. Prisoners with disabilities should be covered by relevant legislation and entitled to accommodations in areas of employment and beyond. As the ACLRC states, "While it would be a challenge to accommodate prisoners ... it would not be impossible."[70]

PROTECTING HEALTH AND RESISTING INJURY

If one only knew about injuries and accidents involving incarcerated workers from court cases and (rare) media reports, it might be reasonable to assume prisoners are largely passive victims. This, however, would be incorrect. Prisoners also resist hazardous work in a wide variety of ways. In her book *Coerced,* a study of coerced labour in the United States, sociologist Erin Hatton provides testimony from a number of prisoners who refused work on the grounds that it put themselves or others at risk.

For example, James D. (a pseudonym), a prison porter, recounts an incident where he refused to serve fellow prisoners pizza that had fallen on the floor, despite being ordered to do so.[71] Similarly, Derrick, a grounds worker, discusses an incident where he refused an order to clean human waste without proper equipment:

> I'm not cleaning that shit ... If you ain't got any special suit for me to wear to clean that, I'm not cleaning that. All you get is some rubber gloves, and you still got your same uniform on, your green uniform ... we had to clean up the septic tanks and all that. I'm not cleaning that shit. You give me a special suit to wear, I'd go in there and clean. I ain't got a problem with it ... [otherwise] no, it's not going down.[72]

Such acts of individual resistance also occur in Canadian prisons, even if they are difficult to chronicle without media attention, and in many cases, a formal institutional response.

To give one recent example, on March 18, 2020, in the early days of the COVID-19 pandemic, a prisoner at the Centre Fédéral de Formation (Federal Training Centre) in Laval, Quebec, made an official complaint about not getting a mask for protection while working for CORCAN, describing his treatment as "callous" and "unprofessional."[73] The complaint was denied, effectively dismissing the issue for others in a similar situation. The refusal decision stated, "There are currently no implemented policies in place to corroborate health services failing to provide you with a mask."[74] It then followed with a contradictory statement: "There is no scientific consensus in regards to wearing a mask preventatively as a recommended measure guaranteeing protection from contracting COVID-19 virus." This seemed to both deny that he was not provided with a mask while suggesting it did not matter anyway. Within months, that prisoner's urgent plea could be considered an unheeded warning, as COVID-19 tore through the facility. It became the site of one of the worst prison outbreaks of COVID-19 in Canada, with over 160 infected and one, Gilbert Dorion, dead.[75]

From time to time prisoners also collectively resist work they deem dangerous. In 1934, prisoners struck, then rioted in the British Columbia Penitentiary after the scaffolding collapse discussed earlier. While the riot was not only a response to the deaths — prisoners demanded both wages and a representative committee — media reports at the time clearly link the disturbance with the incident. Similarly, the successful union drive at the meatpacking plant at the Guelph Correctional Centre (GCC) in 1977, discussed in more detail in Chapter 6, was significantly motivated by concerns over health and safety.[76] In fact, the successful unionization of prisoners at GCC caused a series of debates about the degree to which prison labour should be normalized in Ontario. In terms of health and safety concerns, NDP MPP Robert Mackenzie would argue in the provincial legislature in 1978 that prisoners in the province's provincial prison industries:

> have every right, where they are engaged in an actual industrial installation, to have some input or some say in terms of the actual safety conditions, and the right to question them. I can really see nothing wrong whatsoever in suggesting that these employees have a committee.... I would sure as blazes like to know, if we are going to run something such as an abattoir or a textile operation, or you name it, that those employees have the right to that kind of protection. I am not at all convinced that it's there as it stands now.[77]

Despite this concern, the normalization of prison labour — and the expansion of legal protections to working prisoners in Ontario — would not come to pass.

More recently, prisoners have also engaged in collective resistance in response to concerns over the COVID-19 pandemic. In provincial jails, these collective actions have mostly taken the form of hunger strikes but some labour strikes have also occurred. For example, on July 28, 2020, prisoners at Joyceville refused work and issued a number of demands. While some demands were broader in scope, most of these related directly to safety concerns in the context of the pandemic. For example, the strikers demanded, "Public health intervention by Public Health Canada and Joyceville CC in response to the COVID-19 pandemic," "Separate canteen and yard access to promote prisoner safety, food security, and COVID-19 safety" and "PPE and appropriate social distancing practices for prisoners working as kitchen staff."[78] It is unclear if any of these demands were met. Joyceville would be the site of a major outbreak, with 160 prisoners and at least four staff members being infected between December 2020 and January 2021.[79]

While the Joyceville strike centred around concern over COVID, it hardly resembles a conventional health and safety work refusal — typically, workers must fear they are at imminent risk of harm to invoke their right to refuse unsafe work. In the Joyceville case, it appears the strike was less a refusal to engage in imminently unsafe work and more of an attempt to exert pressure on prison administrators by withholding labour the institution replies upon.

Because they are generally excluded from labour and employment protections, prisoner workers do not have the statutory right to refuse unsafe work that many Canadians have. Despite this, there are some examples of prisoner workers refusing unsafe work even though they lacked formal legal protections.

On September 8, 2020, prisoners on a vehicle cleaning detail at the Edmonton Institution for Women refused work on the grounds that they faced an undue risk of contracting COVID-19. In an internal communication, a CSC staff member reported:

> As of today, our inmate cleaners are refusing to do the cleaning of Vehicles [sic] until the current protocol has changed. Currently, the process requires the vans to be cleaned by them at a time when the vans cannot be deemed to be safe. They are asking why the van is safe for them to go into but is deemed not safe for others to use. I support their concern and think that we should evaluate the process.[80]

While the ultimate outcome of the Edmonton Institution for Women work refusal is unknown, that prisoners received the support of at least some staff members is significant.

Issues of workplace health and safety will continue to persist in Canadian prisons under existing conditions. Given that working conditions and living conditions are inseparable in prison, many of the health and safety issues plaguing Canadian prisons and jails — such as asbestos, violence, unsafe transportation and communicable diseases — should also be thought of as workplace health and safety issues. The exclusion of prisoners from legal health protections applying to those outside of prisons, and subjugation to the lower standards of correctional law, leads to fewer health protections for prisoners. All these conditions form the background for the working lives of prisoners. The legal cases of prisoner work injuries, as well as scholarly analysis of them, show that prisoners face substantial barriers to success in civil cases, and the trend appears to be increasing barriers and less success.

———

Unionization of prison labour and the end of discriminatory exclusions from health and safety legislation would undoubtedly lead to some better health and safety outcomes for working prisoners (and by extension all prisoners). Better health and safety policies would also benefit non-incarcerated correctional staff; mould and asbestos do not discriminate on the basis of criminal convictions. Moreover, injured, unhealthy and mistreated prisoners certainly create more strain for prison healthcare staff and guards. Still, labour scholars have clearly demonstrated that nominal health and safety laws don't necessarily mean workers are able to meaningfully enforce their rights.[81] This is why a union for prisoners, like unions for workers outside, is critical. To better understand the extent of the barriers prisoners face to achieving unionization, it is necessary to look back at the historical background of prisoner workers, which informs the ideological foundation for their exclusion from legal protections.

4

"SWEAT THE EVIL OUT": THE EVOLUTION OF CANADIAN PRISON LABOUR

The history of prison labour, like the history of the penitentiary, is a history of failure. Throughout history, prison labour has been justified for its punitive, rehabilitative and cost-saving qualities. As we've already discussed, prison labour is not an effective punishment. Indeed we, along with many other commentators, are skeptical about the effectiveness of punishment as a response to crime writ large. Prison labour schemes have similarly failed to effectively rehabilitate prisoners. Their success in terms of revenue generation is more mixed but, on the whole, it's clear that prison labour has never been the cash cow many of its proponents envisioned — although the cost savings for prison administrators are real.

This chapter is a brief overview of the history of Canadian prison labour. It's not comprehensive — we simply don't have the space to write a definitive history of prison labour here. Instead, we give a general account of the evolution of prison labour in Canada and touch on some of the most important issues and themes that arise from that history; for example, the ways justifications for prison labour change — and stay the same — over time. This chapter will first discuss the centrality of prison labour in the development of the penitentiary system, the establishment of which marked a key shift in theories and practices of crime and punishment. Next, we discuss some of the specific forms prison labour has taken, such as convict leasing, as well as sentences to "hard labour" before examining the emergence of contemporary prison industries and prison labour schemes after the Second World War. Despite the significant changes to corrections in Canada over the last

150 or so years, the underlying ideology and practical considerations supporting it remain remarkably the same in the contemporary period. Religious justifications for prison labour have become secularized but prison labour continues to have strong moral undertones. Profit-seeking has (largely) been replaced with more modest, but equally important, claims of "cost recuperation." Perhaps most significantly, prison labour is no longer officially justified as effective punishment — instead, it is understood to be a central component of rehabilitation regardless of its efficacy.

THE OLD MODES OF PUNISHMENT AND THE BIRTH OF THE PENITENTIARY

Prisons, as we know them, haven't always existed. Before the dawn of the penitentiary system in the early nineteenth century, criminals were punished in a variety of ways, but imprisonment was largely understood as temporary — prisoners were held while they awaited their punishment. These punishments might be death sentences, corporal punishment or "transportation" (banishment to penal colonies).

Following the lead of their neighbours to the south and across the North Atlantic, jurisdictions across British North America (Upper and Lower Canada, Quebec and the Maritime Provinces) undertook significant legal and social reforms in the first half of the nineteenth century. As part of these reforms, the criminal law, inherited from — and shaped by — imperial Britain, was amended in key ways. The British criminal law was sometimes known as the "Bloody Code" due to the number of offences that could result in a death sentence. Like England, the criminal codes of pre-confederation British North America included a large number of capital offences.[1] Between 1820 and 1840, criminal codes were amended to reduce the number of offences — including some quite minor, such as property offences — that could result in a death sentence.[2] For example, in 1831 the colony of New Brunswick removed the death sentence for all forms of theft, further reducing the number of capital offences over the course of the next decade.[3] In 1833, the Legislative Assembly of Upper Canada passed a criminal law reform bill that reduced the number of capital offences from 150 to 12.[4] Reliance on corporal punishment also decreased in the same period.

Due to these factors, as well as others such as increase in crime and disorder (perceived or real), judges looked to viable "secondary punishments." As a result, imprisonment as punishment for crime increased in frequency and duration. In response to this need for new, effective and more humane punishment, social reformers proposed new institutions, first among them the penitentiary.

Penitentiaries differed from older forms of confinement in key ways. As noted, unlike dungeons, lockups and jails (or "gaols"), which were understood as places of temporary confinement while legal processes played out and appropriate punishments could be arranged, penitentiaries were conceived of as places of punishment. Penitentiaries, however, were not merely sites of punishment — they were also places for *reform*. This idea that wrongdoers could be remoulded into productive and law-abiding subjects stood in stark contrast with earlier European social theories that saw human nature as immutable and guided by providence. It also differed from biological determinist conceptions of criminality, promoted by theorists such as Cesare Lombroso, that saw crime as inherent to certain types of people — conceptions imbued with assumptions about class and race.[5] Of course, it must be said the idea that crime is associated with certain classes or races of people persists to this day. Still, it was a tremendously significant shift in logic to understand human beings as moldable and criminal behaviour as able to be overcome through the proper application of punishment and reformative activities.[6]

As the "Auburn" and "Pennsylvania" systems emerged as model penitentiary systems in the United States in the 1820s, reformers and government authorities in pre-Confederation Canada looked to both for inspiration. The Auburn and Pennsylvania systems were named after the locations that they were developed — the Penitentiary at Auburn, New York, and the Eastern Penitentiary in Philadelphia, Pennsylvania. Both shared several key features such as confinement to cells and enforced silence. Both emphasized religious contemplation (penance) and self-reflection. While the models differed in some other ways — for example, over the utility of variety in meals — they were most significantly distinguished in their approach to work. Initially, labour was not a component of the Auburn system, which emphasized strict isolation — although it would later be integrated into the model. In contrast, the Pennsylvania system allowed for congregate labour (the "congregate system") during the day and confinement to cells at night. This arrangement offered the potential for industrial rather than smaller-scale artisanal production.[7] As such, it promised to be more cost-effective and was the dominant model taken up by governments in British North America.[8]

As Dario Melossi and Massimo Pavarini have shown, the appeal of industrial production in prisons just as the Industrial Revolution was taking off was not simply coincidence.[9] The growth of industrial capitalism in Canada brought with it increased urbanization and new (and worsening) social problems, including crime. Work discipline — or the installation of "habits of industry" to use the phrasing of the day — was widely touted as the cure to growing issues of pauperism, vagrancy and petty crime. The means by which to develop these habits and forge a disciplined labour force capable of working Canada's newly built factories and workshops took different forms and were pursued by what historian Rainer Baehre has phrased "social welfare asylums."[10] Some of these new institutions were alleged to be primarily ones of social welfare — such as poorhouses and workhouses. Others were explicitly colonial and "civilizing" in aim, such as Indian residential and day schools. Still others, such as penitentiaries and industrial schools, were primarily concerned with responding to crime through deterring would-be wrongdoers and reforming those who got caught. As Baehre explains, "In replicating the productive process of the emerging industrial marketplace, the penitentiary was not only a place of incarceration and secondary punishment, *but an instrument of resocialization.*"[11] Put another way, the penitentiary was broadly understood to be a factory: although penitentiaries produced an assortment of products — shoes, twine, brooms and more — the real goal of the penitentiary-factory was the production of disciplined workers.

All of these social welfare asylums combined elements of social welfare and punitive or coercive power and all were influenced by dominant Christian, and especially Protestant, notions of the virtue of work, as well as Victorian ideas of the moral uplift inherent in labour and toil.[12] All served as means of social control. Prisons, of course, exerted this control more or less nakedly in moments of rebellion and protest — such as in the cases of the Métis rebellions or the 1919 Winnipeg General Strike.[13] In more mundane times, however, these carceral-social welfare institutions wrapped themselves in grand notions of modern science — in particular, the emerging field of "penology," the scientific study of crime, punishment and prisons — and righteous morality that obscured their brutality and service to ruling-class interests.

Labour, of course, was only one of several elements aimed at the reformation of the convict within the walls of the penitentiary. Religious contemplation was long understood to be a key ingredient in the recipe of reform — the penitentiary, after all, derives its name from the word "penance." Education, too, was understood to play a vital role. Still, these latter elements cannot be easily separated from the labour. Education was often understood by prison administrators as instrumental. While literacy, for example, could be understood as good in itself, it also has the potential to aid convicts in their reintegration into the labour force. As James E. Muirhead and Robert Rhodes have noted, there is a basic assumption that "improving literacy will reduce recidivism by improving employability."[14] Similarly, while religious instruction is not reducible to ideological labour discipline, the equation of labour and productivity with moral goodness and virtue is undeniable — after all, sloth is a deadly sin and idle hands are the devil's workshop. Baehre's study of the St. John Penitentiary, which operated in Saint John, New Brunswick, from 1842–80, demonstrates the way that commitments to labour manifested in notions of religion and morality in administration of the penitentiary:

> In its attempt to resocialize the convict the penitentiary regimen was based on the belief that "society" had demonstrated "the value of labor, not only as a means of support, but as an auxiliary of virtue." The "main end and object" of the St John Penitentiary, according to its commissioners, was "the amelioration of the morals of its inmates, and *the encouragement of industry*." The central element of the rehabilitative and economic success of the penitentiary was legitimated in the biblical doctrine "Thou shalt labour" and in the systematic application of the work ethic.[15]

Not all administrators believed that religion and education were of equal importance. While labour was almost always the central activity of the penitentiary, religion and education were believed to be "distractions that took prisoners away from their work" by some prison wardens.[16] The reason for this may have been ideological, but it also could have been a practical consideration. Unlike religious contemplation or educational instruction, labour has the potential for revenue generation.

Prison labour was also foundational to the Canadian prison system in another key way: convict labourers constructed and renovated most of Canada's early penitentiaries. Before discussing the economic considerations of Canadian prison labour in more detail, it is instructive to consider the history of sentences to labour *as punishment*.

HARD LABOUR

Because of its promise to deter future criminal acts while reforming the criminal into a productive citizen, sentences of hard labour played a critical role in the Canadian justice system for well over a century. But punitive sentences to "hard labour" failed to effectively deter criminal behaviour and reduce crime. Such sentences were often brutal, merciless and inhumane. However, they were sometimes productive.

In 1800, well before Canadian Confederation, York, Upper Canada (now part of Toronto) passed a "Stump Act," aimed at assisting the fledgling community clear tree stumps from its roads. The law allowed those convicted of public drunkenness to be sentenced to remove one or more stumps from the town's streets. The law appears to have been effective in clearing roads of stumps, and similar laws were passed in other Upper Canadian towns.[17] While stumps were cleared for the public good, the community service sometimes came at a cost to employers who were "occasionally greatly inconvenienced" when their employees were forced to remove stumps rather than work their regular jobs.[18]

Sentences of hard labour, however, were not always so inconvenient for employers, such as in cases where it was imposed on employees who stole from their bosses.[19] Indeed, in some cases thieving workers were sentenced to work for their employers as restitution. This was the outcome of the trial of Patrick Quinn who was found guilty of stealing $25 from his employer, Martha Christopher, a farmer in Osgoode Township, Ontario, in 1928. Quinn was sentenced to twenty days of "honest toil" by the Magistrate overseeing the trial.[20]

Throughout Canadian history, convicts would be sentenced to hard labour for a wide variety of offences including drunk and careless driving,[21] unlawfully selling alcohol,[22] domestic assault,[23] manslaughter,[24] obstructing police,[25] forgery[26] and more. Women and young offenders also faced sentences of hard labour.[27] When the First World War began, a new Order in Council was passed, making "trading with the enemy" an offence. Those who breached the ordinance could face two years of hard labour, as well as fines and additional prison time.[28]

The logic behind the sentence of hard labour was mostly self-evident: it was used in the Criminal Code of Canada (Criminal Code) or other government acts to deal with those seen as lazy, drunk or otherwise criminal, to "sweat the evil out of their systems."[29] In other cases, the logic for a sentence of hard labour was less clear. While re-education through labour is most associated with communist regimes in Russia or China, sentences to labour were also applied in matters of political crimes in Canada. For example, sentences of imprisonment with hard labour were meted out to members of the Communist Party of Canada after the organization was declared illegal in 1931.[30] In 1935 unemployed demonstrators participating in the On-to-Ottawa Trek faced similar sentences.[31] In 1947, Robert Kent Bowley, the Canadian director of the United Textile Workers of America was sentenced to two months in prison "with hard labor" after being convicted of charges related to the picketing of a textile plant in Lachute, Quebec. In sentencing, the presiding judge declared that the sentence "was the ransom for the slavery you tried to impose on willing and free Lachute workers."[32] Such a statement reveals the way the Canadian state understands the virtues of work: from the perspective of the employer. The main concern is there are workers capable of generating profits for capitalists, but the conditions of those workers are of little concern.

More than just offences under the Criminal Code, hard labour was also imposed in cases of unlawful possession or trafficking of liquor into the 1950s. Similarly, punishments of hard labour could be handed out to violators of several provisions of the Indian Act before its modernization in 1985.[33] In 1953, the welfare section of the Ontario Municipal Association passed a resolution calling for legislation to be passed that would see deserting husbands have their wages garnished and face sentences of hard labour. W.J. Grummett, MPP for Cochrane South and member of the Co-operative Commonwealth Federation (a precursor to the NDP), backed the proposal declaring, "desertion is a more abominable crime than robbery."[34] Grummett argued that desertion was not only a crime against a husband's family, it was criminogenic — alleging that 90% of Ontario's prison population had "origins in homes broken by the desertions of a father or mother."[35]

Breaches of municipal bylaws could also result in sentences of hard labour. For example, those found guilty of setting off fireworks in the Township of York, Ontario, could find themselves subject to "a $50 fine or 21 days imprisonment with or without hard labour," well into the 1960s.[36] In 1975, the Township of West Lincoln, in the Niagara Region of Ontario, enacted a bylaw aimed at discouraging drivers from driving the wrong way down the town's only one-way street. The bylaw imposed a penalty of a $300 fine or "a term in jail at hard labour," for violators.[37]

Hard labour remains on the books — although only for some less common offences. For example, those who violate the Foreign Enlistment Act may face a fine, or imprisonment "with or without hard labour," or both.[38] While the sentence of hard labour is no longer routine, and labour is no longer formally assigned as punishment, assumptions about the value of labour in personal reformation remain.[39]

PRIVATE INTERESTS AND EARLY PRISON PRODUCTION

Many contemporary critiques of the "prison industrial complex" tend to focus on the growth of for-profit prison construction and management and the exploitation of prison labour by private corporations since the rise of "mass incarceration" in the 1980s and 1990s. But there is a much broader web of private and public interests involved in the political economy of punishment. Politicians of various ideological stripes campaign (often cynically) on "tough-on-crime" agendas, and prison spending is a ripe opportunity for "pork barrel" politics — a way to bring government contracts and jobs to specific electoral districts.[40] Prison staff and their unions also have clear interests in expanded prison systems and increased correctional budgets.[41] The private sector's involvement isn't limited to private prison companies and firms that employ prison labour — financiers and architectural firms, and construction, security, technology and food service companies, along with many others, benefit from lucrative correctional contracts. While private involvement in corrections may have increased and taken new forms over the past several decades, it is by no means new. A longer historical view makes this clear. Such a view also helps explain how "state-use" production, where the good and services produced in prison are sold to government departments and agencies or used directly by the correctional system itself, came to characterize almost all prison labour schemes in Canada.

Before delving into this history, it is helpful to discuss four different forms of prison labour that involve private interests: convict leasing, contract, piece-price and public accounts. At different times Canadian prisoners have worked under all of these systems and some, like contract and piece-price, continue to be marginal nodes of the broader constellation of prison labour in Canada. Convict leasing, also known as "affermage" or "lease labour," is perhaps the most well known, conjuring images of chain gangs in black-and-white striped uniforms in the American South. In a convict-leasing arrangement, private employers lease prisoners from administrators, typically at a fixed rate per worker per unit of time.[42] Generally, employers (or "leasees") are responsible for the supervision and custody of prisoners, who often work off of prison grounds. Convict leasing is notorious for its brutality, especially in the Postbellum South.[43] In a contract system, outside entrepreneurs hire prisoners who typically work in facilities on prison grounds. Supervision at work is the responsibility of the private employer, but custodial duties remain the responsibility of the prison. Contractors typically provide raw materials and typically pay an hourly rate for labour. This money might go to prisoners as wages, but it also may simply go to prison coffers. In a piece-price system, private buyers purchase completed products made to their specifications at a set price — typically per unit produced. They can then sell these finished goods as they see fit. Supervision and custody of prisoners, as well as the costs of materials and machinery, is borne by the prison system. Finally, in a public accounts system, all aspects of production — and entrepreneurial risk — are borne by the prison. The goods and services produced through a public account system can then be sold through private — or public — retailers.[44]

While these systems differ in key ways, they all directly involve private interests. Due to this fact, all have faced opposition from labour and capital who have decried "unfair" competition with prison labour and prison-produced commodities. Experiments with different forms of private involvement have occurred throughout history — and continue to this day. However, whenever a new proposal for increased private involvement in prison labour occurs, similar debates and criticisms inevitably re-emerge, and the state-use status quo more or less holds firm.

To better appreciate why this is the case, it is necessary to consider the history of private involvement in prison labour in more detail.

As the second Industrial Revolution took hold in Canada, new methods of production and technologies were introduced into penitentiaries.[45] Outfitting industrial shops within the penitentiaries was not cheap, and where they could, governments turned to private financing to facilitate the design and construction of prison industries. Indeed, corporate involvement in prisons and prison industries stretches back to the pre-Confederation period. The public-private partnerships that emerged at this time were largely failures both in terms of rehabilitative and economic goals. They were also marked by corruption, graft and giveaways of public monies to private business.

In the case of the Ontario Central Prison, a provincial institution operating in Toronto between 1874 and 1915, industrial capacity was designed to meet the needs of a specific manufacturer, the Canada Car Company (CCC).[46] The CCC, a producer of railway cars, had invested a quarter of a million dollars as part of a seven-year contract to manufacture goods within the prison. Under this contract system agreement, the CCC agreed to pay fifty cents per prisoner per day to the government. As Joseph Gondor Berkovits explains, "Not even the long-term convicts at the Kingston Penitentiary earned more for their jailers than forty cents a day. (No wages, of course, were paid to either the federal or provincial inmates themselves)."[47]

Unfortunately for prison administrators, the CCC went bankrupt a mere ten months after the Central Prison opened. Not only did the company fail to pay "a cent in wages," the government actually paid $15,000 to the company in an out-of-court settlement. The company quickly reorganized into a new entity and succeeded in securing a contract to produce woodenware products at the prison. While the situation was far from ideal, as Berkovits notes, "What was the province to do? Here was a brand new, half-million-dollar facility, filled with over three hundred convicts suddenly having nothing to do."[48]

The Central Prison's plans for prison labour was unsuccessfully opposed by the Toronto Trades Assembly.[49] Prison labour had long been of enormous concern to workers who feared immiseration if forced to compete with convicts toiling under threat of lash. As Bryan Palmer has chronicled, between 1833–1836, "mechanics" — skilled tradesmen — in Kingston agitated against the establishment of Kingston Penitentiary, fearing that prison labour would undermine their trades and economic standing.[50] As the trade union movement developed over the subsequent century, prison labour remained a central concern. At its inaugural meeting in 1873, the Canadian Labour Union (CLU) appointed a committee on prison labour. The CLU objected especially against teaching trades to convicts, which undermined the craft unionist strategy of taking wages out of competition by limiting admission into the trade. After the demise of the CLU in 1878, its successor organization, the Canadian Trades and Labour Congress, continued to oppose prison labour — albeit with few immediate results.[51] But it was not only labour who feared competition with incarcerated workers. Industrialists and business owners who did not contract prison labour — and who begrudged competition that did — also played a critical role in curtailing and restricting the forms prison labour schemes could take.[52]

Pressure from interest groups was only one factor in the curtailment of private exploitation of prison labour in the early twentieth century. A statement by W.J. Hanna, provincial secretary of Ontario in 1907, noted the potential revenues that could be generated by convict leasing — which existed in Ontario from 1874 to 1905 — was limited by the difficulty the province had in getting leasees to pay their labour bills. In 1909 Ontario would formally adopt a state-use system for prison industry and agricultural programs. The rest of the country would follow suit over the next several decades. A 1934 report by the League of Nations noted "over 99 per cent of work" performed in Canada's federal prisons was for state use.[53] While new efforts at increasing private involvement in prison industries have been made from time to time, such as the case of the abattoir at the Guelph Correctional Centre that is discussed in more detail in Chapter 6, prison production in Canada continues to overwhelmingly occur for state use. Thus far we have mostly focused on the ideological and economic considerations for Canadian prison labour throughout history.

VOCATIONAL TRAINING AND MODERN PRISON INDUSTRY

Mobilization for the Second World War had a considerable impact on Canadian corrections, as it did on the rest of society. The outbreak of the war caused the adoption of recommendations set out in the *1938*

Royal Commission to Investigate the Penal System of Canada, better known as the *Archambault Report,* to largely be put on hold, dissipating the pressure to change a correctional system "on the brink of reform."[54] Significantly, prisoners and guards were allowed to enlist in the armed forces and prison industries were retooled and expanded to support wartime needs.[55] As John Kidman, executive secretary of the of the Prisoners' Aid Society of Montréal, states in his 1947 book, *The Canadian Prison: The Story of a Tragedy:*

> In the late war the penitentiaries went far beyond their ordinary production of clothes and shoes for their own inmates, and filled contracts for war clothing, leather goods and equally in the matter of farm produce. But the urgency of the situation made it easier for them to figure without disturbing the open labour market.[56]

These factors meant that throughout the war, Canadian prisons "had a surplus of work."[57] As Kidman explains, by the end of the war:

> the 'industrial shop' has now become an integral part of any big penal institution. The smithy, the carpentry, the bakery, the laundry, the leather goods, the mail-bag, the shoe and clothing shop mostly have their place, and it is now one of the puzzles of the warden and his classification board how to fit their men into these shops.[58]

Changes to Canadian imprisonment at the conclusion of the war were not limited to prison industry and agriculture. In the aftermath of the Second World War, new developments in penology and behavioural science, along with new emphasis on human rights and international law, ushered in a new set of reforms in corrections — although many of the recommendations of the *Archambault Report* would not be implemented.

The development of vocational training programs in the late 1940s marked an important shift in the conceptualization of prison labour by prison authorities. Punishment was no longer an explicit aim of such programs. Rather, vocational training programs — and eventually all prison labour schemes — were now conceived of as first and foremost rehabilitative. D.J. Halfhide, the chief vocational officer of the Canadian Penitentiary Service explained the aims of vocational programming in 1954:

(a) To assist in rehabilitation through trade training, so that upon release many will be able to find employment in a trade of his own choice.

(b) To give technical training equivalent to that received by apprentices in the trades, as required by apprenticeship regulations.

(c) To provide actual work experience into the trades.

(d) To develop work habits acceptable to employers of Labour.[59]

Many vocational opportunities were offered in federal prisons. For example, prisoners could be trained in carpentry or upholstery in Dorchester Penitentiary (New Brunswick), barbering or plumbing in Collins Bay Penitentiary (Ontario), painting and decorating at Saskatchewan Penitentiary or diesel mechanics and draughting at the British Columbia Penitentiary. The 1956–57 *Annual Report of the Commissioner of Penitentiaries* lists eighteen trades programs available in five federal penitentiaries (one in each region). While most institutions with vocational programs offered half a dozen trades or less, the Federal Training Centre in Quebec offered the vast majority (twelve).[60] Still, only a tiny fraction of federal prisoners had access to such training. Many institutions offered no programs at all. Even where programs existed, only a small number of prisoners participated. In 1960, only 333 prisoners out of a total population of 6,344 were enrolled in vocational programs.[61]

Multiple factors contributed to the low participation rates. In the 1950s, participants in vocational programs had to have at least a grade eight education, be under thirty years of age and not be recidivists, leaving a substantial portion of the population ineligible. Even prisoners who met the necessary criteria and were determined to be "reformable" struggled to secure placements. As most federal prisoners were serving sentences of less than four years, many prisoners would not be able to complete trades training before release. Budgetary concerns and competing institutional needs were other factors. Shop space, instructors and equipment all cost money. Significantly, vocational programs sometimes ran up against institutional labour needs. As explained by Chris Clarkson and Melissa Munn, trades training was also limited by "demand for prisoners to serve in the prison operations, maintenance and construction departments."[62] In other words, if too many prisoners were studying small engine repair, who would cook the meals, clean the floors and maintain the grounds?

The excitement accompanying the establishment of vocational programming soon wore off. In 1966, *Globe and Mail* columnist Scott Young quoted some troubling statistics in a column on Canada's prison training programs. According to J. Ciale, a professor of Criminology at the Université de Montréal, one study on the efficacy of trades training found less than 9% of released prisoners who received vocational training obtained employment in that field upon release. Ciale further reported that "of the 2,764 inmates released from St. Vincent de Paul and Federal Training Centre, 68 per cent were back in jail within five years — and trades training had no influence whatever on whether a man made a success outside, or was returned eventually for some other crime."[63] As the 1960s wore on, a vocational training programs — along with all other correctional programming — would increasingly face a different type of challenge in the form of prisoner protest and organizing.

THE MACGUIGAN REPORT

Canadian prisons were in a state of near-constant turmoil in the 1970s. Strikes, riots, hostage-takings and other "disturbances" occurred regularly; upheavals and uprisings rocked both the federal and provincial prison systems. By 1976 the "prison explosions were almost constant; hardly a week passed without another violent incident."[64] In response the federal government struck a Parliamentary Sub-Committee to investigate the penitentiary system and produce a report of findings. The report, known as the *MacGuigan Report,* after its chair, Liberal MP Mark MacGuigan, was released in 1977. This report transformed the dominant approach to 'rehabilitation' in corrections, which had previously been envisioned as a social issue and shifted responsibility for "reform" away from prison authorities and onto individuals.[65] The *MacGuigan Report* covered issues of work and employment training in detail. The report emphasized that coercion alone was ineffective in meeting correctional aims. Instead, prisoners needed to also be offered *incentives* to change their mindsets, lifestyles and behaviours. Work remained key to the rehabilitative process:

A prison that has not solved the problem of prison labour cannot be said to be operating an institution of correction and reform. There is little chance of reforming an inmate who, upon
his release, is unwilling, unable, or unfit to accept employment.
In most cases, it is only by inspiring the inmate to pursue creative and productive work habits that any lasting value will be
obtained from the expense of imprisoning him.

   We therefore believe that every inmate who is physically capable of working should be required to work, and the situation
in which large numbers spend most, or perhaps all, of their
time in enforced idleness should not be permitted. The employment facilities in the institutions should, so far as possible, be
designed to meet the individual training needs of inmates and
should duplicate the production methods of industry in free society, so that an inmate, upon his release, will have a reasonable
hope of being a competitive member of the labour market.[66]

Or, said more simply: "Work is necessary for personal reformation."[67]

   Given the authors' emphasis on incentives, the report recommended that there should be "a meaningful correlation between the amount
of work done by an inmate and the pay he receives."[68] Reductions in
pay in cases of poor performance were also recommended.[69] Despite
the emphasis on incentives, the *MacGuigan Report* fell far short of ad-
vocating the normalization of prison labour. Most critically, the report
does not break with the notion that coercion of prison labour is justifi-
able: "Wilful refusal to work without just cause should be treated as a
disciplinary matter."[70]

   The report also made several specific recommendations related to
institutional maintenance work, industries and vocational training.
Favouring the employment of prisoners in productive industries, the authors conceded that institutional maintenance work was important for
some prisoners "not suited" to industrial work. While "food service and
preparation, storekeeping, clerical services, mechanical services, plant
maintenance and repair, laundry and janitorial services" were "not all in
great demand in society," they were "to a certain extent marketable."[71]
Furthermore, while marketable skills were one consideration, the authors
also emphasize that institutional maintenance work "is necessary if we
are to keep the operational costs of our institutions as low as possible."[72]

The report took issue with trades training, which echoed earlier criticisms of federal vocational programming. The *MacGuigan Report* authors were concerned with the quality and applicability of training programs, noting a "complaint commonly heard from ex-inmates is that the vocational training they received in our institutions was in fact useless to them once they were released."[73] Employers did not recognize experience or credentials earned within vocational programs and equipment and production processes were outmoded, leading to additional issues of applicability. Furthermore, prisoners trained in a particular trade did not necessarily have an opportunity to ply that trade while serving the remainder of their sentences, leaving them with little work experience — and many were paroled or otherwise released before training programs were completed.[74]

The *MacGuigan Report* was particularly harsh in its criticisms of federal prison industries, which were "not producing at anything like their potential."[75] Prison industries were plagued by "outmoded means of production" and incentive pay was too low to sufficiently attract and motivate workers.[76] The *MacGuigan Report* supported the findings of an earlier *Report on Prison Industries Re-Orientation* (1973), which recommended that prison industries more closely resemble industries in the "outside economy," the provision of "adequate" salaries commensurate with skill and experience, the institution of productivity bonuses and "the right of the workshop foreman to select his staff."[77] While some of these changes were being taken up by the Penitentiary Service (as the CSC was then known), the *MacGuigan Report* emphasized the urgency of the overhaul of prison industries and other prison work schemes. Reflecting these findings, report recommendation 41 states:

> There must be a graduated system of incentives based on labour productivity. Incentives should include bonuses for piecework and improvements, and earned remission. Inmates who work either inside or outside penitentiaries should be required to pay room and board at reasonable rates and to contribute to the support of their families to the extent that these demands are compatible with their retaining a financial incentive to work.[78]

Much of the recommendation would be taken up by the early 1980s; however, many of the problems the reforms sought to address would linger on.

On the issue of the prison industry, the *MacGuigan Report* recommended that the Penitentiary Service follow jurisdictions like the United States in centralizing and modernizing industries: "A national prison industries corporation should be established, and the full cooperation of business and labor enlisted in providing guidance and implementation towards the fullest possible work opportunities in penitentiaries."[79] This recommendation would form the basis for the reorganization of prison industries into a new centralized entity — CORCAN.[80]

PERSISTENT PROBLEMS: THE BIRTH OF CORCAN

CORCAN was established in 1980 as a reorganization and rebranding of federal prison industries.[81] While the name was new, many of the problems identified in the *MacGuigan Report* continued to plague Canadian prisons. Furthermore, new issues around organizational jurisdiction and accounting arose as staff and prison administrators worked out how the new entity would fit into the existing prison bureaucracy. The new program also came with considerable costs. A private firm, Tetrad Marketing/Sales Limited, was contracted to handle sales and marketing; in addition to spending on equipment, raw materials and staffing costs, a new inmate payment scheme (which totalled $8.4 million for the 1981–82 fiscal year) came into effect.[82] Despite the increase in pay, which would presumably attract more participants, the reorganization of federal prison industries did not immediately result in more prisoner employment. In 1981–82, industries employed an average of 1,223 prisoners — while the average for the two previous years was "about 1,175."[83]

Problems would continue to persist over the next several years. The *Third Annual Report of the Inspector's General Branch,* covering the 1982–83 fiscal year, noted several issues related to federal prison work and prison industries. Under a section titled "Areas that need improvement," the report found "Institutions generally experienced difficulty finding sufficient 'meaningful' work for employable inmates, so as to ensure that they were kept fully employed." Furthermore, the report noted that even when work placements were available, they were not always taken up: "There appears to be a generalized lack of enthusiasm on the part of inmates for industrial job placements." When prisoners did take job placements, there were significant quality control issues with the products they produced. Furthermore, CORCAN billing "was a concern for various institutions and regions and was itself the subject of a separate management review. The process proved to be cumbersome and time consuming, serving to cause, among other concerns, significant delays in invoicing and payment for goods." Furthermore, "some of the financial controls over the industrial operation [were] still inadequate."[84]

Even though prison industries had been running in Canadian penitentiaries for nearly a century, basic gaps in managerial policies remained an issue. The 1983–84 annual report of the Inspector's General Branch noted, "Some institutions lacked local control over attendance records and overtime-limits." Similarly, preventative maintenance of industrial equipment was noted as an area of concern:

> The Service has a considerable capital investment in farm and industrial equipment. To ensure that optimal value is received from these assets, there is a requirement for a regular and formal preventive maintenance program. What programs were in place tended to be informal and lacked documentation, and accordingly we were unable to confirm that acceptable standards of maintenance had been provided.[85]

In the 1980s CORCAN experimented with a number of new industries, products and services. Examples include data entry and processing,[86] solar panel assembly[87] and micrographic production.[88]

Federal prisoner work programs entered a particularly controversial phase in the late 1980s when the use of prisoner labour was made available to CSC staff to serve their individual needs as part of a "hire a prisoner" program. As part of the program, prisoners reported doing a variety of jobs for prison staff, including shovelling snow off their roofs, electrical work, landscaping and even helping to build homes. The program, which amounted to a modern-day convict-leasing scheme, soon faced considerable scrutiny. In 1988, the *Toronto Star* reported that prisoners at the federal Beaver Creek Institution described the program as "slave labour." A prison staff member acknowledged that even though the program was described as voluntary, "are you going to say no to the guy who decides about your passes, who decides if you get to see your wife and kids on the weekend?"[89] Prisoners were doing work for prison staff at far less than the prevailing industry wages — the *Toronto Star* reported that prisoners trained as carpenters could make $10 per hour, but the going rate for an outside carpenter was twice to three times that amount.[90] While the formal "hire a prisoner" program would be discontinued, similar — and even more exploitative — practices would continue to occur.

In 2001, the *Province* reported, "An internal investigation at B.C.'s most permissive prison has uncovered a network of corrupt staff exploiting a tax-funded inmate work program for their own benefit."[91] Similar to the program in Beaver Creek, the investigation at Ferndale Institution confirmed earlier allegations that prisoners were tasked with performing work on the houses of prison staff, among other things. Work included putting up a retaining wall, landscaping, hanging up Christmas lights and repairing staff cars. However, unlike in the case of Beaver Creek, it appears these activities were unsanctioned and represented plain corruption by CSC staff. The *Province* reported at least one case in which a prisoner was not paid for their work. Whether they were ever paid is unknown. In addition to the blatant exploitation of prison labour, the investigation found plants, cleaning supplies and gardening equipment from the prison's nursery had also gone missing. The investigation was initiated after the discovery that former Saskatchewan Minister of Energy and Mines, Colin Thatcher, who was serving a life sentence for killing his wife, was allowed to have his horse brought onto the prison grounds to ride while working at the prison's for-profit ranch. Needless to say, this was not officially approved but an example of favouritism.

Both the Beaver Creek and Ferndale controversies reveal something very important about the nature of prisoner labour. Due to the enormous power imbalance between staff supervisors and prisoners, staff were able to extract major personal benefits from access to prisoner labour. While the incidents were eventually reported, the fact is that extremely exploitative activities were able to take place due to the absence of protections for prisoner workers and lacking oversight of staff. If prisoners' pay and working conditions were improved, the incentives for such exploitation would diminish. If prisoners had a union, they would have had a stronger process for raising grievances and better protections against retaliation for whistleblowing. The episodes also call into question the so-called rehabilitative character of prisoner labour, which we will critically evaluate in more detail in Chapter 6. If prisoners are performing work clearly for the benefit of prison staff, any argument about the work being primarily rehabilitative should fall flat.

CORCAN

CORCAN was incorporated and restructured as a Special Operating Agency in 1992. This move gave CORCAN additional bureaucratic and budgetary autonomy and "freedom to enter more fully into partnerships with the private sector."[92] In the 1990s, CORCAN continued its efforts to modernize by seeking International Organization for Standards (ISO) certification and implementing new measures for "offender work performance."[93] CORCAN initiated a number of new ventures, including the opening of "community industries" — workshops located off of prison grounds and new joint enterprises with the private sector (mostly non-profits).[94] Despite these changes, age-old issues of providing sufficient work to meet "offender needs" persisted. As one CORCAN operations manager explained in 1995:

> This year, the link between sales and production has come to the fore as CORCAN, in order to divest itself of high inventories, has had to significantly reduce production allocations. The outcome is that many plants are faced with idle machines and idle inmates at a time when Wardens are demanding that inmate employment in CORCAN be increased. As each institution's inmate population increases, the pressure is exerted on CORCAN to find additional inmate employment opportunities and, of course, the necessary revenue stream to fund the additional work. The events of this year are not an anomaly in terms of the future for CORCAN.[95]

This is yet another example of CORCAN's dual mandates — offender training and "rehabilitation" on the one hand, and profit-seeking on the other — coming into direct conflict.

CORCAN would also face other external challenges at this time in the form of renewed complaints of unfair competition from private businesses — especially furniture makers who argued they could not compete against CORCAN's bids for contracts to furnish government offices. The complaints had merit — in some cases, competitors had no opportunity to bid on contracts due to CORCAN's preferred status with the federal government. Critics in the business community, such as Canadian Federation of Independent Businesses, pointed to this advantage and the low pay of prison labour as factors undermining Canadian businesses and "taking jobs away from the productive sector of the economy."[96] As one furniture industry manager put it, "Why do I need to pay the federal government my taxes for them to come back and compete directly against me and I don't make any money?"[97]

While acknowledging that, at times, CORCAN had prioritized cost recovery over training goals, CEO Sudin Ray asserted the organization was now more "correctional mandate focused" and denied that prison industries represented meaningful competition with the private sector. Ray further argued that the constraints of CORCAN's dual cost-recovery/rehabilitation mandate should be factored into conversations about the organization's competitive position, as CORCAN faced unique costs related to supervision and overhead: "It's not a level playing field because you are dealing with people who are not necessarily the most motivated workforce in the country."[98] In further responding to critics, officials denied that CORCAN's prices undercut competition.[99] CORCAN could have muted critics by simply matching the wages of private industry. However, this solution was neither pursued nor discussed.

———

After reviewing the history of Canadian prison labour, it is clear the cyclical debates, schemes, problems and conflicts that appear and reappear in relation to prison labour do so because of the fundamental contradictions that bedevil prisons in Canadian society. Competition over jobs is a basic feature of capitalist labour markets. As long as most people in society have to maintain employment to ensure they can keep a roof over their head and food on their table, there will be tension around people in prison having these things guaranteed — even if they are inadequate and even if they come with all the pains of imprisonment. As such, it is not surprising that many workers resent publicly funded jobs and training programs for prisoners that they don't have access to. Something similar can be said about counselling, mental health and other services. It is for this reason that the struggle to improve the lives of people in prison must be connected to broader struggles to improve the situation of all working people. This is the historic mission of the labour movement and the reason we believe the labour movement and prison justice movement have common cause.

5

WHAT ARE THE ALTERNATIVES?

Prison labour has faced — and continues to face — intense scrutiny, seemingly from all sides. Reformers want programming improved — generally through minor tweaks. Abolitionists want imprisonment, and with it prison labour, abolished outright. Free marketeers want to end the existing system of production for state use that governs prison industries and expand the private employment of prisoners. "Tough-on-crime" politicians want a return to sentences of "hard labour" and chain gangs. With the exception of the latter point, prisoners have, at different times, supported all of these positions. So what is to be done?

In this section, we consider alternatives to the prison labour schemes that exist in Canada. "Minor tweaks" don't warrant any real discussion; the minor reforms of the last forty plus years show the failure of such an approach. Labour in Canadian prisons, like systems of incarceration in general, require a radical overhaul. Other proposals — like chain gangs — only require a brief discussion. Such revanchist proposals can, and should, be dismissed on legal and moral grounds. Beyond their dubious legality and immorality, advocates of such positions must also ignore the evidence proving such programs ineffective.[1] Other proposals for reform warrant discussion in more detail even if we disagree with them in substance.

As long as it exists, prison labour can and should be utilized for the public good — although this requires some considerable nuancing. Ultimately, we argue that unions for prisoners are needed to ensure prisoners have a clear collective voice, backed by real power, in debates over the work they do and how they do it.

REFORM OR ABOLITION?

Abolitionists generally argue prison labour should be immediately abolished along with prisons themselves. As we will argue in more detail in the next chapter, we believe that a prisoners' union could be an incredibly powerful vehicle for changing prisons. At minimum, a strong prisoners' union could be a potent tool to improve conditions and ensure some measure of accountability from the prison system. It could be a central player in a longer battle for the abolition of prisons.

While it is not a common position among prisoners or the prison justice movement, there are those who argue for the immediate and wholesale abolition of prison labour on the grounds that prison labour is "exploitative." For example, a petition posted to Change.org in 2016 stated:

> Prison labour is a form of modern American slavery used by multiple large corporations across the world. Under the 13th amendment to the United States Constitution, slavery was merely reformed rather than abolished.
>
> An example of one of the most extreme cases of prison labour happens in Texas and Florida, where prisoners are forced to work in fields without any pay. Companies like McDonald's, Wal-mart and many more use slave labour to cut down on production costs despite being more than able to use other ways. Racial justice in the USA cannot be achieved until prison labour is abolished completely.[2]

The petition, which at the time of writing has garnered over 260,000 signatures, also includes a list of firms in the United States that utilize prison labour, suggesting consumers should boycott them. The abolition of prison labour without major reforms to the prison system would have severe and negative effects on prisoners. In fact, since the inception of the penitentiary, prisoners have decried "idleness" in the forms of unemployment, underemployment and make-work as inhumane and undermining their chances of successful reintegration upon release. Throughout history prisoners have demanded better work and improved working conditions, not the elimination of work in prison.

As we've already discussed in some detail, given the economics of Canadian incarceration, some form of income from employment, savings or family support is needed for prisoners to eke out a bearable existence. Money is needed for hygiene products. It is used to buy food items to supplement low quality prison meals. It is also critical for maintaining relationships through phone calls and letter mail. As such, Canadian prisoners have consistently agitated for higher wages (and reduced canteen, phone and other costs). Low prison pay has largely been justified by politicians and administrators for reasons of "less eligibility," which we discuss in Chapter 1. Many argue prisoners should not make as much or more money than "free workers" working similar jobs. But prisoners have advocated for the normalization of prison labour and expansion, not curtailment of prison employment programs. Prisoners would be better able to defend their rights in all arenas if they were entitled to economic rights and responsibilities, such as the payment of income taxes, held by the average person in Canada.

That said, it is also clear that prisoners do not want work for work's sake. When prisoners in BC's Oakalla provincial prison engaged in a sit-down strike in July 1975, they demanded more access to job training and employment programs. In the words of the Oakalla protesters:

> There is no chance of rehabilitation here. There isn't anything here that inmates can do that will develop our minds. All our vocational shops were closed a few years ago. They say the reason for this is that people working here aren't interested in continuing this type of training. We demand the availability of job training.[3]

A year later, in 1976, around 350 prisoners at Archambault Institution in Sainte-Anne-des-Plaine, Quebec, engaged in a four-month-long work strike — one of the longest in Canadian history. The strikers, who styled themselves the "Archambault Guys," released a manifesto of demands. The demands were sweeping. In the words of criminal defence lawyer and strike mediator Robert Sacchitelle, the manifesto contained "well-structured demands which aim at nothing less than a complete change in the very philosophy of the maximum-security institution."[4] A considerable amount of the manifesto concerns work. The Archambault Guys decried the institution's existing employment programming as "bullshit" designed to "keep them in a routine where they [prisoners] have nothing to do and nothing to think."[5]

Instead of meaningful work, existing vocational and employment programming merely served to make "guys have to learn to obey their boss, to do as they're told."[6] As such, the Archambault Guys called for the abolition of "make-work" jobs and "places to store the extra guys" workshops. They demanded trades education that could lead to "a degree of professional competence and some 'outside' recognition."[7] Critically, these programs would be developed and overseen with the participation of prisoners' representatives. They further demanded prisoners be able to freely pursue trades that interested them, as well as better windows in prison workshops, routine health and safety inspections, access to workplace injury insurance, the abolition of the existing pay scale and pay increases.[8]

While the Archambault Guys did not call for a labour union, their demand to participate in the design and running of vocational programs can be seen as analogous to the practice of "codetermination," which sees workers' representatives involved in some management decisions. This practice is particularly associated with Northern European social democratic countries and relates to many historical efforts by prisoners to "democratize" the prison. It's clear prisoners do not want their work to be abolished while their imprisonment continues. Rather, they want it to be stimulating, safe and reasonably remunerated. While demands for improvements to prison labour schemes may not directly advance struggles to abolish the prison, we do not believe they are in conflict with such aims. In fact, as we've stated before, the normalization of prison labour and the creation of a prisoners' union would represent a non-reformist reform with the potential of dramatically rebalancing power within the prison system.

PRIVATIZATION

Arguments for more private involvement in prison labour are typically made by those who support "freer markets" in response to social problems. These include market fundamentalists, such as libertarians and neoliberals, but also many mainstream liberals and conservatives. However, not all arguments for privatization of prison labour schemes are the same. Critically, such proposals can be divided into two main camps — those that advocate for the full normalization of prison labour and those that do not. Unfortunately, the most common are those arguing for increased private control over prison labour while maintaining a myriad of exemptions and barriers to workers' rights. Typically, these proposals see prisoners work for less than minimum wage or below the prevailing rates in "free" industry, have severely restricted opportunities for advancement and continue to be subject to a number of coercive policies and practices. In the worst cases these might include direct punishments or barriers to early release in response to poor work performance or refusals to work. For example, in the late 1990s, Cornell law professor Stephen P. Garvey proposed increasing private involvement in prison industries and the elimination of laws limiting the ability to sell prison-made goods on the open market. To make this proposal politically feasible, Garvey suggests a special income tax on prisoners' wages could be used to redistribute money to workers whose jobs are lost due to competition with prison labour. This is a roundabout way of saying that prisoner wages should remain below those prevailing in industry. While Garvey mentions some commentators have argued for full labour rights for prisoners, including the right to unionize, he does not take a position on the question.[9]

Historically, the exploitation of prison labour by private capital was nothing short of barbaric. Convicts leased to private employers died at notoriously high rates. This was not an accident, as employers were free of the normal disincentives preventing them from working prisoners to death. Employers leasing convicts did not own prisoners as slaves, and thus did not lose property if one died. They likewise did not tend to suffer from replacement costs — if one died, they could simply "get another."[10]

More recently, as noted above, a number of companies in the United States such as Whole Foods and Victoria's Secret have come under fire for using prison labour. Critics of these companies point to the racialized nature of imprisonment in the US and the links between slavery and mass incarceration, as well as poor pay, dangerous working conditions and the coercion involved in prison labour.[11] Unfortunately, the result of campaigns to shame companies for utilizing prison labour have typically had the effect of simply ending contracts between companies and correctional systems. The companies seek out cheap labour elsewhere and incarcerated workers' situations stay the same or are perhaps made worse by unemployment.

This point is worth emphasizing. The idea that prison labour should be constrained, rather than improved through expanded labour rights, has the potential to be disastrous for prisoners. Beyond loss of wages, the cost savings associated with prison work schemes would have to be made up elsewhere by prison administrators. It is undoubtable that increasingly austere prison budgets would come primarily at the expense of prisoners. This is not meant to justify massive prison budgets. Rather, it is simply a recognition that, in the current context, cuts to prison budgets typically result in costs being downloaded on to prisoners and programming and service cuts, rather than reductions in spending on things like staffing or security.

Despite criticisms of private business exploiting prison labour, prisoners have sometimes argued for *more* extensive involvement of private employers in the prison system. Many of the demands of prisoners during the infamous Attica prison rebellion of 1971 related to work. The rebels at Attica demanded the parity of their wages with outside workers, access to worker compensation schemes, the right to join and form unions, unionized vocational training opportunities and to end the practice of punishing prisoners who refuse to work or engage in strikes. Demand number seven is worth quoting at length:

> We demand that industries be allowed to enter the institutions and employ inmates to work eight hours a day and fit into the category of workers for scale wages. The working conditions in prisons do not develop working incentives parallel to the many jobs in the outside society, and a parolled prisoner faces many contradictions of the job that adds to his difficulty in adjusting. Those industries outside who desire prisoners should be allowed to enter for the purpose of employment placement.[12]

The demand that private employers be allowed to operate in prison by some of the most radical prisoners in American history might strike some as surprising. However, when understood in the context of other demands around pay and unionization, it makes perfect sense. Prisoners want access to "good" jobs just like other workers.

Similar calls can be found in Canada. At times prisoners have argued gainful employment should be a priority even if the normalization of prison labour does not occur. In one example, a prisoner writing in

The Outlook, the prisoner-run magazine at Warkworth Institution, suggested "tax-free" export processing zones be set up in Canadian prisons. Referencing similar schemes in Taiwan, the author suggests that such an arrangement, along with "reasonable labour costs and low rent" could incentivize manufacturers to invest in prison production. In exchange, employers would only have to "guarantee a continuous training plan." The author, who, it should be acknowledged, admits the notion is "just a passing thought," argues such a scheme could "save millions of [tax] dollars, and as a very important by-product, thousands of inmates could learn a trade, the work ethic, and leave these institutions with sufficient funds from their labour to get started in society."[13] In a slightly earlier — and less radical — example of private management of prison industry, the takeover of the government-run abattoir at Ontario's Guelph Correctional Centre by a private meatpacking firm seemingly enjoyed support from prisoners there. Notably, the privatization of the abattoir at GCC in 1974 came with industry wages for incarcerated workers. They would go on to unionize with CFAW in 1977, something discussed in more detail in the next chapter.[14]

CO-OPS AND SOLE PROPRIETORSHIPS

Other forms of private enterprise with some support — and which have been experimented with at different times — are sole proprietorships and prisoner cooperatives. Sole-proprietorship schemes allow prisoners to produce and sell goods, typically art and handicrafts, and keep some portion of the profit. Prisoner cooperatives are businesses that are collectively owned and operated by prisoners or ex-prisoners. Prison-based cooperatives currently exist or have previously existed around the world, including Puerto Rico, Bolivia, Italy and Ethiopia. They typically exist as small-scale and artisanal operations, usually producing art and handicrafts; however, some produce a diverse array of products and services including furniture, agricultural goods and trades work.[15]

Advocates of prisoner cooperatives argue that beyond providing an income, co-ops encourage the development of transferable skills and foster self-esteem and dignity among their members. Furthermore, proponents of prison co-ops claim they substantially reduce recidivism.[16]

Some, such as Greg McElligott, have argued prisoner cooperatives could also serve as a means to democratize the administration of prisons and advance the cause of prison justice:

> It would use traditional cooperative structures — voluntary membership, democratic control, a commitment to skill building and community, cooperation with other co-ops, and so on — to deliver work, training, and programming to prisoners in a way that minimizes coercion and maximizes autonomy. These goals run directly counter to those of the supermax prisons that are the flagships of mass incarceration.[17]

This democratizing potential was also identified by those involved in early prisoner-cooperative experiments in Canadian prisons. For example, the Native Extraordinary Line of Furniture (NELOF) cooperative was established in 1974 by members of the Native Brotherhood, an Indigenous prisoner-run organization, in the federal Mountain Institution in Agassiz, BC.[18] The NELOF produced Indigenous handicrafts and built custom furniture, later expanding to include a printing operation to produce advertising material for the co-op. The NELOF was supported by the Mountain Institution administration and the organization was given workshop space within the institution, as well as permission to seek financing, tools and materials from outside groups and supporters.[19]

Indeed, the NELOF was granted an extraordinary amount of autonomy by prison administrators. A 1975 Department of Justice report on the Native Brotherhood described the situation this way: "There was no need for a non-native shop 'instructor,' since in fact he could do little in the way of instructing. Instead, knowledgeable and skilled members of the Brotherhood act in this capacity, teaching their skills to other members."[20] Furthermore, as described by a report on the Native Brotherhood prepared for the Department of Justice in 1975:

> The group does its own "policing," (all within the confines of the group) and responsibility for the selection of workers rests with those "in charge" of the group, namely, the Executive Committee. The Committee hires "new" people at a definite hourly rate, and, in keeping with standard business practices, fires those who are not producing within their ability or whose

behaviour continuously reflects adversely on the overall well-being and operation of the workshop.[21]

The NELOF was governed by a board of directors made up of "Native members of the community" and members of the Mountain Institution Native Brotherhood, who maintained a controlling number of votes. It is unclear if prison administrators had any vetting process for incarcerated board members but all accounts seem to suggest that the Native Brotherhood maintained a high degree of autonomy in relation to the NELOF.[22]

The NELOF is not simply — or even primarily — a story of workers' self-management, prison entrepreneurialism or cooperative economics. The Native Brotherhood understood the NELOF to be a means to allow Indigenous prisoners to connect (or reconnect) to their Indigeneity while incarcerated at a time when Indigenous programming was rare or non-existent. A 1976 article in *Con-versely,* the Mountain Institution magazine, put it this way:

> As an entirely inmate operated commercial project, it [NELOF] is providing all involved with an ample opportunity to learn the intricacies of business, planning, production, sales, maintenance, etc. The daily problems remind all that there is nothing simple or easy about living in a white man's world. The lessons learned will serve them well when they are released to earn a living in a commercially oriented society.[23]

While other attempts have been made to provide "culturally specific" employment programming to Indigenous offenders — such as CORCAN's fur and shearling program — lack of prisoner control has rendered such efforts vulnerable to accusations of cultural exploitation.[24]

Throughout its existence the NELOF impressed administrators, observers, and prisoners alike. An announcement of the co-op's end in the pages of the Mountain Institution's *Off the Wall* magazine bemoaned its loss:

> Operated solely by Native prisoners, NELOF was unique in the CSC: it was the only truly rehabilitative project in the prison system worthy of the name. During the seven years of its existence, NELOF was home to some of the most creative and skilled Indian

artists in the country. Alas, like so much else of the heritage of our Indian brothers, NELOF has gone the way of the buffalo.[25]

The NELOF — praised by prisoners, administrators and community members alike — clearly shows the importance of prisoners' control over their labour, as well as programming more generally.

The NELOF was not the only experiment in prisoner cooperatives during this period. Others include Chandelles St. Francois Ltd., a decorative candle-making enterprise that began in the Montée St-François Institution (now part of the Federal Training Centre) in Laval, Quebec, in 1979. A 1981 report described the endeavour:

> All direct expenses incurred by inmate owners (for example, rental, transportation, supplies) are charged to the company. In addition, $5.50 per day is recovered from each owner for room and board plus $1.65 per day for canteen expenses.
>
> Demand for the candles produced by the firm is substantial. Major clients are a number of boutiques and drug stores. In addition, the company participated in a fund raising campaign on behalf of a Centre for the Mentally Retarded. A 12 day sales campaign generated $22,000 in sales and resulted in a donation of $12,000 to the centre.
>
> The entire operation is labour intensive and lucrative. Gross sales for a six month period, for example, were $63,272 while net profit realised in that period was $25,272. This amount was distributed among the participants (10) according to the number of hours worked.
>
> Inmates involved in this business venture are finding it a challenging and rewarding experience. Some have forwarded money to their families for support and all participants leave the program with substantial savings.[26]

Like the NELOF, the circumstances around the end of the Chandelles St. Francois Co-op are not well documented. The Chandelles St. Francois Co-op appears to have been dissolved in 1985.[27]

These experiments demonstrate the potential for prisoner-run businesses. However, as businesses, the co-ops were subject to many of the mundane challenges faced by start-ups and small businesses and they faced added difficulties in the form of prison bureaucracies. These issues continue to prove to be substantial barriers for successful prisoner-run businesses. The failure of a later prisoner co-op, InsideArt, provides some additional insight into these challenges.

In 1997, CSC adopted Commissioner's Directive 737, "Inmate-Operated Business Enterprises," which allowed prisoners to establish small businesses. (Some provinces, such as Alberta, also allow prisoners to establish businesses).[28] A few years later, in 2003, the Mountain Institution would host another prisoner co-op, InsideArt. InsideArt was a marketing cooperative for artists who produced paintings, wood carvings, stained glass and other artistic goods. The co-op was made up of a handful of prisoner-artists and several "outmate" staff people. InsideArt sold goods directly to the public through craft fairs and its online store (which is still viewable through the Internet Archive).[29] The organization also donated artwork to a number of charities to assist their fundraising efforts.[30] The challenges faced by InsideArt were significant and instructive for any future attempts at a prisoner-cooperative enterprise.

As mentioned, prisoner-run co-ops (and sole proprietorships) contend with all of the normal issues facing start-ups and small businesses, which are known to fail at very high rates. If they are prison based they must also deal with the restrictions and red tape imposed by the prison bureaucracy. If they are "inside-outside" organizations, as InsideArt was, they must establish functioning governance structures under these same constraints. InsideArt member Dean Roberts explained the barriers created by prison administrators:

> On all these levels [of the CSC] down to middle management, they said, "We like this concept. It's great." But when it came down to the practical level, nobody had figured how to make the thing work … They wouldn't give us regular contact. We couldn't communicate with our board of directors. We were constantly getting problems sending product to the co-op. There was no policy in place for dealing with profits for the co-op.[31]

Stacey Corriveau, a non-incarcerated community economic development manager and project coordinator for InsideArt, explained that red tape forced the co-op to adopt a "4:1 rule" in its planning. The 4:1 rule reflected the reality that everything that "needs doing in regular business takes at least four times as long in prison due to the paperwork and communication with CSC that was required."[32]

In response to these issues, InsideArt restructured itself as a "multi-stakeholder" cooperative in 2006, increasing the role of former prisoners in the organization's governance structure. This streamlined communication and decision making and allowed greater participation by "high-profile" supportive organizations.[33] A later analysis of the project noted the restructuring had the effect of granting "members who were former prisoners the role of stewards for the members who were prisoners and thus removed the centre of democratic decision-making away from its prisoner members."[34] This tension between prisoner producers and non-prisoner staff and supporters was substantial. Prisoner members expected that, after an initial period of support, the reins of the organization would be handed to them. The non-prisoners (and former prisoners) involved in the project worried that a longer period of mentorship was necessary for the co-op to be successful. As summarized by Corriveau, the cooperative principles of autonomy and independence "abutted against the push for profits, fast."[35]

Despite prisoner control being reduced, the co-op would fail to become self-sustaining. Throughout its existence InsideArt was supported by funding from the Co-operative Development Initiative, a joint program between the federal government, the Canadian Co-operative Association and the Conseil canadien de la coopération et de la mutualité. In 2007 InsideArt failed to secure additional external funding and ceased operations shortly thereafter.[36]

Some, such as McElligott, have suggested the financial pressures placed on prisoner co-ops could be reduced through tax incentives as is done in some jurisdictions, such as Italy.[37] Such incentives could be justified by the reduced costs borne by the correctional system if a co-op was successful in providing income to prisoners and reducing recidivism — not to mention the social benefits of reduced crime. Although it is not exactly clear why he believes this to be the case, McElligott also argues that co-ops could productively alter the relationships between prisoners and guards:

A major goal of democratic administration, as I understand it, is to unleash creative skills now suppressed by various forms of hierarchy. For this reason it is difficult to imagine exactly what will emerge from prisoner co-ops and how COs [correctional officers] might connect in other ways with the needs of the new organizations. Certainly their jobs, too, would be more oriented toward co-op production and the diffusion of co-op skills would affect them as well. They might eventually be drawn into the prison co-ops in some new membership category. Rather than COs, they might begin to see themselves as "reintegration specialists" or "production facilitators." In any case, simply being in close proximity to the developing co-ops would be an education, a training opportunity, in itself. Ideally, former COs and prisoners would begin to work out new ways of relating to one another and to the broader public that relied much less on hierarchy and coercion.[38]

While it would be nice if this were the case, it is not clear why guards, who routinely resist reforms that undermine their authority and job security, would support this dramatic change in the operations and administration of corrections.

There are other issues besides the financial risks associated with prisoner entrepreneurialism and potential guard opposition to prisoner cooperatives. Indeed, we believe many of the left-wing critiques of workers' cooperatives apply to prisoner co-ops.[39] We don't wish to overstate this point, given the miserable situation that incarcerated workers find themselves in. However, it's valuable to consider how, despite their potential to create "less alienating and less exploitative workplaces,"[40] co-ops are still subject to competition and market pressures. So, despite being worker owned it is possible that, at times, what is best for the business is not necessarily what is best for the workers.

PRODUCTION FOR PUBLIC GOOD

In his proposal for Canadian prisoner co-ops, Greg McElligott emphasizes the need for prison production to be oriented toward "socially useful goods and services that are not currently being provided by anyone else." This is important to avoid the criticisms of unfair competition from labour and capital that resulted in the establishment of the state-use system. Elaborating on the point, McElligott argues prisoners' co-ops could play a role in "production of new green technologies, as these are encouraged among fair trade producers, and might be subsidized by friendly governments." Ultimately, for McElligott, "the struggle for a more democratic economy might be linked here to the struggle for a greener one as well."[41] In this assertion, McElligott points to the truly radical potential of prisoners' co-ops. Understood this way, co-ops could not only radically alter corrections; they could also play an important role in a broader shift to a lower carbon and more just economy for workers.

The notion that prison labour should deployed based on an understanding of social utility rather than maximum cost recuperation have long been held by prisoners themselves. At times administrators have also held such a view, and it is no surprise that programs resulting in meaningful contributions to society have been popular. A 1983 *Globe and Mail* profile of the children's toy workshop in the Ontario Correctional Institute, a provincial jail in Brampton, Ontario, provides a clear example. In the lead up to Christmas, prisoners in the Ontario Correctional Institute, with the support of others from the Vanier Centre for Women in Milton, produced trucks, rocking horses and other toys. Once finished, the toys were distributed to children by the Salvation Army and the Hospital for Sick Children. Participants in the program were required to also participate in treatment programs and perform institutional maintenance work, such as laundry and grounds work. In addition to developing soft skills and learning some carpentry basics, participants clearly appreciated the "helping others" aspect of the work.[42] As one participant interviewed in the profile stated, "I love making the toys. Besides reminding me of my kids — I love making things for kids — I know the needy kids need these toys so badly." Another notes, "For once in my life I'm really enjoying something."[43]

While considerations of social utility can make prison labour more meaningful for workers, the utilization of prison labour for the "public good" has also been used to justify low wages, terrible conditions and outright abuse. Chain gangs of prisoners digging ditches or building roads can be said to be the good for public; however, appeals to the public good are insufficient to justify the drudgery, humiliation and exploitation evident in such arrangements. Similarly, CORCAN partnerships with charities such as Habitat for Humanity, Parks Canada or Frist Nations' housing development initiatives may be more desirable than ones with for-profit corporations, but they should not justify sub-minimum wages and the exclusions of CORCAN workers from labour, employment standards and occupational health and safety laws.

As can been seen in unionization campaigns in social services and the charitable sectors, participating in socially useful work does not lessen the desire of workers to have voice in the workplace. There is nothing democratic about existing prison labour programs, and prisoners do not have any say in what they produce and how they do it. Co-ops, as dis-cussed by McElligott, would provide workers with a considerable say in their work. The unionization of prison labour would be another way to give incarcerated workers a stronger voice.

It should be acknowledged that prisoner co-ops are not incompatible with prisoners' unions. If a prisoners' union could be organized, that un-ion could choose to pursue self-managed prison industries or workers' co-ops. Prisoners currently working do so as workers in capitalist em-ployment relationships, even if this is obscured by the language of reha-bilitation. A prisoners' union would provide the organizational basis for prisoners to exercise power to support a variety of demands, including broader goals of prisoners and the prison justice movement.

THE NEED FOR PRISONERS' UNIONS

While there is a long history of efforts to establish representative bod-ies of prisoners, the idea that prisoners should be organized into trade unions was only put into practice in the 1960s and 1970s.[44] There are several reasons for this.

The growth of public sector unionism and public sector labour mili-tancy — including labour activism by guards — served as an impor-tant source of inspiration for prisoners.[45] The 1970s also represented a high point of the prison reform movement, which included a radical wing with substantial influence.[46] In the aftermath of the Attica pris-on rebellion in 1971, in which thirty-two prisoners and eleven guards were killed, prison organizers increasingly looked for methods capable of winning gains without triggering the level of state violence that fol-lowed riots and hostage-takings. As a result, prisoner union organizing efforts spread across the United States.[47] Campaigns were also taken up in the UK and Canada.[48] Prisoners' labour unions were also appealing for prisoners who saw themselves as part of a broader working class. By asserting economic rights, prisoners attempted to utilize the legal labour relations system to limit the control of administrators. At their most basic, demands to form and join unions came into direct conflict with administrative control over the right of prisoners to associate.[49]

Organizations that have been called "prisoners' unions" take several distinct forms. Some, such as the California Prisoners' Union, were political unions — essentially prisoners' rights organizations — that attempted to negotiate with prison administrators. These are distinct from prisoners' labour unions, such as the North Carolina Prisoners' Labor Union or the Ohio Prisoners' Labor Union, which conceived of themselves as representing prisoners as workers vis-a-vis their employer (who was most often also their jailer).[50] Obviously, there is considerable overlap between these categories. Political unions might take up issues of prison labour. Similarly, trade unions, including prisoners' trade unions, might raise issues that go beyond the immediate issues in a given workplace.

Prisoners' unions can also be categorized in other ways. Some are "inside-based" — made up entirely (or at least primarily) of currently incarcerated people — such as the Canadian Prisoners' Labour Confederation.[51] Others, such as the Canadian Prisoners' Union Committee were "outside-based" and run by lawyers, staff and volunteers who may or may not have ever been imprisoned.[52]

Prisoners' unions have also differed considerably in their ideology, strategic approaches and tactical repertoires. Some, such as the Industrial Workers of the World's Incarcerated Workers Organizing Committee, conceive of themselves as revolutionary anti-capitalist organizations; however, most have espoused a more traditional "bread and butter" conception of trade unionism.[53] This sometimes meant tension between prisoners' unions that conceived of prisoners as workers who were more or less exploited in the same ways as other workers, and prison activists who saw the prison as an extension of slavery and prisoners as "slaves" — conceptions with different racial and political implications. That said, it should be noted that many prisoner labour unions in the United States have been majority Black and/or Black led.[54]

For a period in the early 1970s, prisoner union organizing was relatively widespread in the United States. One study found that by 1973, prisoners in at least forty-four institutions in twenty different states had formed or attempted to form a union.[55] In Washington, Massachusetts and Maine, prisoners' political unions were able to win some level of recognition from authorities. This recognition was not without pushback. In 1976, the California Prison Guards' Union threatened a mass wildcat strike if the state followed through on implementing a tentative agreement reached with the California Prisoners Union, effectively stymieing prisoners' organizing efforts there.[56]

Notable prisoners' labour unions formed in New York, Ohio and North Carolina. Some won support from organized labour. In the case of New York, prisoners at the Green Haven Correctional Facility won the backing of District 65, an affiliate of the Distributive Workers of America.[57] The North Carolina Prisoners' Labor Union (NCPLU) received backing from the state-level AFL-CIO; however, none of these unions would succeed in winning formal certification or negotiating a collective agreement.[58] In 1977 the United States Supreme Court ruled against the NCPLU, declaring prisoners did not have a constitutional right to join or form unions. While some prisoners' unions attempted to organize after this ruling, 1977 marks the end of the main period of prisoner union organizing in the United States.[59]

Prisoner union efforts also occurred in Canada. A wave of prison strikes in the summer of 1975 led to the formation of an organization called the Prisoners' Union Committee (PUC). The PUC was an outside-based organization, largely made up of lawyers and activists who had cut their teeth in the student, anti-war and women's movements. While "outside-based," the PUC did have strong connections to prisoner activists and organizers. By July 1975 over three hundred prisoners in BC had signed a petition demanding the provincial and federal prison systems recognize the PUC as their bargaining agent. Striking prisoners in Ontario prisons made similar demands, and PUC organizers reported to media that they were also in contact with prisoners in the Prairies and New Brunswick.[60] By the end of the summer of 1975, prison protest tactics shifted, and a number of large riots marked the end of the strike wave and the PUC's organizing efforts.

The PUC, however, would not be the last prisoner union effort in Canada. In 1977, prisoners working in the abattoir at GCC, a provincial jail in Ontario, would be successful in establishing a local of the Canadian Food and Allied Workers Union and negotiating a series of collective agreements with their employer, the private firm contracted to run the abattoir. Later, between 2010 and 2015, a group of prisoners would unsuccessfully attempt to form a union for prisoners in the federal prison system, the CPLC. These cases are examined in more detail in the next chapter.

———

We have outlined some proposals to reform prison labour: abolition of prison labour, privatization and the development of prisoner worker co-ops. These examples emphasize the need for unionizing prisoner workers, and some past examples demonstrate their potential. While prisoner union campaigns have, for the most part, achieved only limited successes, the efforts described above show how prisoners have understood unionization to be a potent means to protect and advance their interests. In the next chapter, we make the legal and strategic case for prisoner labour unions.

6

THE CASE FOR PRISONERS' LABOUR UNIONS

History demonstrates that prisoners' unions are possible. As we've already mentioned, provincial prisoners at GCC were able to successfully certify a union in the late 1970s. The situation of the incarcerated workers at GCC, however, was unique in many ways. Prisoners worked for a private employer, the Guelph Beef Centre, who operated the jail abattoir under a new and experimental program. They also unionized at a time when the labour movement was much more powerful than it is today. Still, the precedent set by the prisoners in Guelph is critically important.

Apart from the Guelph case, prisoners have faced a legal system that has denied they are employees. Most recently, prisoners have been placed into a legal limbo by federal labour boards in 2013 and 2015, which held that prisoners did not have jurisdiction when faced with applications for union certification.[1] This means prisoners are not legally viewed as employees and have been effectively relegated to the status of "participants" in rehabilitation programs. However, recent cases at the SCC regarding the right to collective bargaining, and breakthroughs in the fight against employee misclassification by gig economy workers, may be turning the tide. The law and labour movements may be reorienting in a way that could put prisoners in a better position for successful unionization.

The political stakes are high for the unionization of prisoner workers. Prisoners are disproportionately Indigenous and Black, often suffer from mental health conditions and disproportionately come from poor backgrounds. As such, the unionization of prisoner workers is the unionization of workers who are severely marginalized by society. The particularly disadvantaged position of prisoner workers compared with their employers places them in a category of coerced, captive and vulnerable labourers, for whom unionization is particularly urgent.

PRISONERS' UNIONS CAN EXIST; ONE ALREADY HAS

As we discussed in Chapter 4, the 1970s was a time of significant upheaval in Canadian prisons. As summarized by the *MacGuigan Report*, "Seven years of comparative peace in the Canadian Penitentiary System ended in 1970 with a series of upheavals (riots, strikes, murders and hostage-takings) that grew in numbers and size with each passing year."[2] This prisoner agitation — both the spectacularly violent and the more mundane — motivated reports and talk of reform.

Although hostage-takings and riots captured much of the popular imagination of the 1970s — for good reason given the blood spilled at Attica and other places — other forms of prisoner activism also proliferated. Prisoners' labour unions were one such form. The idea is relatively simple. If prison labour was and is necessary for prison systems to function, withholding that labour in an organized manner would give prisoners the ability to pressure administrators and government to concede demands. Prisoner labour organizers have also viewed the legal employment and labour regime as a potential means to limit the unilateral power of administrators. Prisoners have demanded the rights to join and form unions, to collectively bargain and to limit the ability of employers to act unilaterally. Just as labour law has limited the discretion of employers, prisoners have argued it could also be used to limit the discretion of guards and administrators.

The strength of organized labour in the 1970s also helps explain why prisoner labour unions became so appealing to prisoners not just in the United States, but also the UK and Canada. In Canada, union density climbed through the 1970s before peaking in 1981.[3] But not only was the labour movement of the 1970s larger, it was also considerably more militant. As Linda Briskin has demonstrated, the frequency of strikes reached their peak in the period between 1974 and 1981. Between 1960 and 1979, the number of workdays lost to strikes increased dramatically, from 32,799 for the period of 1960–64 to 139,688 for the period of 1974–79. The number of workers who participated in strikes also rose significantly over the course of the 1970s.[4]

The growth of public sector unionism over the 1960s and 1970s is also significant. The passing of the Public Service Staff Relations Act ushered in a frenzy of public sector worker organizing, including by prison guards. Prison guard unions quickly established themselves as both militant and politically significant.[5] The flexing of guard union muscle made a considerable impact on prisoners concerned with improving their own situations.[6]

In 1977, prisoner workers at GCC working for a privately managed abattoir located on prison grounds shook the foundations of power relations at their institution. Alongside non-incarcerated coworkers, prisoner abattoir workers unionized to form Canadian Food and Allied Workers Union Local 240, establishing the first certified union of incarcerated workers in Canadian history. Although the union local only lasted approximately a decade, it was of enormous importance. The unionization came about through the right political and administrative pieces falling into place, along with a receptive labour movement.

In 1969, the Ontario Ministry of Correctional Services initiated a program to allow temporary absences for prisoners to work outside of provincial jails. Following the success of the Temporary Absence Program, in 1974 the Ministry established Outside Managed Industrial Programs (OMIP). OMIP saw private firms operate within provincial correctional institutions, employing prisoners as workers. These programs were not instituted out of respect for prisoners' rights, but more so for the correctional bosses to offset costs of incarceration by having private entities pay prisoner wages, as well as enabling institutions to charge for room and board. They were also very much in keeping with the long-standing idea of prison administrators that if prisoners engaged in work, they were less likely to reoffend.[7] The OMIP initiative was also motivated by the government's interest in expanding prison industries as a means to recoup costs. The private management of the abattoir at GCC was the pilot project of this program. Other OMIPs would later be established related to catering and food services, automotive parts and electric wheelchair production, and more. By 1981, seventy-five provincial prisoners in Ontario were employed by Outside Managed Industrial Programs.[8]

Organized labour's approach to the possibility of prisoners working in outside industries was initially lukewarm. Ontario Federation of Labour Secretary-Treasurer Terry Meagher described the abattoir program as "a worthwhile undertaking," but Meagher, along with other labour leaders who were consulted by the Ministry of Correctional Services, raised concerns about the program undercutting industry wages and the possibility of prisoners being used as scab labour if there was a strike of outside workers.[9] These concerns were at least temporarily alleviated with the unionization of the OMIP at GCC.

After collecting union authorization cards, the Canadian Food and Allied Workers had to take up a considerable fight to win labour board certification. The employer, the Guelph Beef Centre, argued, "the control exercised over them [the prisoners] by the institution deprived them [the prisoners] of a normal employee-employer relationship." The Ministry of Correctional Services neither officially supported nor opposed the certification but raised concerns about prisoners having access to a normal labour grievance process, which could undermine correctional authority.[10]

In their ruling, the Ontario Labour Relations Board decided that prisoners working for the Guelph abattoir were "employees" working in similar conditions to their non-imprisoned counterparts. They also ruled that despite the "rehabilitative" character of their work, prisoners performed an essential service for the company that would otherwise have to be sought elsewhere. Finally, they held that prisoners, if not included in the bargaining unit along with their non-incarcerated coworkers, would be likely to be used by the company as scabs in the event of a strike. This was determined to be a labour relations problem best avoided.[11] For these reasons the union, CFAW Union Local 240, was certified.

The union was able to win some important gains for the GCC abattoir workers, both incarcerated and non-incarcerated — but prisoner workers, who made up the majority of the bargaining unit, undoubtably benefitted the most. Pay differentials between incarcerated and non-incarcerated workers were eliminated in the unions' first collective bargaining agreement. Most significantly, unionized prisoners "gained freedom of movement to attend union meetings and increased freedom of association to join the union and hold union office, and, critically, they won the ability to (potentially) keep their jobs upon release."[12] This is a fundamental point worth reiterating: through unionization, prisoner workers can achieve the power to transform their conditions beyond what they could achieve through other means. The Guelph example is a mere snapshot of what could be possible on a larger scale.

A STEP BACK: THE CPLC VS. THE FEDERAL LABOUR BOARDS

The victory at Guelph did not result in the mass unionization of Canadian prisoners — although several other organizing efforts have occurred since. Of these, the campaign by the CPLC, which went public in 2011, is worth examining in detail.

The CPLC was founded by David Jolivet and several other prisoner workers in Kent Institution, a federal penitentiary in Agassiz, British Columbia. On October 18, 2011, Jolivet requested permission to access offenders in other cell blocks to sign cards in support of the CPLC's certification drive. Ten days later, the warden denied the request, saying that the CPLC was not an organization recognized by the CSC. Jolivet complained that denying his request was an "unfair labour practice" under the Public Sector Labour Relations Act (PSLRA).[13] The case was heard through the Public Service Labour Relations Board (PSLRAB). The two issues were: (1) whether the prisoner workers were unjustly excluded from "employee" status due to the rehabilitative aspect of their program and, (2) whether they were excluded from collective bargaining rights due to a lack of employee status in the federal public service. The ruling stated:

> I do not have sufficient evidence to determine that offenders in federal penitentiaries who participate in employment programs are employed. However, even if they are considered employed in the common law sense of the word, I cannot find that they are employees within the meaning of subsection 2(1) of the PSLRA … it is clear that to be employed in the public service, a person must have been appointed by the [Public Service Commission] to positions created by the Treasury Board.[14]

The creation of public service jobs, according to the PSLRAB, required a specific two-step process, with no exception, where the federal government's Treasury Board officially creates jobs and the Public Service Commission then appoints candidates. In saying this, the board was asserting they had no jurisdiction to decide whether there was an employment relationship.

However, the decision on whether there *could have been* an employment relationship was more nuanced. While the ruling at the PSLRAB rejected employee status for Jolivet and his coworkers on the jurisdiction issue, the board appeared to leave the door open to a future case for prisoner workers as employees by suggesting rehabilitation could coexist with an employment relationship. The board put considerable emphasis on the significance of the Guelph abattoir certification decision, noting that despite the rehabilitative character of their work, the prisoners at the abattoir were "integral" to the commercial operation and failure to include them along with their non-prisoner coworkers would have undermined the union's ability to represent the non-incarcerated employees thus creating conditions ripe for scabbing.[15] Ultimately the board found:

> Evidence of the nature and purpose of the work, the working conditions, and the work's integration into the employer's operations, among other factors, would be critical to such a determination. In this case, I do not believe that I have sufficient evidence that would allow such a determination to be made. For example, I have no real evidence of the nature of the work performed by offenders in federal institutions or the integration of that work into the respondent's operations.[16]

Essentially, the ruling on whether there could have been an employment relationship — in spite of the jurisdiction issue — suggested possible success if sufficient evidence had been presented. The CPLC appealed the decision to the Federal Court of Appeal, but was again denied.[17] The appeal court decision affirmed the ruling of the PSLRAB: "prisoners participating in work programs organized by the Correctional Service of Canada have not been appointed to a position in the federal public service. As a result, they are not 'employees' within the meaning of the Act."[18]

After Jolivet was unsuccessful with the PSLRAB, the CPLC took their fight to the Canadian Industrial Relations Board (CIRB), the labour board for the federal private sector. The facts of this case were the same: prisoners were denied access to sign up coworkers from other cell blocks, and they made an unfair labour practice complaint.[19] This time around, the CPLC focused specifically on CORCAN prisoner workers. They asserted that CORCAN is a Crown corporation, so this made the prisoner workers employees under the Canada Labour Code.[20] The CIRB would have none of this argument:

at best, any potential employment relationship the prisoners might have with Treasury Board, Correctional Service Canada or with its agency CORCAN, would necessarily constitute employment by her Majesty in right of Canada such that the Board is without jurisdiction to entertain the complaint further.[21]

The CIRB went on to say that CORCAN is not a Crown corporation because it was not created as one.[22] In stating this, the CIRB basically threw prisoner workers — like a hot potato — back to the public service for *potential* employee status in a future case, on the grounds that the CIRB had no jurisdiction to deal with them.

The subject of employee status would come up again at the 2018 federal court case of *Guerin v. The Attorney General of Canada*.[23] In this case, federal prisoners were challenging the 30% wage cuts to federal prisoners that were instituted in 2013. Prisoners argued CORCAN workers were either part of a federal "work, undertaking or business" under the Canada Labour Code or they should be considered employees under the common law.[24] The judge rejected the argument that prisoners working in CORCAN were covered by the code, saying CORCAN was part of a federal department, not a federal business. He then added that prisoners could not be employees under the public service in any case, citing Jolivet's case at the Federal Court of Appeal.[25] Yet again, prisoner workers were rendered non-existent under federal law.

The decision further picked away at prisoner employee status, repeating the refrain that prisoners are in rehabilitation program for their own benefit, rather than in an employment relationship.[26] It added that employee status cannot be created under the common law for federal workers if they did not exist under any federal legislation, placing them in complete limbo.[27] Section 78 of the Corrections and Conditional Release Act (CCRA) was also applied:

78 (1) For the purpose of

(a) encouraging offenders to participate in programs provided by the Service, or

(b) providing financial assistance to offenders to facilitate their reintegration into the community, the Commissioner may authorize payments to offenders at rates approved by the Treasury Board.

In the judge's opinion, this section is *only* about payment for participation in programs, *not* payment for work:

I do not see how payment as encouragement to participate in programs, including some that are not in any way associated with institutional work or work for CORCAN, could transform into remuneration for the work done, as the applicants argue but have not demonstrated. In the penitentiary, work can take on the character of a privilege.[28]

He said the only way around this barrier is to render section 78 of the CCRA unconstitutional, which he noted the prisoners did not argue.[29] This could be an avenue to attack in a future case, but it would be useless without also having a tribunal or court with jurisdiction to hear the argument.

The Guérin case came to the Federal Court of Appeal (FCA) in 2019,[30] which upheld the federal court ruling. However, along the way the appeal court noted that the correct way for an employee to complain about the pay cuts would have been through filing a complaint with an inspector under the Canada Labour Code.[31] This is contradictory because by the FCA's own reasoning, prisoners do not fall under the code. The FCA justices also added that the prisoners made a fundamental error by failing to state in which federal business they were a part when they claimed employment under the code.[32]

Between the two *Jolivet* decisions and the *Guérin* decision, prisoners have been left in utter limbo. They have been rendered mere participants in a rehabilitation program, rather than employees. Collectively, these rulings have resulted in a legal paradox where prisoners who work do not have jurisdiction under any federal labour board but have been told what they should have done to make their case.

The unending barriers federal prisoners have faced in their efforts to unionize or even be covered by minimum employment standards are the result of an ideology that refuses to accept prisoner workers as employees. Prisons in Canada exist within a capitalist social order. Capitalism requires control and discipline of the most vulnerable working class and unemployed people, which necessitates prisons. Prisons are filled with predominantly poor and racialized people, a holding pen for an otherwise volatile pool of surplus labour that may be more apt to resist the social order if left free.[33] Prisons also act as a reminder — and a threat — to working-class and unemployed people to not deviate from the social order. As we will cover, while the political pressure to keep prisoners down is high, prisoners can still win employee status and the right to unionize if the right conditions are in place and arguments are made by asserting rights under the *Canadian Charter of Rights and Freedoms* as well as international law. Before moving on to the case for prisoner worker unionization, it is important to return to the subject of rehabilitation, to detail the content of this legal barrier to be overcome.

THE REHABILITATION BARRIER

The Corrections and Conditional Release Act (CCRA) lays out the purpose of the correctional system in section 3, including rehabilitation:

> The purpose of the federal correctional system is to contribute to the maintenance of a just, peaceful and safe society by
>
> (a) carrying out sentences imposed by courts through the safe and humane custody and supervision of offenders; and
>
> (b) assisting the rehabilitation of offenders and their reintegration into the community as law-abiding citizens through the provision of programs in penitentiaries and in the community.

For something so central to corrections, no definition of rehabilitation appears *anywhere* in the CCRA or the Corrections and Conditional Release Regulations (CCRR). Commissioner's Directive 726, "Correctional Programs," which incorporates all rehabilitation programming, does not define rehabilitation either. The CSC considers prisoners' jobs to be part of "programming" — another buzzword for rehabilitation. It states the purpose of the programming is "to ensure offenders receive the most effective correctional programs at the appropriate time in their sentences to promote their rehabilitation and to prepare them for reintegration into the community."[34] CORCAN refers to rehabilitation on their website, stating:

> CORCAN is a key rehabilitation program of the Correctional Service of Canada (CSC). It contributes to safe communities by providing offenders with employment and employability skills training while incarcerated in federal penitentiaries, and for brief periods of time, after they are released into the community.[35]

However, CORCAN is careful to ensure they call the work, "employment and employability skills training," rather than actual employment. It is very similar to how many employees are wrongly classified as independent contractors so employers can justify escaping minimum employment standards. But gig workers and other misclassified employees have begun to win victories against this label, including Foodora (now defunct) food delivery workers.[36]

CSC has also been careful in their framing of pay for prisoners. The CCRA tries to explain prisoner pay as some form of reward for participation or social assistance to support prisoners for their eventual release rather than wages. However, the payments are nowhere near sufficient to support prisoners for release. As we addressed earlier, the highest wage possible for prisoner workers is $6.90 per day minus deductions. Considering the whole point of the pay, according to CSC, is to set a prisoner up to be a contributing member in society upon release, denying funds for self-development is a problem. Low pay doesn't just mean less money for a person to get back on their feet. It also means postsecondary education, something with the potential to dramatically improve a person's employability, is out of reach for many prisoners. As put by Correctional Investigator Ivan Zinger in his 2019–20 report, in addition to lack of internet access and few opportunities for paper-based correspondence courses,

> Offenders must fund their own post-secondary education which is difficult given the challenges associated with applying for government grants, only a very few bursaries are available through universities/colleges, inmate pay has not changed in over thirty years and deductions have increased leaving very little for postsecondary education. It is clear that pursuing anything beyond high school behind bars is challenging. There are only a handful of individuals in any one institution pursuing post-secondary education and often with limited to no assistance from CSC.[37]

As Zinger stated, inmate pay rates have not increased in over thirty years, compromising the ability to afford post-secondary education. In fact, the overall "take home" pay has decreased due to inflation and the 2013 implementation of deductions designed to offset the costs of imprisonment. As we detailed in Chapter 2, these wage cuts, which amounted to a 30% reduction in pay, led to nationwide prisoner strikes in 2013. According to law, rehabilitation and reintegration are fundamental purposes of the correctional system; rehabilitation is supposed to be a step toward reintegration. However, neither are theoretically possible without sufficient pay to survive on the outside.

CORCAN jobs, theoretically designed to set prisoners up for employment upon release, form the basis of the Employment and Employability Program (EEP) of CSC. The stated purpose of the EEP is "To provide the framework for offender opportunities to develop employability skills and acquire employment experience in preparation for reintegration into society."[38] Additionally, CSC has to "ensure that a range of programs, employment and vocational opportunities addressing the identified needs of offenders is available." According to these policies, the EEP is *supposed to be* for the benefit of prisoners.

The EEP has been strongly criticized for being dysfunctional. In his 2019–20 report, Correctional Investigator Ivan Zinger stated the EEP "does not fully support the acquisition of marketable skills [and...] does not adequately address the need to ensure that prison employment opportunities match current labour market trends." He added, "CORCAN needs to update, adapt and change to meet the demands of today's job market." And the "policy and strategy, taken together, essentially maintain status quo rather than advance employment skills."[39]

The previous Correctional Investigator, Howard Sapers, noted in his 2013–14 report, "A policy specific to employment and employability has yet to be developed." In other words, there was no clear direction for the EEP and no clear accountability in setting prisoners up for release and entry into a viable job market. Sapers found the EEP to be falling short of its stated purpose as of his 2014–15 annual report, where he recommended CSC focus on training through in-demand areas, Red Seal trades, apprenticeships and information technologies.[40]

In February 2021, a lifer at the federal Bath Institution in Ontario, Ghassan Salah, put together a list of problems with the EEP. Salah's criticisms of the EEP, which requires that employment programming be assigned to prisoners regardless of need, include inadequate pay and the absence of meaningful career counselling available for federal prisoners. Most of the jobs assigned to prisoners "do not provide any marketable and transferable job skills, are not useful to the current job market demand and are not readily linked to formal employment." Relatedly, the "EEP program does not provide a path to employment through certified vocational training programs or through formal post-secondary education. On the rare occasions when vocational programs are available, they do not reflect the current job market or demand." Finally, prisoners are forced to fend for themselves upon release: "The CSC fails to help prisoners released into the community who are still under CSC jurisdiction to find training or employment. In fact, the CSC places the onus on incarcerated prisoners to present valid employment opportunities as part of their release plan before being supported for parole."[41] Given all of this, Salah proposes:

> Since the CSC is very adamant that employment for prisoners in federal correctional institutions is a program and not employment, then the CSC must be held accountable to all its commitment and obligations beginning with the fact that the EEP must provide marketable job skills and be relevant to the current job market. *This means that every institutional position for prisoners should lead to some form of formal training and certification by an accredited institution to be useful for the prisoner and be readily linked to formal employment. This also means that any work in the institution that does not have any employment and employability enhancing value should not be a part of the EEP and should be offered as general employment for minimum wage pay.*[42]

In summary, based on the observations of the current and former correctional investigators and prisoners themselves, the EEP is not serving the so-called training and reintegration purpose that CSC sets out. We can speculate about any number of possible reasons for the disconnect.

For one, CSC's own research tends to show prisoners are actually getting employment in areas related to their "training" upon release.[43] As put by Irene Klassen, director of the EEP in the early 2000s:

> Over 1,000 offenders have been employed each year, with the number growing from 1,036 in 2001–02 to 1,194 in 2002–03

and by year end 2003–04 1,193 male offenders and 70 women offenders found employment using these services in the areas of construction, general labour, hospitality, janitorial services, manufacturing, call centres and food and beverage services. In the simplest of terms, the EEP equals job readiness.[44]

Leaving aside the marginal increase in employment over the period discussed, this assertion stands in stark contrast to the findings of the Office of the Correctional Investigator and research commissioned by the CSC itself. A 2014 assessment of CORCAN outcomes found "There was no overall association between CORCAN participation and direct reductions in recidivism."[45] While the study did find a small improvement in successfully obtaining work for men who had worked for CORCAN, women who participated in CORCAN were no more likely to find work upon release than those who didn't.

CSC's analysis also leaves out who is and isn't getting CORCAN jobs. For reasons we discussed in Chapter 2, the prisoners who get the jobs are those already most likely to find employment upon release because the process self-selects for success rather than assisting those with the greatest challenges. While CORCAN stresses that it trains prisoners with identified needs related to employment, its own 2013–14 annual report states only 10% of the prisoners who worked for CORCAN that year had a "high" level of employment needs.[46]

To reiterate, there are significant racial factors at play. As former federal prisoner Rick Sauvé stated at the 2021 Canadian Association of Labour Lawyers conference that many Black and Indigenous prisoners cannot get the better jobs, or sometimes any jobs, because they are defined as being part of a "security threat group."[47] If prisoners are considered higher security threats, they will not be eligible for many programs, including higher-level jobs most likely to help them get employment on the outside. Sauvé, who has assisted hundreds of prisoners with parole hearings and programming over the years, relayed the story of an Indigenous prisoner he worked with who could not get any employment on the inside. He described another person who went in during his teenage years and was still in prison in his fifties. This person could not get sufficient programming or employment in prison, so when he got out, he was unable to get established. Not surprisingly, he ended up back in prison. The racialization in the distribution of prison work opportunities and of "successful outcomes" upon release is a big reason why any numbers released by CSC about the results of EEP need to be closely scrutinized.

It is possible that some proponents of EEP think the point of the jobs is for CSC to instill labour discipline rather than labour skills, such as enforcing a nine-to-five schedule and conforming to the will of an employer. Such sentiments are clear in the amount of stress CSC puts on the development of "soft skills." For example, a 2014 article published by CSC that profiled a reintegration training program aimed at helping federal prisoners find work in the resource extraction sector emphasizes "the program addresses areas such as self-management, life skills, basic computer skills and career preparation."[48] Profiles of CORCAN success stories routinely emphasize the how prisoners successfully developed good habits and attitudes. As one such profile states: "He is a very good worker and a fast learner. He is resourceful, respectful and shows initiative. He is becoming more and more social and very respectful."[49]

With this thinking, the actual outcomes for prisoners — whether they are actually getting jobs in fields for which they were trained — is irrelevant. In this sense, the work has a punitive aspect, where prisoners only get what they deserve, rather than what they need. Finally, a more cynical view is that CSC is fully aware the programs do not function as rehabilitative, but they are useful for CSC: they produce things of value that CSC can sell, that keep the institutions running and that keep prisoners busy.

Institutional labour makes up over 80% of all prisoner labour, but is not geared for outside employability. But these low-level jobs are still considered rehabilitative by default, since CSC claims *all* work done by prisoners is part of programming, not employment. As pointed out by Salah previously, how is it justified that prisoners doing this kind of work are not at least paid minimum wage, considering the jobs do not have any real impact on employability upon release but are instead benefiting the institution?

Salah, in the letter mentioned previously, also brought up concerns over labour being coerced, because failing to participate affects the prospects for a prisoner to be released:

> Refusal to participate in work assignments is usually reflected
> on prisoners pay levels, [Security Reclassification Scale] score,

correctional plan completeness and compliance and prisoners' motivation levels. Refusing to participate in employment also affects the three categories prisoners are rated on for institutional placement, transfers to lower security, temporary absences and parole. In some institutions it can affect which living units prisoners can apply to live in. In effect, prisoners are required to work for years on end (sometimes over 25 years) for no apparent benefit to themselves. Speaking for myself, none of the employment positions I have worked in provided any transferable skills or were relevant to the current job market.[50]

The EEP has not been found to support rehabilitation, and if the work is not being done voluntarily, there is no basis to suggest that those released are in any way prepared for the job market, as a free worker, upon release.

As for work done by prisoners in provincial institutions, there is an even more extreme disparity. As noted in Chapter 2, provincial prisoners are not paid for their work but may be offered incentives such as canteen credits. While all the work done is portrayed as rehabilitative, there is no basis for how the work accomplishes this objective. As we described in Chapter 2, provincial prisoners perform work including: making licence plates, preparing food, performing laundry services, cleaning up provincial parks, doing small construction jobs for non-profit organizations and helping firefighters combat forest fires. They do this work for, at best, very minimal pay and often for canteen credits or no compensation at all.

Failure to participate in work in provincial jails could result in not being released at the statutory release date of two-thirds of a sentence on account of bad behaviour. It is hardly a choice if the consequences of not doing so include longer incarceration. Labour has to be voluntarily given, without punishment for refusal, for the labour to not be coerced and to have any semblance of being rehabilitative.[51]

OVERCOMING THE BARRIERS TO UNIONIZATION

Two barriers must be overcome for prisoner workers to unionize: first, the exclusion of an employment relationship due to prisoners' work being seen as *rehabilitation rather than employment*, and second, the *exclusion of prisoner workers from employee status* under federal and provincial legislation.

Rehabilitation has been used as a barrier by correctional administrators, governments, courts and tribunals to justify excluding prisoners from employee status. We argue it is both possible and necessary to overcome this barrier. As we will explain, the work of prisoners is essential for the functioning of prisons, necessitating that prisoners are employees. It is necessary for prisoners to be seen as employees, with the same legal protections of their non-incarcerated counterparts, because they are among many other precarious and vulnerable workers for whom legal protections are crucial to avoid extreme exploitation. Other workers in vulnerable positions include gig economy workers, migrant workers, sex workers and many others who are on the margins of society when it comes to protection of their rights. The labour movement's validity among the most vulnerable workers will depend on whether the most vulnerable workers are included in union organizing campaigns moving forward.

There is Canadian legal precedent for including workers in a prison rehabilitation program as employees: the case of the Guelph abattoir workers. While the political context of that case has been discussed, the legal issues are important to understand as well, to see a way forward in a future case of prisoner worker unionization. The employment relationship was part of a licence agreement between GCC and the company Guelph Beef Centre, with the point on rehabilitation as follows, "The parties hereto recognize that the operation of the Abattoir forms an essential part of the Licensor's prisoner rehabilitation."[52] In its decision, the board rejected attempts by the provincial government to exclude the prisoner workers from employee status based on the rehabilitative aspect of their work:

> There can be no doubt that the rehabilitative aspect of the work, which the prisoners perform while under the control and direction of the respondent, is the primary value of the license agreement from the Ministry's point of view. But from the point of view of the respondent, which is the alleged employer, the services provided by the prisoners are an integral and significant part of its meat-packing operation.[53]

Clearly, if the services are "integral and significant" to the employer's operation, the prisoners had to be employees.

In cases where a rehabilitative work program exists, facts that support an employment relationship (including control by the employer, payment of wages, the authority to hire and fire and the authority to discipline) of the work needs to be balanced against facts that support a rehabilitative program (including training, education and self-development). In *Fenton v. British Columbia* (1991) (*Fenton 1991*), patients of the Forensic Psychiatric Institute participated in a rehabilitative work program.[54] The case was about whether Forensic Psychiatric Institute inmates in British Columbia were entitled to the statutory minimum wage, which required they had to be employees, not just beneficiaries of a rehabilitation program. Psychiatric Institute inmates are in a very similar situation to prisoner workers. *Fenton 1991* held that the "real economic benefit" test was required to determine if an employment relationship exists despite a rehabilitative character of the work:

> Many programs, undeniably of significant therapeutic purpose and effect, might provide some incidental economic benefit to the institution. Indeed provision of some economic benefit is difficult to avoid. The test should be whether there is real economic benefit flowing to the institution from the work programs…. [Whether] the programs are presently carried on at cost and yield no real economic benefit.[55]

The workers in the *Fenton 1991* case did not succeed in gaining employee status; however, the case remains important because it created the legal test for whether there is an employment relationship between an institution and the participants in a rehabilitation program run by the institution, called the "real economic benefit" test. Before addressing this issue, it is important to note that workers with disabilities have long suffered the same form of superexploitation as prisoners, dating back to asylum workers in the nineteenth century working for nothing.[56] The workers in the *Fenton 1991* case were working within "sheltered workshops." These are segregated workplaces, often presented as "training programs," where workers with disabilities work for less than minimum wage because the work is supposedly for their own benefit. As of 2015, both workers with disabilities in Royal Canadian Legion sheltered workshops as well as CORCAN workers in prison were making pin-on poppies. The sheltered workshop workers were making an abysmal piecemeal rate of $0.01 per poppy while the prisoners were making no more than $4.83 per day.[57] These payments are supposed to be understood not as wages but a reward for participation in an effort to justify how far below the legal minimum they fall.

It is easy to argue that the nature of all work is both for the benefit of workers (earning money) and their employer (labour). However, there are some workers for whom there is something to gain beyond wages — for example rehabilitation or education — which has been used as a barrier to employee status. It is helpful to consider other workers who have such a dual purpose to their work, but who have also been successful in gaining employee status: students who work. None of the cases discussing whether an employment relationship exists for prisoner workers have broached this analogous subject.

In *St. Paul's Hospital (Re)(St. Paul's)*,[58] the British Columbia Labour Relations Board decided that interns at a hospital, who were fulfilling their work requirements as employees and as students for their educational program, were employees who had the right to join a union:

> the working and educational functions of the house staff in the Hospital are largely overlapping and inseparable. Indeed, that is the raison d'être of any program of clinical education. But that fact is still no barrier to the legal coexistence of both employee and student status.

Similarly, in *University of Toronto (Governing Council)* (*U of T Case*), Post-Doctoral Fellows (PDFs) were vying for recognition as employees to access collective bargaining rights. The issue was whether the "student" aspect of their work diminished their status as employees. The Ontario Labour Relations Board (OLRB) decided the PDFs were employees. Regarding the effect of student status, the OLRB stated, "The fact that work provides an opportunity to learn ... does not transform what would otherwise be an employment relationship into a non-employment relationship."[59] Today, thousands of PDFs are unionized across Canada. In another example, *Hotwire Electric-All Inc.* (*Hotwire*), a co-op student was held to be an employee. The OLRB stated, "Spinosa was clearly a student, however, that is not all he was. His enrollment ... had an educational purpose which was to participate in the electrical trade through work related experience in a manner not dissimilar to other electrician apprentices."[60]

The worker-student cases make the point that an employment relationship *can coexist* with an educational objective or with a benefit achieved by both the worker and employer. Analogously, the fact that prisoner workers are both in rehabilitative programming as well as performing work, whether through CORCAN or institutional labour, should not inherently disqualify them from status as employees. If students can have a dual character to their employment, study and work, how is it justified that prisoners cannot be engaged in rehabilitation and work at the same time? Though the real economic benefit test in *Fenton 1991* does allow for some aspect of rehabilitation in an employment relationship, too much weight has been given to rehabilitative aspects based simply on correctional administrators calling programming rehabilitative. In contrast, the cases where students were successful in establishing themselves as employees considered both the student and employee characteristics.

The question of employee status has also been raised for other precarious workers in recent times, namely gig economy workers who are engaged in a fight for recognition as employees rather than independent contractors in Canada and around the world. In February 2020, after a battle with their employer at the OLRB, Foodora food delivery workers were successful in unionization when the OLRB determined that they were "dependent contractors" — a class of worker entitled to collective bargaining rights under Ontario's Labour Relations Act — not independent contractors as the company insisted. In *Canadian Union of Postal Workers v. Foodora Inc. (Foodora),* the tribunal found "The courier is a cog in the economic wheel — an integrated component to the financial transaction. This is a relationship that is more often seen with employees rather than independent contractors."[61] This was a major decision, with the OLRB noting it was its first case addressing the employee status of gig economy workers.[62]

The employee status of prisoner workers boils down to the "real economic benefit": whether their labour is *substantially* to the benefit of their employer or themselves. This should not be an all or nothing scenario — as demonstrated by the example of students — but a matter of the overall character of the work. CSC describes institutional labour as follows: "Institutional employment programs include activities such as maintenance, custodial duties or kitchen work. By contributing to institutional operation and maintenance, offenders help to reduce the costs to the government of their incarceration and rehabilitation."[63] By CSC's own description, the work of prisoners in institutional maintenance provides an economic benefit to CSC because it reduces the costs of incarceration, specifically labour costs. CSC saves on labour costs by having prisoners do the work instead of outside workers, who would have to be paid at least the legal minimum wage — if not much more.

In the case of prisoner workers in CORCAN, CSC clearly articulates the value of prisoner labour to growing business operations:

> Successful business operations have created surpluses that have been re-invested in capital equipment or vocational training opportunities for offenders … In recent years, CORCAN has … begun to market its products and services to a greater number of departments.[64]

In both the case of institutional labour (provincial and federal) and CORCAN industries, a real economic benefit can easily be demonstrated: prisoner labour is *necessary* for the operations to continue and — in the case of CORCAN — to grow. Of course, in a tribunal or court, an enormous evidentiary record would be needed for proof, but for now it suffices to say reducing costs of incarceration and growth of business operations on the backs of prisoners are strong indicators of a real economic benefit. As made clear in the reasoning in *Fenton 1991*, there can be both a rehabilitative purpose for the worker and a real economic benefit for the employer.

If there is any ambiguity about whether there is a real economic benefit, the matter should be resolved in favour of an employment relationship on account of the vulnerability of unprotected workers, as noted in SCC case of *Re Rizzo & Rizzo Shoes Ltd.* (*Rizzo*).[65] Increased vulnerability or precariousness results in a more pressing need to include these workers under the protection of employee status. In 2012, the Law Commission of Ontario (LCO) published a report, titled *Vulnerable Workers and Precarious Work.*[66] The report noted level of earnings, employer-provided benefits, degree of regulatory protection and degree of control or influence as key factors to measure precariousness. Additionally, the authors pointed out characteristics such as immigration status, racial characteristics, gender or other aspects of marginalization also influenced precariousness. There is no doubt prisoners fit the category of precarious or vulnerable in all these aspects, perhaps most significantly in their lack of regulatory protection since they are not afforded the basic protections of employee status. The racialized and otherwise marginalized status of prisoners — being disproportionately Indigenous, Black, suffering from mental health conditions, coming from poverty, etc. — adds to their degree of vulnerability or risk of abuse by their employer. Another factor of increased vulnerability not directly noted in the LCO report is the lack of access to media, which is a huge barrier prisoners face.[67] Non-incarcerated workers routinely turn to media to shine the light on the bad behaviour of their employers. While prisoners do speak out to media from time to time, they face considerable obstacles. These circumstances should work to enhance the urgency of recognizing employee status for prisoners who work.

In *Rizzo,* the SCC determined employee status resulted in minimum protections, so courts should interpret employee status "in a broad and generous manner. Any doubt arising from difficulties of language should be resolved in favour of the claimant."[68] A generous interpretation of prisoner workers, considering their high degree of vulnerability, is to see them as employees.

The SCC has also recognized the necessity of collective bargaining as a way for employees to overcome their power imbalance relative to employers. In a 2015 decision, *Mounted Police Association of Ontario v. Canada,* Chief Justice (at the time) McLachlin discussed the importance of the right to unionize — as part of the right of freedom of association under s. 2(d) of the *Charter* — stating:

> By banding together in the pursuit of common goals, individuals are able to prevent more powerful entities from thwarting their legitimate goals and desires. In this way, the guarantee of freedom of association empowers vulnerable groups and helps them work to right imbalances in society. It protects marginalized groups and makes possible a more equal society.[69]

Freedom of association rights under the *Charter* serves to "right imbalances in society" between the more powerful employers and weaker individual employees. In the case of prisoner workers, the imbalance is tipped quite significantly in favour of employers who have disciplinary power that normal bosses could only dream of. A necessary precondition to righting this imbalance is recognizing prisoner workers as employees, since only employees are recognized as having collective bargaining rights.

RECOGNITION OF PRISONER WORKERS BY A LABOUR BOARD

If federal prisoners are found to be employees, then they must be included under either the federal public service or private service. There is only one option for provincial prisoners, which is the labour board in whichever province the institution lies. This may have been one of the reasons for the success of the Guelph abattoir workers — less bureaucracy and fewer technical barriers to legislative inclusion. Because of this, it may be that a concerted effort by provincial prisoners can yield more success in the short term. We will focus discussion on federal prisoners here because their situation is more complicated.

In the legal battles waged by the Canadian Prisoners' Labour Confederation, David Jolivet and his fellow workers were told they were not public service employees because they had not been appointed to the federal public service, resulting in the PSLRAB denying the CPLC union certification.[70] The PSLRAB relied on the SCC case of *Canada (Attorney General) v. Public Service Alliance of Canada (1991)*, which ruled, "There is quite simply no place in this legal structure for a public servant without a position created by the Treasury Board."[71]

But why doesn't the Treasury Board then "create" positions for prisoner workers? Shouldn't exclusion or inaction be a problem that violates rights of prisoner workers? The SCC has repeatedly ruled in support of *inclusion* of employees to protect collective bargaining rights under the *Charter*. The case of *Dunmore v. Ontario (Attorney General)* (2001) dealt with exclusion of agricultural workers from collective bargaining rights under Ontario's Labour Relations Act, deciding "underinclusive state action … sustains the violation of fundamental freedoms."[72] They elaborated that such action was unconstitutional because it "delegitimizes associational activity and thereby ensures its ultimate failure."[73] In *Ontario (Attorney General) v. Fraser*, the SCC found it was unconstitutional if state action resulted in a "substantial impossibility of exercising their freedom of association."[74] In a similar vein, the majority in the SCC case of *Machtinger v. HOJ Industries Ltd.* held that an interpretation leading to securing "protections to as many employees as possible, is to be favoured over one that does not."[75]

More recently, in *Mounted Police 2015,* the SCC may have opened the door for inclusion of prisoner workers as employees — which may be the only time police have ever opened a door in a helpful way for prisoners. In this case, Royal Canadian Mounted Police (RCMP) employees were challenging their exclusion from collective bargaining rights in the federal public service. They were specifically excluded from the definition of "employee" in the Public Service Labour Relations Act (PSLRA), which stated an "employee" did not include RCMP employees.[76] The reason for excluding the RCMP employees from the PSLRA, according to the Attorney General of Canada, was to "maintain and enhance public confidence in the neutrality, stability and reliability of the RCMP by providing a police force that is independent and objective."[77] The SCC majority rejected this argument, finding that there was no rational connection between those objectives and "total exclusion from meaningful collective bargaining," noting this exclusion was an unconstitutional infringement of their right to freedom of association.[78]

Prisoner workers are not formally excluded, like RCMP employees were, but are omitted entirely from existence in the public service. If they are part of the federal public service, as is suggested in the *Guerin 2018* case, it should be unlawful to exclude them, just as was the case for RCMP employees. There is a basis for this argument. The SCC ruled in *Dunmore* that total exclusion from legislative protection could be considered interference with a protected freedom (freedom of association).[79] In the case of *Health Services and Support – Facilities Subsector Bargaining Assn v. British Columbia,* which finally constitutionalized the right to unionization in Canada, the SCC decided the right to freedom of association "may place positive obligations on governments to extend legislation to particular groups ... There must be evidence that the freedom would be next to impossible to exercise without positively recognizing a right to access a statutory regime."[80] That certainly sounds like the case for prisoner workers.

By denying prisoner workers status under the PSLRA, Canada has interfered with their constitutional rights under the *Charter.* This should make the exclusion an unjustifiable infringement of prisoner workers' rights. Without inclusion, prisoner workers face the "impossibility" of access to collective bargaining rights under the *Charter.*

If prisoner workers are not found to be public service employees covered by the PSLRA, then all of them (institutional labour and CORCAN industries) should be covered by the definition of an employee of a "federal work, undertaking or business" in the Canada Labour Code.[81] The federal court case of *Dart Aerospace Ltd. v. Duval* provides an overview of the requirements to fit under this section: (1) where the employer is engaged in work inherently under federal jurisdiction through the Canadian Constitution Act, and (2) if the nature of the work is not inherently federal, it is essential to the functioning of the federal work.[82]

All "employees" of the CSC fall under the federal Department of Public Safety and Emergency Preparedness.[83] CSC is under federal jurisdiction because it is part of "The Establishment, Maintenance, and Management of Penitentiaries" of the Constitution Act.[84] An employee is part of a "federal work, undertaking or business" if their work is considered "integral" to it. Federal prisoners' work is integral to the corrections regime because, in CSC's own governing law, the work is rehabilitative, and rehabilitation is an integral objective of CSC under the CCRA and the CCRR.

Unlike the PSLRA, no prior creation of positions is required under the Canada Labour Code. If a new federal "work, undertaking or business" arises, such as a new telecommunications company, those employees are eligible for inclusion under the code's labour protections.

Any federal employee must fall under the PSLRA or the code; there is no way around it. As soon as "employee" status has been reached, prisoner workers must fall under either regime. No employee should be left in limbo simply because of the government's failure to include them under any legislation. SCC rulings in favour of other workers, highlighted above, support this position. Due to the vulnerable nature of prisoner workers, including experiences due to racism, mental health conditions and other marginalized statuses, they especially should not be left out of legal protection as employees.

THE ISSUE OF GUARD UNIONS

Guards and their unions will likely prove to be a substantial barrier to a successful prisoner unionization effort. While in rare circumstances guards and prisoners have found their interests aligned, such as in opposition to private prisons, all too often guards have viewed organized prisoners as a threat to their own power. Speaking of the possibility of a prisoners' union in the 1970s, the editors of *Transition*, the prisoner-run magazine based in the Saskatchewan Penitentiary, noted:

> The possibility of a tie-in to existing public service unions should be looked at. If the bulls [guards] and the cons could develop an alliance of some sort the bargaining power of both could increase considerably. As it now stands, the bull's union may try to block a prisoners' trade union.[85]

Prisoners have clearly recognized both the power of guard unions as potential allies and the power of the guards' union to stand in their way.

The position of guards' unions in the broader labour movement poses an additional challenge. The fact that Canadian guards are represented by public sector unions — such as the Public Service Alliance of Canada and the Canadian Union of Public Employees, and larger union centres such as the Confédération des syndicats nationaux — means that trade union centres, national unions or union locals, may be hesitant to support a fledgling prisoners' union.

LIVING CONDITIONS AS WORKING CONDITIONS

Migrant farm workers in the Seasonal Agricultural Workers Program (SAWP) — outside of prison — face a situation very similar to prisoner workers.[86] Just like prisoner workers, they are tied to their employers because they are on closed work permits and housed by their employers. In contrast to prisoner workers, SAWP employers have obligations for housing conditions through the program:

> Employers must provide TFWs [temporary foreign workers] with adequate, suitable and affordable housing as defined by the Canadian Mortgage and Housing Corporation. The hous-

ing can be either on-farm (for example bunkhouse) or off-site (for example commercial establishment). Employers must ensure the occupancy of each accommodation location does not exceed the maximum occupancy permitted. They must also ensure that sufficient housing will be made available for all TFWs per approved accommodation from the date of arrival to the date of departure.[87]

The reality for SAWP workers is that the housing conditions are miserable.[88] However, they still are able to make complaints to Employment and Social Development Canada as employees for failure of their employer to provide the minimum standard in housing, even while at the peril of retaliatory repatriation for making complaints. The key is that these complaints, while specifically about housing, are actually about working conditions, from which the employer-provided housing are inseparable.[89] The obligation is part of the employment relationship.

In the case of prisoner workers, even though their employment relationship includes deductions for "housing," there is no legal precedent to connect prison living conditions to prisoner working conditions. However, with unionization, there should be a very strong basis for prisoner workers to put their living conditions on the bargaining table as working conditions. They are nearly inseparable. Obviously, prison conditions matter to whether the prisoners are fit to work.

HOW PRISONERS COULD UNIONIZE

If workers want to form a union they have two options: start an independent organization or obtain the assistance of a local or national. Either way, workers must mount resources for an organizing drive; sign union cards and invite coworkers to join the effort, aiming for a strong majority before making the application to certify. Perhaps the matter is taken to a vote. If so, they must win the vote to win the union. If the employer tries to interfere with organizing efforts, workers may file an unfair labour practice. If the unfair labour practice is particularly serious the labour board may award union certification on that basis.

For prisoners, each of these steps come with substantial barriers. Thus far, the barriers have only been overcome in the case of the Guelph abattoir. In contrast, stumbling blocks faced by the CPLC proved to be impassible. While there were a number of important differences between these two unionization efforts, the fact that the workers at Guelph had support from an established trade union, while the CPLC did not, is worth considering in more detail.

The CPLC was a prisoner-initiated and inside-based campaign. The union was its prisoner members and a lawyer, Natalie Dunbar. In statements to the media, the CPLC explained it was moving forward as an independent labour organization to avoid putting an established union "in an awkward political position over the controversial nature of the request" to take on their campaign.[90] Still, the CPLC also sought support from established unions, although they did not have much success in this endeavour. While some labour organizations had sent private messages of support, none were willing to publicly back the CPLC.[91] This was not the first time the Canadian labour movement declined to support prisoners' labour struggles. Efforts to get the Public Service Alliance of Canada to support prisoner organizing efforts in 1974 went unheeded.[92] So did calls by federal prisoners for representation by the Canadian Labour Congress in 1983.[93]

Without established union support, the effort had to be financed by CPLC supporters, who made a maximum of $6.90 per day before pay cuts came into effect in 2013. Because the CPLC was not sanctioned by CSC, the union also ran into considerable red tape that complicated dues collecting and banking.[94] While the CPLC faced difficulties in relation to finances and resources, it also quickly found itself politically isolated after the campaign went public in 2011.[95] Without an outside support network, inside-based organizations are vulnerable — lockdowns and solidarity confinement can effectively kill organizing efforts. Furthermore, limitations on communications between prisoners in different institutions can stymie efforts considerably. What would have happened if the CPLC had substantial resources to mount a thorough legal case to confront the rehabilitation barrier and make full arguments for inclusion under either federal labour board, all with a large, public campaign behind them? The results could have been quite different.

In a 1974 editorial on the topic of prisoners' unions in the pages of *Transition*, a prisoner magazine with an editorial board spread across Canadian federal prisons, the authors made a forceful case that any successful prisoner union would need the backing of established unions:

> A lot of cons will say 'to hell with the big unions,' but the fact is that without their support, either individually, or through the Canadian Labour Congress, chances of a union being formed and recognized are slim and chances of it being effective are damn near nil. Take it or leave [it] the big unions are essential.[96]

While uncommon, there are precedents for union support for incarcerated workers. In 1956, the Western Pulp and Paper Workers declared, "We would like to see every inmate working, 40 hours a week, at regular union wages for whatever work he or she is doing, and we would also like to see inmates learning a trade if they wish … and be compelled to join a union made up of all the inmates."[97] As already discussed, the Canadian Food and Allied Workers made history in 1977 when they successfully organized prisoner meatpackers into a union.

Beyond the issue of the potential "controversial nature" of union drives for prisoners, there are also mundane financial reasons why unions might decline to support a prisoners' union. Unionizing prisoner workers would not result in an enlarged dues base for a parent union because prisoners make little to nothing. The costs of a campaign and the costs of servicing prisoner union locals would almost certainly be more than whatever would be brought in through dues. Simply put, money would have to be invested into a prisoners' union to keep it viable.

A large, established union with ample resources to serve an impoverished local — such as the Canadian Food and Allied Workers — could provide adequate support for a prisoner labour union, but they would have to do this in the interest of solidarity. As Sam Gindin has argued, "Unions that are narrowly focused on their dues base, rather than building the power of the working class, are unlikely to mobilize the energy, resources, cross-union cooperation, community support and strategic creativity needed to unionize in these more difficult times."[98] It is for this reason that a prisoners' union also has something to offer the labour movement. Taking up the struggles of the most marginalized and oppressed workers in society would necessarily require a shift in thinking about what the labour movement is and who it is for. As Gindin and others have argued, "unionism with a class sensibility" is necessary if the labour movement is going to reverse its obvious decline.[99] The formation of a prisoners' union would not itself revive the labour movement, but to take up the struggles of working prisoners, unions would necessarily have to shed their sectionalism in favour of broad solidarity and defence of the working class.

To win support for a prisoners' union, union members would have to compel their organizations to get behind the struggle of prisoner workers. Likely, support would have to come from social justice departments of unions or perhaps resolutions from organizing committees to support prisoner worker drives despite the losses. For reasons of prestige, genuine concerns for social justice, or some blending of both, it is possible an established union might decide to throw its weight behind vulnerable workers and take up the struggle to organize the dungeons of Canada.

However, if this is to happen, there remains a larger challenge related to popular opinion. Over the years, most of society, including working people, have tended to assume prisoners deserve to be where they are.[100] In the late 1990s, an Angus Reid poll revealed that 69% believed sentences were not harsh enough.[101] As federal prisoner and prisoner rights activist Peter Collins noted in the lead up to the 2013 federal prison strike, "We're in prison and we're not a big sympathy-grabber."[102]

But very recently, after the fallout related to the murder of George Floyd and the increased attention on police killings and the targeting and jailing of Black and Indigenous people in Canada, public opinion may have begun to shift. In the context of recognizing that systemic racism results in a greater number of Black and Indigenous people incarcerated, a 2020 Angus Reid poll revealed that 59% believed it was better to support crime prevention and rehabilitation over longer sentences.[103] Movements against systemic racism and colonialism must reckon with prisons, including by supporting the struggles of working prisoners. That said, it would be naïve to think long-held opinions could suddenly shift for the long term without the possibility of suddenly shifting back.

A campaign to get behind prisoner workers will require significant public education efforts by prisoners and prison justice organizers to humanize the labour struggles of prisoner workers. This would have to take place in conjunction with on-the-ground organizing efforts by prisoners. Prisoners should not have to take on the risks of organizing without outside support or infrastructure. Of course, no amount of support can substitute for the desire of prisoners to pursue unionization. History shows that prisoners have consistently agitated for unions, even if these efforts haven't tended to succeed.[104] In our view, the question is less about *if* prisoners will once again seek union representation, and more about *when* they will do it.

COUNTERING ARGUMENTS AGAINST PRISONER WORKER UNIONIZATION

A key argument of prison justice advocates and abolitionists is to reduce or eliminate funding to prisons so the injustices of prison, including the exploitation and dehumanization of prisoners, is not supported with public monies. In January 2021, a number of organizations across Canada favouring defunding of prisons released the following a statement in light of increasing COVID-19 numbers across Canada, noting an opportunity to decarcerate:

> STOP investing more public or private money into policing and prison infrastructure
>
> STOP increasing budgets to hire more police and prison officers
>
> STOP building new police stations, detachments and headquarters, courthouses, jails, prisons, penitentiaries and immigration detention centres
>
> COMMIT to dramatically cutting municipal, provincial and federal funding for carceral infrastructures.[105]

Following this line of thinking, defunding would first stop the expansion of the carceral system and then slowly starve prisons out of existence. Money diverted from the carceral system would be invested into community services and alternatives to incarceration. However, the argument to defund is, unfortunately, not necessarily consistent with demands for improving working conditions and wages for prisoners. Clearly, improvements to wages and working conditions would require an increase in government funding or private investment for those specific purposes.

As far apart as these views appear on the surface, in our view there is substantial common ground. We do not support the thickening of prison bars and fattening of prisons as a whole, but the opposite. We support prisoners in their fight for better conditions, including working conditions and pay. There is a major difference between supporting prisons and supporting prisoners, especially when it comes to supporting prisoners' efforts to unionize. Through unionization, prisoners would gain more power than they would through other means to realize demands for improvements. This includes ensuring any work they do actually prepares them for timely release. A union would give prisoners an independent organization through which to assert themselves politically.

The idea of making any improvements to prison working conditions through unionization was criticized by former US federal prisoner and prison justice organizer James Kilgore:

> Unionization is one frequently proposed solution to the plight of incarcerated workers. In considering unions, the question becomes: do we put resources into improving prison working conditions or do we fight to get people out of prison? Suddenly raising people's pay rate from ten cents an hour to a living wage would require massive increases in corrections budgets or, in the absence of large-scale decarceration, a huge reduction in employment inside prisons. Moreover, since many non-prisoners are also part of the marginalized sector of the working class who don't earn a living wage or belong to unions, unionizing prison workers could essentially be creating a situation where prison offered economic advantages over the labor market on the street.[106]

Kilgore raises important points that have to be dealt with to make a case for why unionization is good for prisoners.

First, "Do we put resources into improving prison working conditions or do we fight to get people out of prison?" At this point, it should be clear we are suggesting there is no doubt that unionization represents a clear strategic choice to improve the working lives of prisoners. The question creates a false dichotomy. Resources should be put into place to improve the working conditions of prisoners, consistent with a strategy to get more prisoners out of jail faster and prevent recidivism. If prisoners are unionized, they are entitled to good faith bargaining with their employers. They can assert their demands for jobs that are more useful for their release; for increased wages *and* reduced costs of phone services and canteen items to ensure they have more resources available for survival upon release; to gain skills in negotiating and other administrative duties required for any union local that can assist in improving their rehabilitative scores; and many other advantages that will actually assist prisoners to get out and stay out. This was a key assertion of the CPLC.[107] Paired with other strategies to reduce prison populations — such as the expansion of parole eligibility and sentencing reform — a prisoners' union could be a key tool in reducing the prison population. Indeed a prisoners' union could be a key player in campaigns for decarceration.

Second, "Suddenly raising people's pay rate from ten cents an hour to a living wage would require massive increases in corrections budgets or, in the absence of large-scale decarceration, a huge reduction in employment inside prisons." This point is based on an assumption of what a union would be focused upon: raising wages. It is a fair point; a big part of what unions do is fight for improved wages. But that has never been the crux of the organized working class's demands. Unions give workers power. This power can — and should be — used to win higher wages, and prisoners' wages should certainly be increased. However, if prisoners unionized, it is likely their focus would largely be on the usefulness of their work for their release, power disparity between them and their institutional bosses, having the institution pay a greater share of the costs of phone and others services, as well as control and discipline issues. In fact, in 1983 when prisoners at the Stony Mountain Institution in Winnipeg sought the assistance of the Canadian Labour Congress, it was not primarily to seek higher wages but to gain the support of the labour movement to assist prisoners in early release.[108]

In the case of any unionized workplace, including public sector ones, workers must be cognizant of the economic position of their employer, lest they bargain themselves out of a job. However, in the big picture, CSC cannot actually get rid of prisoner workers. Prison work cannot be offshored — and there are real limits to strategies that other public sector employers may deploy to reduce costs, such as sub-contracting. Prisoners are essential to the functioning of the correction system in both material and ideological terms. The labour of prisoners reproduces the prison and its programming day after day and serves as activity that can be labelled "rehabilitative." This means prisoners could potentially be in a good position to win higher compensation, which could translate into increased pressure on correctional budgets. This gets to the crux of the issue: a prisoners' union could be a means to challenge *how* public monies are spent on corrections, not just how much money is spent.

———

Apart from some bureaucrats and a handful of employment program supervisors whose jobs depend on the status quo, it seems no one is happy with the state of prison labour in Canada. Despite this widespread discontent, there are few proposals for reasonable alternatives. This applies as much to proposals that seek to improve the situation for prisoners as it does to those motivated by pecuniary interests and unconcerned with human rights. While every few years it seems like some enterprising politician pledges to "make crime pay" by ramping up the (private or public) exploitation of prison labour, such schemes inevitably run up against the same interests and arguments that resulted in the existing state-use compromise. On the other hand, calls to abolish prison labour ignore the battles prisoners have fought to ensure they have access to work and wages — even if meagre. The reality is, so long as there are prisons, prisoners will work. Some innovative proposals, such as prisoner co-ops do acknowledge this reality; however, history demonstrates the challenges these types of experiments face. The problem from the point of view of prison justice is less that cooperatives are difficult to start and sustain and more that, even if successful, they don't necessarily alter power relations in the prison. Prisoners' unions, even with all their own challenges, do have this potential.

CONCLUSION

AND JUSTICE FOR ALL?

Despite all the hardships and challenges, prisoners have won gains through strike action. Some of these victories have been substantial and have had significant impacts on correctional policy — such as the implementation of wages for prisoners in the aftermath of the 1934 British Columbia Penitentiary strike. Other times, victories are more modest. Still, it is critical that prisoners do, from time to time, withhold their labour to pressure prison authorities on issues of concern. On the morning of June 27, 2011, federal prisoners at the Collins Bay Institution (CBI) in Kingston, Ontario, went on strike. A CSC media release stated prisoners "have refused to attend any of their work programs or correctional programming." The release also stated administrators had met with the elected Inmate Committee and management was "working toward having all inmates return to their regular program assignments as quickly as possible."[1]

Prisoners' demands included dryers and ice machines in units that did not already have them, as well as bug screens, ceiling repairs, even distribution of "double-bunks," improved ventilation in the prison weight room and action on unacceptable levels of prisoner unemployment. On June 29, Collins Bay Warden Julie Blasko penned a memo to the Inmate Committee indicating the prison would concede to all of the prisoners' demands. The memo stated new dryers had been purchased and the administration was actively looking to purchase an ice machine. The prison's double-bunk plan was "modified to ensure equal distribution of the double-bunks within all units." An inventory of bug screens had been taken and orders had been put in for new screens. Ceiling work had been approved and the ventilation system in the weight room would be upgraded. A working group was stuck to address unemployment. With these concessions in hand, the strikers returned to work on June 30.[2]

A subsequent memo by Julie Blasko, written on July 15, 2011, confirmed the administration had followed through on its promises. Dryers had been installed and an ice machine had been purchased. New bug screens were being delivered by the supplier. The double-bunking plan had been changed and a new ventilation system had been installed in the weight room. Ceiling work was approved and would be completed by CORCAN, who would hire additional prisoner workers for the project. Furthermore, the prison would institute a new central hiring system to help address issues of unemployment. A new position of "Inmate Employment Clerk" was created to "help facilitate discussions between the prison population and administration," and the administration would consider several other proposed "inmate positions."[3]

This strike isn't remarkable for what prisoners won — which were hardly life changing concessions. The strike is notable because prisoners won it so decisively. It clearly shows the potential for prisoners to exercise economic power successfully. The economic and institutional impact of the strike was real and immediate. On the first morning of the strike CBI managers were asked to "provide all available staff to the kitchen to assist in meal preparation." Management also solicited staff for volunteers to work weekend kitchen shifts, presumably at overtime rates, if the strike continued.[4] The 2011 CBI strike, like other examples before it, demonstrates that prisoners can win demands through strike action. Formal organization — a union — would allow for even greater coordination and strategy by prisoners. We argue, for this reason, a prisoners' union would significantly shift the balance in Canadian prisons and, as such, represents a strategically important "non-reformist reform." We also think a prisoners' union would have a number of other important implications. However, before we get to these, we would like to briefly summarize our arguments so far.

THE PRISON LABOUR PROBLEMS

Prisons have failed to use work programs to "sweat the evil out." Over the course of the history we have documented, government and prison administrators tried to position prisoner labour as a moral good, both in terms of punishing laziness and to change prisoners into law-abiding individuals imbued with the industriousness to make it in the outside world — the capitalist world. Both objectives failed. The moral basis of prisoner labour was never based on any assessment of the reasons why individuals ended up in prison, which had to do with poverty, minimal education and racial and other biases. Virtue and moral goodness cannot be imposed through punishment.

While prisons have aimed to instill industriousness in prisoners, it has not significantly supported setting up prisoners for a life outside of prison. Pay cuts, increased costs and rising prices for phone calls, stamps, hygiene items and food, means prisoners face increasingly difficult circumstances upon release. Moreover, the kinds of jobs done in prison have no correlation with the jobs prisoners would be eligible for upon release, and their criminal records deny them work opportunities that would otherwise be available.

Prison labour can be dangerous, resulting in injury, illness and death. While prisoners have made gains around access to medical care, significant issues persist. Prisoners' legal exclusions render them unacceptably vulnerable. This is true in general, but also specifically relevant to issues of workplace health and safety. Prisoners deserve all the protections the law affords to regular employees. Prisoners also deserve an active say in their conditions of work. A union is the best means to this.

Federal and provincial employment programs — and specific prison industry programs like CORCAN — have failed to adapt to the needs of prisoners. Administrators have ignored the concerns from prisoners about the ineffectiveness of the programs and the racial biases in who is even able to obtain the better jobs. As we covered in Chapter 2, there is a major problem with selection bias in the findings of correctional administrators about the so-called effectiveness of rehabilitation programs. Those prisoners most likely to succeed are given the best job placements in prison, which counteracts the idea of rehabilitation. In fact, the state of scientific corrections in Canada significantly undermines the debates around determinations of effective programming — CSC's calculation of recidivism does not include new convictions that lead to provincial custody, meaning statistics on recidivism significantly underestimate its occurrence and there is no reliable measure of recidivism in Canada.[5] The assertion that rehabilitative programming is effective when there is no objective measure to determine if that's true simply defies logic. Altogether, the issues apparent in Canadian prison labour are significant — however, many could certainly be addressed at a bargaining table through negotiations by a union.

The relationship between so-called "free labour" and prisoner labour has been mixed at best. Historically, the labour movement has opposed the use of prisoner labour out of concern that it undermines wages and takes away jobs from "free" workers. Humanitarian concerns over the use of prison labour have also been routinely made by the labour movement; however, these have generally not been made as forcefully. Presently, there is no substantial issue with prisoner labour acting as any meaningful competition to free labour. There is no clamouring of free workers to do the work of prisoners. Like with the work of migrant workers, including intensive agricultural labour, there is no actual competition in the domestic labour market. That being said, we disagree with prisoners being relegated to work that is of little use. There have been examples of late where prisoner work has been extremely socially useful such as the production of PPE during the COVID-19 pandemic. We argue there needs to be more socially useful work for prisoners, such as employment in the production of green technology, but it should all take place in the context of improved working conditions and access to full labour rights.

We highlighted alternatives to the present system, including privatization, co-ops and prisoner entrepreneurialism. The history of privatization in the prisons is a history of barbaric practices, including convict leasing. We do not support increased exploitation of prison labour by private employers — however, history demonstrates that the employment of prison labour by private interests does not always result in worse conditions for workers. The case of the Guelph abattoir, which was a privatized operation, shows prisoner unionization is not inconsistent with private industry — indeed, it was the involvement of a private employer that created the legal conditions that made certification possible. There is also a history of prisoners' cooperatives, such as the Indigenous prisoner owned and operated NELOF, that point to the potential for radically different prison industries than those that currently exist. New experiments with prisoner cooperatives could result in better wages and working conditions for prisoners. As prisoner-owned entities they also could contribute to developing a range of skills and capacities that existing prison industries appear incapable of doing. Prisoner co-ops have their own limitations — they would need to be adequately resourced and find ways of overcoming the bureaucratic barriers that contributed to the demise of earlier co-op efforts.

The importance of developing alternatives to the present form of prisoner labour — most crucially unionization — cannot be overstated. In the history we have recounted, the notorious examples of convict leasing and "hire a prisoner" initiatives reveal how abusive the system is without prisoners having a meaningful say and leverage over their working conditions. In the "hire a prisoner" programs at Beaver Creek Institution in Ontario and Ferndale Institution in British Columbia, guards took huge advantage in conditions some prisoners called slave labour.

As we detailed in Chapter 1, Canada is supposed to follow its international legal obligations to protect prisoners' rights under the *Mandela Rules*. We highlighted a number of the rules that Canada is not following in the treatment of prisoner workers. In revisiting the *Mandela Rules*, we can say unequivocally that they are not being followed:

- "prisoners have the opportunity to work" (Rule 96);

Prisoners do not all have the opportunity to work, nor to the fair distribution of jobs. Jobs in prisons are gendered and there is higher unemployment among Black and Indigenous prisoners than their white counterparts.

- "So far as is possible, the work must maintain or increase the prisoners' ability to earn an honest living after release" (Rule 98);

No prisoner is well placed to earn an "honest living" upon release. With their paltry wages — which continue to shrink through inflation and rising costs of living — prisoners have little to support themselves honestly upon release. Furthermore, rising costs of services, including phone costs, mean prisoners have a more difficult time maintaining community connections. Altogether these conditions have been correlated with more recidivism.

- "The organization and methods of work in prisons shall resemble as closely as possible those of similar work outside of prisons, so as to prepare prisoners for the conditions of normal occupational life" (Rule 99);

The Employment and Employability Programs (EEPs) are disconnected from the realities of the outside world. Ghassan Salah, whose concerns with the EEPs are highlighted above, has been emphatic about the urgent need to listen to prisoners and focus on preparing prisoners for release because the existing job placements are not doing this. The Correctional Investigator has also stressed the need for the programs to be more effective in preparing prisoners for the outside world. Furniture and textile manufacturing, two central components to CORCAN, are hardly growth industries.

- "The interests of the prisoners and of their vocational training, however, must not be subordinated to the purpose of making a financial profit from an industry in the prison" (Rule 99);

The example of the controversy with the redevelopment of prison farms raises the spectre of a for-profit industry, with the possibility of a large-scale industrial goat milk operation for export. This story needs to be closely followed by all who are concerned about prisoners being exploited for profit. It also appears the Wallace Beef abattoir operation is making a profit from prisoner labour through depressed wages. However, even putting these examples of private employment aside, one could reasonably argue CORCAN and other prison industry programs routinely subordinate "the interests of prisoners and their vocational training" to maximize revenues. This is not the result of nefarious intentions among prison industry managers. Rather, it reflects the contradictory nature of prison industries' dual mandates for maximum profits and maximum "rehabilitation."

- "Unless the work is for other departments of the government, the full normal wages for such work shall be paid to the prison administration by the persons to whom the labour is supplied, account being taken of the output of the prisoners" (Rule 100);

Again, the Wallace Beef example shows this rule is not being followed. Partnerships with non-profits such as Habitat for Humanity also appear to fall outside of this stipulation.

- "The precautions laid down to protect the safety and health of free workers shall be equally observed in prisons" (Rule 101);

Prisoners have not been afforded the safe level of protections in health and safety as free workers. As we elaborated in Chapter 3, prisoners have suffered asbestos-filled workplaces; have had to deal with work environments with a risk of hepatitis C and tuberculosis, among other infections; have had to work in congregate environments during the spread of COVID-19 without the same level of safety precautions outside workers are provided; and have suffered serious injuries without appropriate compensation.

- "There shall be a system of equitable remuneration of the work of prisoners" (Rule 103).

Clearly, prisoners do not receive remotely equitable remuneration. Working full time at the highest pay level in the federal system results in $6.90 per day before deductions. Prisoners' work is not being valued for what it is worth but only to "reward participation." If the work that people are doing on the outside is compared to the pay in prisons, prisoners make far less than their counterparts. As an example, the average rate of pay for a furniture maker in Canada is $21.25 per hour based on 2019 industry statistics.[6]

THE UNION SOLUTION

As we have outlined, prisoners need organizational structures that do at least two things. For one, the structures need to reduce the isolation of prisoner workers from "free" workers by making tangible connections between them. If prisoners unionize, it will be very difficult to maintain that they are not a part of the labour movement along with all other workers. Secondly, through unions, formal legal protections must be available, including the right to collective bargaining with the employer, where the employer has to show up at the bargaining table in good faith according to *Charter* rights. The bundle of rights also includes the right to a grievance procedure to deal with possible violations of collective agreements. It would also include the right to access administrative tools to reach an agreement. If prisoners were unable to win the right to strike, they could at the very least achieve the right to binding arbitration. This would mean that if the parties could not come to a negotiated resolution for the collective agreement, an arbitrator would decide what is fair.

Prisoner unions would not just be about working conditions but also the broader "conditions of confinement." Prisoner unions would represent a fundamental shift in the relative power between prisoners and their administration or bosses. We have called this a non-reformist reform because of the fundamental shift in power balance it would represent.

Ultimately, if we want to achieve prison justice, we have to change the capitalist society in which prisons exist. The power to make that change will have to come from organized working-class people, including prisoners. Some precarious workers like baristas, rideshare drivers and food couriers are making important breakthroughs and unionizing. This could also be a key moment for other vulnerable workers like prisoners to be supported in their organizing efforts. This solidarity should go both ways. As scholar and activist El Jones has asserted:

> People in prison are largely there for crimes of poverty, mental health and addiction. So I hope that people living in poverty recognize we are dealing with a common oppression here, and that we should all have access to these things, and to deprive part of the population doesn't give others more rights.[7]

Prisoners have never stopped trying in their efforts to unionize. We detailed the efforts of prisoners at GCC, working at the Guelph abattoir, unionizing with the CFAW Union Local 240 in 1977. They were successful and were able to achieve pay parity with their non-incarcerated coworkers, as well as important provisions for entitlement to jobs upon release. This continues to be one of the most powerful examples in Canadian history of the impact of organized prisoner workers. Without being organized together with free workers at the same workplace, being considered as equals in all senses possible, except for the fact of their incarceration and those impacts, shows so much about what is possible. Decades later, federal prisoners attempted to organize through the CPLC, but only hit a series of brick walls.

The failures of the CPLC make it all too clear the law is not on the side of prisoners who seek unionization. However, it is also the case the law was never on the side of any workers who wanted to unionize. There has always been a fight — nothing was given and everything was won through struggle.[8] Lawyers, advocates, and unions must support prisoners as they wade through the fog of "rehabilitation" and climb over barriers set by labour boards that have continued to deny them jurisdiction. They have to fight for their rights and make the case. The case does exist, but it will be a very intense battle to assert it. Labour tribunals and judges have demonstrated the refusal to see prisoners as having the same fundamental human rights as free workers to unionize. This bias has to be defeated. It can be with enough support behind prisoners in their fight.

We realize this is not a simple task. It would require unions to reconceptualize their understanding of who counts as a worker and what constitutes the working class in Canada. It would also require unions to think in *class terms* about the fundamental ways in which Canadian society is structured. It would also require rethinking the role of police and prison guards in the labour movement. At a practical level, a project of organizing prisoners would challenge the predominant bean-counting organizing approach that considers a campaign viable only if potential dues income exceeds organizing and servicing costs.

The prison justice movement has not, thus far, been primarily concerned with issues of prison labour. This is entirely understandable given the range of life-and-death issues that haunt Canadian prisons. Solitary confinement, use of force, lack of access to harm reduction supplies and medical services and other injustices need to be addressed urgently. When issues of prison labour have been taken up by the prison justice movement, it has tended to be in response to major policy changes, such as the 2013 pay cuts or the closure of prison farms. Again, we understand why this is the case. Resources are limited, there are only twenty-four hours in a day and priorities have to be made. Still, we believe that prison labour and prisoners' unions have incredible strategic potential. It is for this reason that we urge prison justice advocates to support prisoner unionization.

Ghassan Salah, the lifer whose work to try and improve conditions for prisoners we highlighted in Chapter 6, has been trying to reinvigorate the conversation around unionization for prisoners in Canada. Through the assistance of outside support, he has recently created an organization, Prisoners United. The website lists a number of projects designed to assert rights of prisoners and bring about improvements prisoners want to see. One of the initiatives he lists is a prisoner's union:

> We are looking into creating a union for prisoners in the Canadian Correctional system. The purpose of the Union is to

advocate for prisoners' rights and provide a unified voice for prisoners in the public square.

The *Prisoners Union of Canada* intend to engage the government through judicial and extra-judicial processes to address the challenges and injustices imposed on prisoners by the Correctional Service of Canada (CSC). Our goal is to enhance the correctional outcome for prisoners while limiting the adverse effects resulting from incarceration. Some of the concerns the Union wishes to address are issues pertaining to living conditions, treatment programs, the appropriate and timely delivery of programs, health services, psychological therapy, meaningful education, vocational training and certification, adequate pay for work, access to community support and family, as well as fair representation on goods and services (i.e. purchasing system, Inmate Telephone System, cable/satellite package).[9]

Combined with the historical and contemporary cases outlined in this book, Salah's organizing is a demonstration that the interest in unionization of prisoners is alive and well.

This book started from the position that prisoners should be understood as workers. Prisoners' exclusion from normal employment standards, occupational health and safety and labour law cannot be justified by arguments of punishment or rehabilitation. Given the injustices faced by prisoners — as workers and in general — it is urgent that those who believe in principles of social justice support their struggles. As we've argued, unionization offers a potential means to improve the lives of prisons but also fundamentally alter the dynamics of prison. The struggle is not a simple or easy one. Labour unions and other community supports need to make prisoner worker unionization a reality, but they must also be there for the organization of all vulnerable workers. Prisoners deserve the same rights and protection of all other workers — and their struggle connects deeply to improving working conditions for all.

NOTES

INTRODUCTION: PRISON LABOUR AND PUNISHMENT

1. Ruth Morris, *Penal Abolition: The Practical Choice* (Toronto: Canadian Scholars' Press, 1995); Michael Jackson, *Justice Behind the Walls: Human Rights in Canadian Prisons* (Vancouver: Douglas & McIntyre, 2002); Paula Mallea, *Beyond Incarceration: Safety and True Criminal Justice* (Toronto: Dundurn Press, 2017); Chris Clarkson and Melissa Munn, *Disruptive Prisoners: Resistance, Reform, and the New Deal* (Toronto, Buffalo, and London: Toronto University Press, 2021).

2. *Corrections and Conditional Release Act*, SC 1992, c 20, ss. 3 and 78.

3. Peter Oliver, *'Terror to Evil-Doers': Prisons and Punishment in Nineteenth-Century Ontario* (Toronto: Osgoode Society, 1998), 93–95.

4. Rainer Baehre, "Prison as Factory, Convict as Worker: A Study of the Mid-Victorian St John Penitentiary, 1841–1880," in *Essays in the History of Canadian Law: Crime and Criminal Justice in Canadian History,* edited by Susan Lewthwaite, Tina Loo and Jim Phillips (Toronto: University of Toronto Press, 1994), 449.

5. Calvin Neufeld, *Bloody Bad Business: Report on the Joyceville Institution Abattoir,* Evolve Our Prison Farms, August 31, 2021: 17, evolveourprisonfarms. ca/wp-content/uploads/2021/09/Bloody-Bad-Business-Joyceville-Abattoir-Report-Evolve-Our-Prison-Farms.pdf.

6. *Guérin v. Canada (Attorney General),* 2018 FC 94, para 130.

7. Mark MacGuigan*, Report to Parliament by the Sub-committee on the Penitentiary System in Canada* (Ottawa: Government of Canada, 1977), 37.

8. United States Constitution, Amendment XIII, Section I, www.senate.gov/civics/constitution_item/constitution.htm.

9. Jordan House, "When Prisoners Had a Union: The Canadian Food and Allied Workers Union Local 240," *Labour/Le Travail* 82 (Fall 2018): 36.

10. For example, see Donald Tibbs, *From Black Power to Prison Power: The Making of Jones v. North Carolina Prisoners' Labor Union* (New York: Palgrave Macmillan, 2012), 152.

11. Dario Melossi and Massimo Pavarini, *The Prison and the Factory: Origins of the Penitentiary System* (40th Anniversary Edition) (London: Palgrave Macmillan UK, 2018), 260.

12.   See Eric Cummins, *The Rise and Fall of California's Radical Prison Movement* (Stanford, CA: Stanford University Press, 1994); Steve D'Arcy, "The Political Vocabulary of the Post-New Left: How Activists Articulate Their Politics and Why It Matters," in *A World to Win: Contemporary Social Movements & Counter-Hegemony,* edited by William K. Carroll and Kanchan Sarker (Winnipeg: ARP Press, 2016), 141–156.

13.   Claire Culhane, "To the Guys at Kent," *Kent Times,* August 10, 1986: 3. Gaucher/Munn Penal Press Collection, penalpress.com/wp-content/uploads/KentTimes_V1_I1_Aug1986.pdf.

14.   See Andre Gorz, "Reform and Revolution," in *Socialist Register 1968,* edited by Ralph Miliband and John Saville (London: Merlin Press, 1968); Thomas Mathiesen, *The Politics of Abolition Revisited* (Abingdon, Oxon and New York: Routledge, 2015).

15.   Sam Gindin, "Rethinking Unions, Registering Socialism," in *The Socialist Register 2013: A Question of Strategy,* edited by Leo Panitch and Vivek Chibber (London: Merlin, 2012), 26–51.

16.   See Mark P. Thomas and Steven Tufts, "Blue Solidarity: Police Unions, Race and Authoritarian Populism in North America," *Work, Employment, and Society* 34:1 (2019): 126–144; Joshua Page, "Politically Realistic Unionism: The California Prison Officers Association and the Struggle Over the 'Public Good'," *WorkingUSA* 15 (September 2012): 377–396.

17.   See Marsha McLeod, "Broken Telephone: How Ontario's Prison-Phone System Leaves Inmates Disconnected," *TVO,* February 11, 2021, tvo.org/article/broken-telephone-how-ontarios-prison-phone-system-leaves-inmates-disconnected. Also see Micheal Spratt, "'Bell Let's Talk' Campaign and the Reality of Ontario's Jails," January 24, 2020, michaelspratt.com/opinion/bell-lets-talk-campaign-and-the-reality-of-ontarios-jails/.

18.   Justin Ling, "The CSC Is Censoring Whistleblower Complaints about COVID-19 in Federal Prisons," *National Post,* April 8, 2020, nationalpost.com/opinion/justin-ling-the-csc-is-censoring-whistleblower-complaints-about-covid-19-in-federal-prisons.

19.   Jordan House, "Making Prisons Work: Prison Labour and Resistance in Canada," PhD dissertation, York University (2020), 239.

20.   For example, see Dan Taekema, "Inmates Protest Against More Lockdowns at Toronto South Detention Centre," *Toronto Star,* June 10, 2016, thestar.com/news/gta/2016/06/10/inmates-protest-against-more-lockdowns-at-toronto-south-detention-centre.html.

21.   See Justin Piché, "Accessing the State of Imprisonment in Canada: Information Barriers and Negotiation Strategies" in *Brokering Access: Power, Politics, and Freedom of Information Process in Canada,* edited by Mike Larsen and Kevin Walby (Vancouver and Toronto: UBC Press, 2012): 234–260.

22.   Standing Senate Committee on Human Rights, *Human Rights of Federally-Sentenced Persons,* June 2021: 41, sencanada.ca/content/sen/committee/432/RIDR/reports/2021-06-16_FederallySentenced_e.pdf.

CHAPTER 1: WHY CARE ABOUT PRISONERS' LABOUR RIGHTS?

1. Department of Justice, "Public Perception of Crime and Justice in Canada: A Review of Opinion Polls," justice.gc.ca/eng/rp-pr/csj-sjc/crime/rr01_1/p4_1. html.

2. Ruth Morris, *Penal Abolition: The Practical Choice* (Toronto: Canadian Scholars' Press, 1995); Michael Jackson, *Justice Behind the Walls: Human Rights in Canadian Prisons* (Vancouver: Douglas & McIntyre, 2002); Paula Mallea, *Beyond Incarceration: Safety and True Criminal Justice* (Toronto: Dundurn Press, 2017); Chris Clarkson and Melissa Munn, *Disruptive Prisoners: Resistance, Reform, and the New Deal* (Toronto, Buffalo, and London: Toronto University Press, 2021).

3. Prime Minister of Canada, "Statement by the Prime Minister of Canada on the 35th anniversary of the Canadian Charter of Rights and Freedoms," April 17, 2017, pm.gc.ca/en/news/statements/2017/04/17/statement-prime-minister-canada-35th-anniversary-canadian-charter-rights.

4. *R. v. Oakes,* 1986 CanLII 46 (SCC), [1986] 1 SCR 103.

5. *Solosky v. The Queen,* [1980] 1 SCR 821, 1979 CanLII 9 (SCC).

6. *Sauvé v. Canada (Chief Electoral Officer),* 2002 SCC 68 (CanLII).

7. United Nations, *Convention Against Torture and Other Cruel, Inhuman or Degrading Treatment or Punishment,* United Nations, Treaty Series, vol. 1465, 85.

8. *R. v. Capay,* 2019 ONSC 535 (CanLII).

9. Canadian Civil Liberties Association v. Canada (Attorney General), 2019 ONCA 243 (CanLII).

10. United Nations General Assembly, *United Nations Standard Minimum Rules for the Treatment of Prisoners (the Nelson Mandela Rules), resolution / adopted by the General Assembly,* January 8, 2016, A/RES/70/175, refworld.org/docid/5698a3a44.html

11. *Gosselin v. Québec (Attorney General),* 2002 SCC 84 (CanLII), [2002] 4 SCR 429.

12. Health Services and Support — Facilities Subsector Bargaining Assn. v. British Columbia, 2007 SCC 27 (CanLII), [2007] 2 SCR 391.

13. See Judy Fudge and Eric Tucker, *Labour Before the Law: The Regulation of Workers' Collective Action in Canada, 1900–1948* (Oxford and New York: Oxford University Press, 2001).

14. Reference Re Public Service Employee Relations Act (Alta.), 1987 CanLII 88 (SCC), [1987] 1 SCR 313.

15. Larry Savage and Charles W. Smith, *Unions in Court: Organized Labour and the Charter of Rights and Freedoms* (Vancouver: UBC Press, 2017). Also see Adam D.K. King, "How the Right to Strike Is Being Eroded in Canada," *Passage,* June 30, 2021, readpassage.com/p/how-the-right-to-strike-is-being-eroded-in-canada/.

16. Barry M. Fox, "The First Amendment Rights of Prisoners," *Criminal Law Criminology and Police Science* 63 (1972): 162–184.

17. Christopher E. Smith, "Black Muslims and the Development of Prisoners'

Rights," *Journal of Black Studies* 24, 2 (1993): 131–146.

18.   Michael Jackson, "Justice Behind the Walls: A Study of the Disciplinary Process in a Canadian Penitentiary," *Osgoode Hall Law Journal* 12, 1 (1974) : 1–103

19.   *Martineau v. Matsqui Institution,* 1979 CanLII 184 (SCC), [1980] 1 SCR 602.

20.   Eric Andrew-Gee, "Prisoners Lose Appeal in Upside-Down Maple Leaf T-Shirt Lawsuit," *Toronto Star,* May 15, 2015, thestar.com/news/gta/2015/05/15/prisoners-lose-appeal-in-upside-down-maple-leaf-t-shirt-lawsuit.html; *Lauzon v. Canada (Attorney General),* 2014 ONSC 2811 (CanLII).

21.   *Corrections and Conditional Release Act,* SC 1992, c 20.

22.   Ewert v. Canada, 2018 SCC 30 (CanLII), [2018] 2 SCR 165.

23.   Jeremy Patrick, "Creating a Federal Inmate Grievance Tribunal," *Canadian Journal of Criminology and Criminal Justice* 48, 2 (2006): 289; Prisoners' Legal Services, "Writing an Effective Grievance," December 2018, prisonjustice.org/wp-content/uploads/2019/01/Federal-Grievance-2018.pdf.

24.   Office of the Correctional Investigator, *Office of the Correctional Investigator Annual Report 2016–2017,* oci-bec.gc.ca/cnt/rpt/pdf/annrpt/annrpt20162017-eng.pdf.

25.   Patrick, "Creating a Federal Inmate Grievance Tribunal": 287–304.

26.   Amanda Bell Hughett, "A 'Safe Outlet' for Prisoner Discontent: How Prison Grievance Procedures Helped Stymie Prison Organizing During the 1970s," *Law & Social Inquiry* 44, 4 (2019): 893–921.

27.   International Labour Organization, "C029 — Forced Labour Convention, 1930 (No. 29)," ilo.org/dyn/normlex/en/f?p=NORMLEXPUB:12100:0::NO::P12100_ILO_CODE:C029.

28.   United Nations General Assembly, *United Nations Standard Minimum Rules for the Treatment of Prisoners (the Nelson Mandela Rules), resolution / adopted by the General Assembly,* January 8, 2016, A/RES/70/175, refworld.org/docid/5698a3a44.html.

29.   Tari Ajadi, Harry Critchley, El Jones, Julia Rodgers, "Defunding the Police: Defining the Way Forward for the HRM," Halifax Board of Police Commissioner's Subcommittee to Define Defunding, halifax.ca/sites/default/files/documents/city-hall/boards-committees-commissions/220117bopc1021.pdf.

30.   Robert Mason, "Wrongful Convictions in Canada," *Parliamentary Information Service Publication No. 2020-77-E,* September 23, 2020, lop.parl.ca/sites/PublicWebsite/default/en_CA/ResearchPublications/202077E. Also see Brigitte Pellerin, "Reviewing Wrongful Convictions," *CBA/ABC National,* October 6, 2021, nationalmagazine.ca/en-ca/articles/cba-influence/submissions/2021/reviewing-wrongful-convictions.

31.   Mason, "Wrongful Convictions in Canada."

32.   Statistics Canada, "Adult and Youth Correctional Statistics in Canada, 2018/2019," December 21, 2020, www150.statcan.gc.ca/n1/pub/85-002-x/2020001/article/00016-eng.htm.

33.   Canadian Civil Liberties Association and Education Trust, "Set Up to Fail:

Bail and the Revolving Door of Pre-trial Detention," July 2014: 1, ccla.org/wp-content/uploads/2021/07/Set-up-to-fail-FINAL.pdf.

34.   Canadian Civil Liberties Association and Education Trust, "Set Up to Fail," 9.

35.   CBC News, "'At Some Point, They Have to Arrest Me': Homeless Man Wants to Go to Jail to Stay Warm," December 24, 2016, cbc.ca/news/canada/manitoba/homeless-man-jail-winter-1.3912199; Associated Press, "Man Says He Wanted 'Three Hots and a Cot,' So He Set Fire," July 31, 2018, wowt.com/content/news/Man-says-he-wanted-three-hots-and-a-cot-so-he-set-fire-489627041.html.

36.   Gresham M. Sykes, *The Society of Captives: A Study of the Maximum Security Prison* (Princeton: Princeton University Press, 1958).

37.   iPolitics, "Verbatim: Stephen Harper's Speech to the Calgary Convention," November 1, 2013, ipolitics.ca/2013/11/01/verbatim-stephen-harpers-speech-to-the-calgary-convention/. Also see Paula Mallea, *Fearmonger: Stephen Harper's Tough-on-Crime Agenda* (Toronto: Lorimer, 2011).

38.   Desmond Devoy, "Forget 'Club Fed': Inside Canada's Aging, Segregated Prisons," *Perth Courier*, February 20, 2017, insideottawavalley.com/news-story/7146391-forget-club-fed-inside-canada-s-aging-segregated-prisons/.

39.   See Office of the Correctional Investigator, *Office of the Correctional Investigator Annual Report 2019–2020*, oci-bec.gc.ca/cnt/rpt/annrpt/annrpt20192020-eng.aspx#fn65-rf; Standing Senate Committee on Human Rights, *Human Rights of Federally-Sentenced Persons*; Andre Marin, "The Code: Investigation into the Ministry of Community Safety and Correctional Services' Response to Allegations of Excessive Use of Force Against Inmates," *Ombudsman Ontario*, June 2013, ombudsman.on.ca/Files/sitemedia/Documents/Investigations/SORT%20Investigations/The-Code-EN.pdf; Simmone Poirier, "Decades of Darkness — Moving Towards the Light: A Review of the Prison System in Newfoundland and Labrador," October 2008, gov.nl.ca/jps/files/publications-ac-report.pdf.

40.   See Brigitte Noël, "Les Prisons Québécoises Sont Surpeuplées, Délabrées et Débilitantes," *Vice News*, February 22, 2017, vice.com/fr/article/78mnda/les-prisons-quebecoises-sont-surpeuplees-delabrees-et-debilitantes; Thomas Rohner, "Inmates of Iqaluit Jail Subjected to 'Shocking' Lengths of Solitary Confinement," *Vice News*, July 12, 2018, vice.com/en/article/zm5vb5/inmates-in-notorious-iqaluit-jail-subjected-to-shocking-lengths-of-solitary-confinement; Independent Review of Ontario Corrections, "Corrections in Ontario: Directions for Reform," Queen's Printer, September 2017, files.ontario.ca/solgen-corrections_in_ontario_directions_for_reform.pdf.

41.   Raizel Robin, "The $1-Billion Hellhole," *Toronto Life*, February 15, 2017, torontolife.com/city/inside-toronto-south-detention-centre-torontos-1-billion-hellhole/.

42.   Robin, "The $1-Billion Hellhole."

43.   Robin, "The $1-Billion Hellhole."

44.   See Office of the Auditor General of Ontario, *Annual Report 2019, Vol-*

ume 3 (Fall 2019), auditor.on.ca/en/content/annualreports/arreports/en19/2019AR_v3_en_web.pdf.

45.   Rosie DiManno, "Why Toronto South Detention Centre is known as Guantanamo South, a $1-billion Hellhole, and the Plea Factory," *Toronto Star,* December 14, 2019, thestar.com/opinion/star-columnists/2019/12/13/toronto-south-detention-centre-a-giant-black-hole-for-those-who-disappear-there-head-of-criminal-lawyers-body.html.

46.   Betsy Powell, "Citing 'Unconscionable' Conditions at Toronto South Jail, Judge Imposes 7-Year Sentence but Says Man Should Face No Further Prison Time," *Toronto Star,* June 11, 2019, thestar.com/news/gta/2019/06/11/citing-unconscionable-conditions-at-toronto-south-jail-judge-imposes-7-year-sentence-but-says-man-should-face-no-further-prison-time.html.

47.   See Mallea, *Beyond Incarceration.*

48.   Emilie Coyle and Jackie Omstead, "The Use of Solitary Confinement Continues in Canada," *Policy Options,* January 18, 2022, policyoptions.irpp.org/magazines/january-2022/the-use-of-solitary-confinement-continues-in-canada/; Jane B. Sprott and Anthony N. Doob, "Solitary Confinement, Torture, and Canada's Structured Intervention Units," February 23, 2021, johnhoward.ca/drs-doob-sprott-report/; Vera-Lynn Kubinec, "'A Dungeon Inside a Prison': Lawsuit Seeks Compensation for Manitoba Inmates Held in Solitary Confinement," *CBC News,* June 1, 2021, cbc.ca/news/canada/manitoba/solitary-confinement-lawsuit-class-action-1.6047810.

49.   Standing Senate Committee on Human Rights, *Human Rights of Federally-Sentenced Persons* 88. Also see Seamus Heffernan, "We Are Feeding Our Prisoners Gruel and Using Hunger As Punishment," *The Line,* November 19, 2020, theline.substack.com/p/seamus-heffernan-we-are-feeding-our?s=r.

50.   Heffernan, "We Are Feeding Our Prisoners Gruel."

51.   Bryan D. Palmer, "The New New Poor Law: A Chapter in the Current Class War Waged from Above," *Labour / Le Travail* 84 (2019): 60.

52.   John Clarke, "A Tale of Two Austerities," *Canadian Dimension,* January 24, 2019, canadiandimension.com/articles/view/a-tale-of-two-austerities.

53.   Edward W. Sieh, "Less Eligibility: The Upper Limits of Penal Policy," *Criminal Justice Policy Review* 3, 2 (1989): 159–183. Also see Peter Oliver, *"Terror to Evil-Doers": Prisons and Punishment in Nineteenth-Century Ontario* (Toronto: Osgoode Society, 1998): 222–223; 245–246.

54.   Paul Gendreau, Claire Goggin and Francis T. Cullen, "The Effects of Prison Sentences on Recidivism," Public Works and Government Services Canada Cat. No.: J42-87/1999E (1999), publicsafety.gc.ca/cnt/rsrcs/pblctns/ffcts-prsn-sntncs-rcdvsm/ffcts-prsn-sntncs-rcdvsm-eng.pdf.

55.   See Adam D.K. King, "Uber's Flexible Work+ Proposal Is a Ploy to Undermine Workers' Rights and Protections," *Passage,* March 16, 2021, readpassage.com/p/ubers-new-flexible-work-plan-is-bad-for-workers/.

56.   See Oliver, *"Terror to Evil-Doers":* 175; Seth Adema, "More than Stone and Iron: Indigenous History and Incarceration in Canada, 1834–1996," PhD dis-

sertation, Wilfrid Laurier University (2016): 81.

57.   See Eugene V. Debs, *Walls and Bars* (Chicago: Charles H. Kerr & Company, 1973), 76–87.

58.   Mental Health Commission of Canada. "Mental Health and the Criminal Justice System: 'What We Heard,'" (2020): 1, mentalhealthcommission.ca/wp-content/uploads/drupal/2020-08/mental_health_and_the_law_evidence_summary_report_eng.pdf; Standing Senate Committee on Human Rights, *Human Rights of Federally-Sentenced Persons,* 14.

59.   *Cell Count,* "Re: Inmate Pay Cut," 73 (Spring, 2014): 5, prisonfreepress.org/Cell_Count/Cell_Count_-_Issue_73.pdf.

60.   Office of the Correctional Investigator, *Office of the Correctional Investigator Annual Report 2013-2014,* June 27, 2014, oci-bec.gc.ca/cnt/rpt/annrpt/annrpt20132014-eng.aspx?pedisable=true.

61.   Eric Thibault, "Federal Inmate Cost Soars to $117Gs Each Per Year," *Toronto Sun,* March 19, 2014, torontosun.com/2014/03/18/federal-inmate-cost-soars-to-177gs-each-per-year.

62.   This calculation is based on figures showing the average annual cost of a federal prisoner was $117,788 for the 2011–2012 fiscal year. Community supervision (probation or parole) has been estimated to cost $18,000 per person per year, resulting in savings of around $99,788. The federal prison population was 14,745 in April 2013. See Thibault, "Federal Inmate Cost Soars"; John Howard Society of Canada, "Financial Facts on Canadian Prisons," August 18, 2018, johnhoward.ca/blog/financial-facts-canadian-prisons/.

63.   See Black Lives Matter Canada, "Defund the Police," 2022, defundthepolice.org/canada/.

64.   See Rose Ricciardelli and Adrienne M.F. Peters, *After Prison: Navigating Employment and Reintegration* (Waterloo, ON: Wilfrid Laurier University Press, 2017).

65.   James Young [pseud.], "Work After Prison: One Man's Transition" in Ricciardelli and Peters, *After Prison:* 25.

66.   See Gendreau, Goggin, and Cullen, "The Effects of Prison Sentences on Recidivism"; Cheryl Marie Webster and Anthony N. Doob, "Searching for Sasquatch: Deterrence of Crime Through Sentence Severity," in *Oxford Handbook on Sentencing and Corrections,* edited by Joan Petersilia and Kevin Reitz (New York: Oxford University Press, 2012): 173–195; Elizabeth Comack, Cara Fabre, and Shanise Burgher, "The Impact of the Harper Government's 'Tough on Crime' Strategy: Hearing from Frontline Workers," *Canadian Centre for Policy Alternatives,* September 2015, policyalternatives.ca/sites/default/files/uploads/publications/Manitoba%20Office/2015/09/Tough%20on%20Crime%20WEB.pdf.

67.   See Mallea, *Beyond Incarceration,* Chapter 1; Webster and Doob, "Searching for Sasquatch: 173–195.

68.   See INCITE! Women of Color Against Violence and Critical Resistance, "The Critical Resistance INCITE! Statement on Gender Violence and the Prison

Industrial Complex," in *Abolition Now! Ten Years of Strategy and Struggle Against the Prison Industrial Complex,* edited by the CR10 Publications Collective (Oakland and Edinburgh: AK Press, 2008): 15–29; Jo-Anne Wemmers, "Restorative Justice For Victims of Crime: A Victim-Oriented Approach to Restorative Justice," *International Review of Victimology* 9 (2002): 43–59.

69.   Judy Fudge, Elene Lam, Sandra Ka Hon Chu and Vincent Wong, "Caught in the Carceral Web: Anti-Trafficking Laws and Policies and Their Impact on Migrant Sex Workers" (2021), gflc.ca/wp-content/uploads/2020/10/MSW-Report-Final-Sept-26.pdf.

70.   Jordan House, "Making Prisons Work: Prison Labour and Resistance in Canada," PhD dissertation, York University (2020): 182.

71.   See Douglas Hay, "Property, Authority, and the Criminal Law," in *Albion's Fatal Tree: Crime and Society in Eighteenth-Century England,* edited by Doulas Hay, Peter Linebaugh, John G. Rule, E.P. Thompson, and Cal Winslow (New York: Pantheon, 1975): 17–63. Also see Harry Glasbeek, *Capitalism: A Crime Story* (Toronto: Between the Lines, 2018).

72.   Barack Obama, "The President's Role in Advancing Criminal Justice Reform," *Harvard Law Review* 130, 3 (2017): 812–866; Adriana Belmonte, "NBA Teams Become Latest Voices on Prison Reform," *Yahoo! Finance,* February 29, 2020, finance.yahoo.com/news/nba-teams-prison-reform-155959725.html;   Asha Bandele, "Jay Z: 'The War on Drugs Is an Epic Fail,'" *New York Times,* September 15, 2016, nytimes.com/2016/09/15/opinion/jay-z-the-war-on-drugs-is-an-epic-fail.html; Steve Everett Baber, "Responses to Mass-Incarceration by Faith Communities," PhD dissertation, Seattle University (2020), scholarworks.seattleu.edu/cgi/viewcontent.cgi?article=1006&context=dmin-projects; Shane Bauer, "How Conservatives Learned to Love Prison Reform," *Mother Jones,* March/April 2014, motherjones.com/politics/2014/02/conservatives-prison-reform-right-on-crime/.

73.   For example, see Tom Cordoso, "Bias Behind Bars: A Globe Investigation Finds a Prison System Stacked Against Black and Indigenous Inmates," *Globe and Mail,* October 24, 2020, theglobeandmail.com/canada/article-investigation-racial-bias-in-canadian-prison-risk-assessments/; Jackson, *Justice Behind the Walls*; Mallea, *Beyond Incarceration*.

74.   Justin Ling, "Houses of Hate: How Canada's Prison System Is Broken," *Maclean's,* February 28, 2021, macleans.ca/news/canada/houses-of-hate-how-canadas-prison-system-is-broken/.

75.   Robert Devet, "Interview: El Jones on Supporting the Burnside Jail Protest," *Nova Scotia Advocate,* August 22, 2018, nsadvocate.org/2018/08/22/interview-el-jones-on-supporting-the-burnside-jail-protest/.

76.   Nancy Macdonald, "Canada's Prisons Are the 'New Residential Schools,'" *Maclean's,* February 18, 2016, macleans.ca/news/canada/canadas-prisons-are-the-new-residential-schools/. Also see Adema, "More than Stone and Iron."

77.   Office of the Correctional Investigator, "Indigenous People in Federal Custody Surpasses 30% Correctional Investigator Issues Statement and Challenge,"

January 21, 2020, oci-bec.gc.ca/cnt/comm/press/press20200121-eng.aspx.

78.   *Corrections and Conditional Release Act,* SC 1992, c 20, s. 79. For an analysis of federal "Aboriginal Correctional Programming," see Jean-Philippe Crete, "A Disciplined Healing: The New Language of Indigenous Imprisonment in Canada," MA thesis, Carleton University (2013). For a discussion of the role of labour in residential schools, see Karen Bridget Murray, "The Violence Within: Canadian Modern Statehood and the Pan-Territorial Residential School System Ideal," *Canadian Journal of Political Science / Revue canadienne de science politique* 50, 3 (September 2017): 760–761.

79.   Quoted in Roger Neufeld, "Cabals, Quarrels, Strikes, and Impudence: Kingston Penitentiary, 1890–1914," *Histoire Sociale / Social History* 31, 61 (1998): 95–96.

80.   Indigenous Corporate Training, Inc., "10 Quotes John A. Macdonald Made about First Nations," June 28, 2016, ictinc.ca/blog/10-quotes-john-a.-macdonald-made-about-first-nations. Emphasis ours.

81.   Jorge Barrera, "Federal Prison Corporation's Selling of Moccasins, Drums for Revenue 'Exploitative,' Says Cree- Metis Artist," *APTN*, November 16, 2016, aptnnews.ca/2016/11/16/federal-prison-corporations-selling-of-moccasins-drums-for-revenue-exploitative-says-cree-metis-artist. For more analysis of the program, see Jean-Philippe Crete, "Punitive Healing and Penal Relics: Indigenous Prison Labour and the (Re)production of Cultural Artefacts," in *The Palgrave Handbook of Prison Tourism,* edited by Jacqueline Z. Wilson, Sarah Hodgkinson, Justin Piché and Kevin Walby (London: Palgrave MacMillan, 2017): 969–988.

82.   Barrera, "Federal Prison Corporation's Selling of Moccasins."

83.   Office of the Correctional Investigator, *Office of the Correctional Investigator Annual Report 2019–2020*; Statistics Canada, "Canada's Black Population: Growing in Number and Diversity," February 6, 2019, www150.statcan.gc.ca/n1/pub/11-627-m/11-627-m2019006-eng.htm.

84.   Standing Senate Committee on Human Rights, *Human Rights of Federally-Sentenced Persons,* 135.

85.   Cordoso, "Bias Behind Bars."

86.   Akwasi Owusu-Bempah, Maria Jung, Firdaous Sbaï, Andrew S. Wilton, and Fiona Kouyoumdjian, "Race and Incarceration: The Representation and Characteristics of Black People in Provincial Correctional Facilities in Ontario, Canada," *Race and Justice* (April 2021), 1–13.

87.   Standing Senate Committee on Human Rights, *Human Rights of Federally-Sentenced Persons,* 45.

88.   Deniz Do, René Houle and Martin Turcotte, "Canada's Black Population: Education, Labour and Resilience," Statistics Canada, February 25, 2020, www150.statcan.gc.ca/n1/pub/89-657-x/89-657-x2020002-eng.htm; Emmanuelle Bourbeau and Andrew Fields, "Annual Review of the Labour Market, 2016," Statistics Canada, April 28, 2017, www150.statcan.gc.ca/n1/pub/75-004-m/75-004-m2017001-eng.htm.

89.   Rick Sauvé, personal communication, August 10, 2021,

90.   Rick Sauvé, personal communication, August 10, 2021; Standing Senate Committee on Human Rights, *Human Rights of Federally Sentenced Persons,* 202.

91.   Office of the Correctional Investigator, "Federally Sentenced Women," March, 14, 2016, oci-bec.gc.ca/cnt/priorities-priorites/women-femmes-eng.aspx.

92.   See Ted McCoy, *Four Unruly Women: Stories of Incarceration and Resistance from Canada's Most Notorious Prison* (Vancouver and Toronto: UBC Press, 2019); Kelly Hannah-Moffat and Margaret Shaw (eds.), *An Ideal Prison: Critical Essays on Women's Imprisonment in Canada* (Halifax: Fernwood Publishing, 2000).

93.   Standing Senate Committee on Human Rights, *Human Rights of Federally-Sentenced Persons,* 39.

94.   Martha Paynter and Emilie Coyle, "In Canada's Federal Women's Prisons, Reproductive Rights Are Under Threat," *Briarpatch Magazine,* February 8, 2021, briarpatchmagazine.com/articles/view/in-canadas-federal-womens-prisons-reproductive-rights-are-under-threat.

95.   Office of the Correctional Investigator, *Office of the Correctional Investigator Annual Report 2019–2020,* oci-bec.gc.ca/cnt/rpt/annrpt/annrpt20192020-eng.aspx#fn65-rf.

96.   Meredith Robeson Barrett, Kim Allenby and Kelly Taylor, "Twenty Years Later: Revisiting the Task Force on Federally Sentenced Women," Correctional Service of Canada, July 2010, csc-scc.gc.ca/research/005008-0222-01-eng.shtml.

97.   Claire Bodkin, Lucie Pivnick, Susan J. Bondy, et al., "History of Childhood Abuse in Populations Incarcerated in Canada: A Systematic Review and Meta-Analysis," *American Journal of Public Health* 109, 3 (2019): 1–11.

98.   Department of Justice Canada, "State of the Criminal Justice System: Focus on Women," (2021): 39, justice.gc.ca/eng/cj-jp/state-etat/2021rpt-rap2021/pdf/SOCJS_2020_en.pdf.

99.   Office of the Correctional Investigator, *Office of the Correctional Investigator Annual Report 2019–2020.*

100. Department of Justice Canada, "State of the Criminal Justice System: Focus on Women," 15.

101. Department of Justice Canada, "State of the Criminal Justice System: Focus on Women," 41.

102. Simon Rolston, "The Hidden Lives and Uncertain Future of Trans Prisoners," *Xtra,* October 6, 2021, xtramagazine.com/power/trans-prisoners-canada-legal-fights-209961.

103. Kathleen Harris, "Canada's Prison System Overhauls Transgender Inmate Policy," *CBC News,* January 31, 2018, cbc.ca/news/politics/transgender-inmates-csc-policy-1.4512510.

104. Quoted in Johann J. Go, "Structure, Choice, and Responsibility," *Ethics & Behavior* 30, 3 (2020): 230–246.

105. See Olivia Stefanovich, "'We're in Trouble': Advocates Urge Ottawa to Help

Close the Access-to-Justice Gap," CBC News, April 18, 2021, cbc.ca/news/politics/access-to-justice-federal-budget-2021-requests-1.5989872; Public Prosecution Service of Canada, "Innocence at Stake: The Need for Continued Vigilance to Prevent Wrongful Convictions in Canada," September 2018, ppsc-sppc.gc.ca/eng/pub/is-ip/index.html.

106. Canadian Bar Association, "Reaching Equal Justice: An Invitation to Envision and Act," November 2013, cba.org/CBA-Equal-Justice/Equal-Justice-Initiative/Reports.

107. See Nancy Macdonald, "Canada's Prisons Are the 'New Residential Schools'"; Cordoso, "Bias Behind Bars"; Jim Rankin, Patty Winsa, Andrew Bailey and Hidy Ng, "Carding Drops but Proportion of Blacks Stopped by Toronto Police Rises," Toronto Star, July 26, 2014, thestar.com/news/insight/2014/07/26/carding_drops_but_proportion_of_blacks_stopped_by_toronto_police_rises.html; Andrea Huncar, "How Systemic Racism Is Factoring into Sentences for Black Albertans," CBC News, March 24, 2021, cbc.ca/news/canada/edmonton/black-indigenous-offenders-gladue-enhanced-pre-sentence-reports-1.5951638; Jeffrey Reiman and Paul Leighton, The Rich Get Richer and the Poor Get Prison (11th edition) (New York and London: Routledge, 2016).

108. See Kelly Hannah-Moffat, "Criminogenic Needs and the Transformative Risk Subject: Hybridizations of Risk/Need in Penality," Punishment & Society 7, 1 (January 2005): 29–51.

109. John Howard Society of Toronto, "Homeless and Jailed: Jailed and Homeless," August 2010, https://johnhoward.ca/wp-content/uploads/2016/12/Amber-Kellen-Homeless-and-Jailed-Jailed-and-Homeless.pdf.

110. Victoria Gibson and Nadine Yousif, "Nearly One in Four People Sent to Toronto's Detention Centres in 2020 Were Homeless — The Worst Rate Seen in Years," Toronto Star, May 7, 2021, thestar.com/news/gta/2021/05/07/nearly-one-in-four-people-sent-to-torontos-detention-centres-in-2020-were-homeless-the-worst-rate-seen-in-years.html?utm_source=Twitter&utm_medium=SocialMedia&utm_campaign=GTA&utm_content=homeless-detention.

111. Office of the Correctional Investigator, Office of the Correctional Investigator Annual Report 2014–2015, oci-bec.gc.ca/cnt/rpt/annrpt/annrpt20142015-eng.aspx#s3.

112. Office of the Correctional Investigator, Office of the Correctional Investigator Annual Report 2014–2015.

113. John Howard Society of Ontario, "Crime and Unemployment: What's the Link? FactSheet 24 (2009), johnhoward.on.ca/wp-content/uploads/2014/09/facts-24-crime-and-unemployment-whats-the-link-march-2009.pdf.

114. Standing Senate Committee on Human Rights, Human Rights of Federally-Sentenced Persons, 41.

115. Nathaniel Lewis, "Locking Up the Lower Class," Jacobin, jacobinmag.com/2018/01/mass-incarceration-race-class-peoples-policy-project.

116. Kyle Duggan, "The Proposed Budget 2017 Lines Canadians Couldn't Stom-

ach," *iPolitics,* July 20, 2017, ipolitics.ca/2017/07/20/the-proposed-budget-2017-lines-canadians-couldnt-stomach/.

117. Bryan Evans, "The New Democratic Party in the Era of Neoliberalism," in *Rethinking the Politics of Labour in Canada,* edited by Stephanie Ross and Larry Savage (Halifax and Winnipeg: Fernwood Publishing, 2012): 48–61; Bronwyn Dobchuk-Land and James Wilt, "Prison Unionism," *Briarpatch,* July 2, 2020, briarpatchmagazine.com/articles/view/prison-unionism.

118. The public sector operates on a different logic but is ultimately still dependent on capitalist production from which it derives tax revenues. For more discussion of the role of the public sector in capitalism and public sector labour relations, see Byan Evans, "When Your Boss Is the State: The Paradoxes of Public Sector Work," in *Public Sector Unions in the Age of Austerity,* edited by Stephanie Ross and Larry Savage (Halifax and Winnipeg: Fernwood Publishing, 2013): 18–30. Social reproduction feminists challenge the notion that the public sector is "unproductive" and emphasize the centrality of the public sector — and the family — in producing the workers needed for capitalist production. See Tithi Battacharya, "How Not to Skip Class: Social Reproduction of Labour and the Global Working Class," *Social Reproduction Theory: Remapping Class, Recentring Oppression* (London: Pluto Press, 2017): 68–93.

119. Steven Bittle, Dean Curran and Laureen Snider, "Crimes of the Powerful: The Canadian Context," *Critical Criminology* (2018) 26: 451–454; Morris, *Penal Abolition,* 15–19.

120. It is difficult to figure out what the exact impact including incarcerated in unemployment calculations would have on unemployment figures. Using December 2019 numbers (which represent more "normal" figures before the beginning of the COVID-19 pandemic), by our calculations, the inclusion of incarcerated people would increase the Canadian unemployment rate by 0.2%. However, this figure is not entirely accurate as not all incarcerated people would necessarily count as part of the labour force — some would be considered retired or otherwise out of the labour force. On the other hand, due to difficulties obtaining work upon release, it is also the case that formerly incarcerated people are more likely to drop out of the labour market and not be included in unemployment figures. More research on incarceration and unemployment statistics is needed.

121. Greg McElligott, "Beyond Service, Beyond Coercion? Prisoner Co-ops and the Path to Democratic Administration," in *From the Streets to the State: Changing the World by Taking Power,* edited by Paul Christopher Gray (Albany, NY: State University of New York Press, 2018): 235.

122. Adam D. Reich and Seth J. Prins, "The Disciplining Effect of Mass Incarceration on Labor Organization," *American Journal of Sociology* 125, 5 (March 2020): 1303–1344.

123. See Aziz Choudry and Adiran Smith (eds.), *Unfree Labour? Struggles of Migrant and Immigrant Workers in Canada* (Oakland: PM Press, 2016). Also see Todd Gordon, "Capitalism, Neoliberalism, and Unfree Labour," *Critical Soci-*

ology 45, 6 (2019): 921–939.

124. CCRA, s. 127(3).

125. *Prisons and Reformatories Act,* RSC 1985, c P-20, s. 6.

126. German Lopez, "America's Prisoners Are Going on Strike in at Least 17 States," *Vox,* August 22, 2018, vox.com/2018/8/17/17664048/national-prison-strike-2018.

127. Karl Marx, "Wage Labour and Capital," in *The Marx-Engels Reader* (second edition), edited by Robert C. Tucker (New York: Norton, 1978): 205.

128. Ken Klippenstein, "Documents Show Amazon Is Aware Drivers Pee in Bottles and Even Defecate En Route, Despite Company Denial," *The Intercept,* March 25, 2021, theintercept.com/2021/03/25/amazon-drivers-pee-bottles-union/.

129. Gordon, "Capitalism, Neoliberalism, and Unfree Labour," 10.

130. Rick Sauvé, personal communication, August 10, 2021.

CHAPTER 2: ALL WORK AND (ALMOST) NO PAY

1. *CTV News,* "First Look at Where Ontario Inmates Make Blankets, Licence Plates," March 17, 2015, london.ctvnews.ca/first-look-at-where-ontario-in-mates-make-blankets-licence-plates-1.2284452.

2. Nova Scotia Justice Correctional Services, "Fine Option Program," (n.d.), novascotia.ca/just/Corrections/_docs/FineOptionsProgram.pdf.

3. *Fenton v. British Columbia* (1991), 56 B.C.L.R. (2d) 170 (B.C.C.A.)

4. D. Owen Carrigan, *Crime and Punishment in Canada: A History* (Toronto: McClelland & Stewart, 1991): 408

5. Kristin Annable, "Manitoba Government Ends Employment Training Program for Provincial Inmates," *CBC News,* May 1, 2018, cbc.ca/news/canada/manitoba/jail-mancor-closes-employment-1.4642073.

6. Patrick Cain, "Canada's Last Military Prison Costs $2M a Year. About Half the Time, It Has No Prisoners," *Global News,* May 23, 2018, globalnews.ca/news/4097208/military-prison-edmonton-empty/.

7. Global Detention Project, "Immigration Detention in Canada: Important Reforms, Ongoing Concerns," June 2018: 18, globaldetentionproject.org/immigration-detention-in-canada-important-reforms-ongoing-concerns.

8. Amnesty International, "Op-ed: Canada Should Get on the Path to Abolishing Immigration Detention," June 18, 2021, amnesty.org/en/latest/news/2021/06/canada-path-abolishing-immigration-detention/. For information on activism against immigration detention, see End Immigration Detention Network, endimmigrationdetention.wordpress.com/.

9. Office of the Correctional Investigator, *Office of the Correctional Investigator Annual Report 2019–2020,* oci-bec.gc.ca/cnt/rpt/annrpt/annrpt20172018-eng.aspx.

10. Correctional Service of Canada, "CORCAN — Employment and Employability," July 9, 2018, csc-scc.gc.ca/publications/005007-3016-en.shtml.

11. Claire Brownell, "Prisoners making $1.95 a Day Want a Raise, Taxpayers Want a Break," *Financial Post,* August 30, 2017, https://financialpost.com/news/court-challenge-to-inmate-pay-places-prison-labour-program-in-the-cross-hairs.

12. CCRA, s. 40.

13. Gregory McMaster, personal communication, February 29, 2020.

14. Correctional Service of Canada, "CORCAN: Overview," November 13, 2018, csc-scc.gc.ca/corcan/002005-0001-eng.shtml.

15. Correctional Service of Canada, "CORCAN: Overview."

16. Government of Canada, *Public Accounts of Canada 2020 Volume III: Additional Information and Analyses,* publications.gc.ca/collections/collection_2020/spac-pspc/P51-1-2020-3-eng.pdf .

17. Alberta Civil Liberties Research Centre, "Keeping the Peace: Prisoners' Rights and Employment Programs," (2014): 102, static1.squarespace.com/static/511bd4e0e4b0cecdc77b114b/t/5d237a13e48a5a0001896e76/1562606102833/6+Keeping+the+Peace+Prisoners+and+Employement+Programs+2014.pdf.

18. *Corrections Act,* RSA 2000, c C-29, s. 17.

19. *Correctional Services Act,* SNS 2005, c 37, s. 59.

20. *General Regulation, NB Reg* 84-257, s. 12(b).

21. *General Regulation, NB Reg* 84-257, s. 15(c).

22. See R.M. Warren, "A Defence of Burwash" *Globe,* September 21, 1920: 6; Andreas Schroeder, *Shaking it Rough: A Prison Memoir* (Toronto and New York: Doubleday, 1976); "Inmates Will Be Foresters in Hallow," *Globe and Mail,* August 14, 1978: 23.

23. Alberta Civil Liberties Research Centre, "Keeping the Peace," 99; Ontario Ministry of the Solicitor General, "Rehabilitation Programs and Services for Offenders," September 14, 2019, ontario.ca/page/rehabilitation-programs-and-services-offenders.

24. *Toronto Star,* "B.C. Thanks Inmates Who Helped During the Province's Worst-Ever Wildfire Season," October 3, 2017, thestar.com/news/canada/2017/10/03/bc-thanks-inmates-who-helped-battle-the-provinces-worst-ever-wildfire-season.html.

25. Alberta Civil Liberties Research Centre, "Keeping the Peace," 99.

26. Alberta Civil Liberties Research Centre, "Keeping the Peace," 101–102.

27. Ministère de la Sécurité publique, "Fonds central de soutien à la réinsertion sociale," (n.d.), solutionmaindoeuvre.ca/.

28. Stéphanie Borgia, "Fonds de soutien à la réinsertion sociale des établissements de détention: Rapport d'activités 2019," cdn-contenu.quebec.ca/cdn-contenu/adm/min/securite-publique/publications-adm/publications-secteurs/services-correctionnels/reinsertion-sociale/rapport_activites_FCSRS_2019.pdf?1624456703, 5–6.

29. Ministère de la Sécurité publique, "Fonds central de soutien à la réinsertion sociale."

30. Ingrid Peritz, "Mexicans, Convicts Work Quebec Farms; They Like It, But at

$4.95 An Hour They're Exploited Critics Complain," *Gazette,* June 4, 1988: A1. Also see Vic Satzewich, *Racism and the Incorporation of Foreign Labour: Farm Labour Migration to Canada Since 1945* (London and New York: Routledge, 1991), 81.

31. Neil Scott, "Training Programs Loss Protested," *Leader Post,* April 2, 2004: B3; Dan Zakreski, "Down on Her Luck," *StarPhoenix,* June 16, 2001: A1.

32. Ashley Martin, "Inmate Kitchen Training to Return; In the Beginning, It Will Only Be Offered at Yorkton Facility," *StarPhoenix,* January 15, 2016: A9.

33. Annable, "Manitoba Government Ends Employment Training Program."

34. *Kingston Whig-Standard,* "Inmates Lose Jobs After TV Show Move," February 22, 2003: 34; Annable, "Manitoba Government Ends Employment Training Program."

35. Annable, "Manitoba Government Ends Employment Training Program"; Bryce Hoye, "Manitoba Looks to Private Sector to Help Reduce Youth Recidivism Through Social Impact Bond," *CBC News,* July 8, 2020, cbc.ca/news/canada/manitoba/manitoba-youth-recidivism-social-impact-bond-1.5642957.

36. Simonne Poirier, "Decades of Darkness — Moving Towards the Light: A Review of the Prison System in Newfoundland and Labrador," October 2008, gov.nl.ca/jps/files/publications-ac-report.pdf.

37. There are many hurdles to jump to qualify for temporary absence programs. For example, see Prince Edward Island Community and Correctional Services, "Adult Custody Information Handbook," 2016: 17, princeedwardisland.ca/sites/default/files/publications/adult_custody_information_handbook_2016.pdf.

38. See Jordan House, "When Prisoners Had a Union: The Canadian Food and Allied Workers Union Local 240," *Labour/Le Travail* 82 (Fall 2018): 13n12.

39. Arielle Zerr, "Inmates Help Clean Up Saskatoon," *StarPhoenix,* September 11, 2013: A3; Charles Hamilton, "Inmates Hard at Work in Urban Camp," *StarPhoenix,* February 4, 2013: A1.

40. Carl DeGurse, "All Should be Welcome in Storm Cleanup," *Winnipeg Free Press,* October 26, 2019: 13.

41. See Thomas Fuller, "Coronavirus Limits California's Efforts to Fight Fires With Prison Labor," *New York Times,* August 22, 2020, nytimes.com/2020/08/22/us/california-wildfires-prisoners.html; Philip Goodman, "Hero and Inmate: Work, Prisons, and Punishment in California's Fire Camps," *WorkingUSA* 15, 3 (2012): 353–376.

42. Luc Gosselin, Prisons in Canada (Montréal: Black Rose Books, 1982); Jordan House, "Making Prison Work: Prison Labour and Resistance in Canada," PhD dissertation, York University (2020).

43. Dan Berger and Toussaint Loiser, Rethinking the American Prison Movement (New York and London: Routledge, 2018), 7. Also see: M.J. Adams, "Chip Away at It," Briarpatch, July 5, 2021, briarpatchmagazine.com/articles/view/chip-away-at-it.

44. House, "When Prisoners Had a Union," 19.

45. Quoted in Aline Nogueira Menezes Mourão, "Understanding the Effects of Carceral Employment Programs in Canada: Exploring the Perspectives of Former Federal Prisoners," Master's thesis, University of Ottawa (2018): 81.

46. See House, "When Prisoners Had a Union," 22.

47. See Jordan House, "The 1934 British Columbia Penitentiary Strike and Prisoners' Wages in Canada," *Active History*, April 26, 2019, activehistory. ca/2019/04/the-1934-british-columbia-penitentiary-strike-and-prisoners-wages-in-canada/.

48. John Kidman, *The Canadian Prison: The Story of a Tragedy* (Toronto: Ryerson Press, 1947), 67.

49. Chris Clarkson and Melissa Munn, *Disruptive Prisoners: Resistance, Reform, and the New Deal* (Toronto, Buffalo, and London: Toronto University Press. 2021), 141.

50. Solicitor General of Canada, *Solicitor General Annual Report 1981–1982* (1982): 67, ojp.gov/pdffiles1/Digitization/89331NCJRS.pdf.

51. "Inside View," *Primetime*, August 1981: 4. Gaucher/Munn Penal Press Collection, penalpress.com/wp-content/uploads/Primetime_Aug1981.pdf; Also see Malcolm Gray, "Meltdown in the Gilded Cage," *Maclean's*, June 15, 1981, archive.macleans.ca/article/1981/6/15/meltdown-in-the-gilded-cage; Malcolm Gray, "Arsonists and Inmates," *Maclean's*, November 30, 1981, archive. macleans.ca/article/1981/11/30/arsonists-and-inmates.

52. Solicitor General of Canada, *Solicitor General Annual Report 1981–1982*, 67.

53. Kirk Makin, "Federal Prisoners' Pay Tripled to Meet Minimum Rate," *Globe and Mail*, April 22, 1981: 23.

54. Damien Cox, "Inmates at Four Penitentiaries Stop Work to Protest Pay Rates," *Toronto Star*, January 24, 1989: A7.

55. *Toronto Star*, "Inmates Dine on Burgers and Fries," January 21, 1989: A13.

56. Kirk Makin, "Low Pay Leads to Thievery in Penitentiaries," *Globe and Mail*, April 17, 1989: A4.

57. Brennan Neil, "'The Prices are Outrageous': Concerns Raised Over Monopoly on Ordered Goods in Federal Prisons," December 19, 2018, cbc.ca/news/canada/montreal/federal-prison-prices-catalogue-1.4950577.

58. Office of the Correctional Investigator, *Office of the Correctional Investigator Annual Report 2015–2016*, oci-bec.gc.ca/cnt/rpt/annrpt/annrpt20152016-eng.aspx.

59. Standing Senate Committee on Human Rights, *Human Rights of Federally-Sentenced Persons*, 254.

60. Ministry of the Attorney General, "Inmate Information Guide for Adult Correctional Facilities," September 13, 2021, ontario.ca/page/inmate-information-guide-adult-correctional-facilities.

61. Borgia, "Fonds de soutien à la réinsertion sociale des établissements de détention."

62. D.C. Fraser, "Protest Underway at Regina Jail Over Recent Cuts to Inmates' Pay," *Leader Post*, May 3, 2017: A2; CTV News, "Some Working Inmates at

Regina Correctional Centre Strike Over Wage Cut," May 4, 2017, regina.ct-vnews.ca/some-working-inmates-at-regina-correctional-centre-strike-over-wage-cut-1.3399137.

63. Cory Charles Cardinal, "Prisons Are Built on Our Backs," *Briarpatch Magazine,* September 2, 2021, briarpatchmagazine.com/articles/view/prisons-are-built-on-our-backs.

64. Tobi Cohen, "Prisoner Purchases Offer Peek at Life Inside the Penitentiary; Inmates Buy Shoes, Games, Body Wash," *Windsor Star,* September 15, 2012: A9.

65. Stark Raven Radio, "Prisoner Strikes" [Audio podcast episode], October 7, 2013, vcn.bc.ca/august10/audio/Oct7.mp3.

66. Sam Cooper, "Rising Threat of Violence: Guards; Prisons: Cuts to Inmate Wages, Benefits Lead to Compounding Dangers in Already-volatile Situations," *The Province,* October 3, 2013, A3.

67. Jordan House, "Making Prison Work," 208.

68. *Province,* "Federal Policy on Crime Just Plain Nasty: Retired Official," October 4, 2013: A26.

69. *Drumheller Mail.* "Inmates Take Strike Action." October 9, https://www.drumhellermail.com/news/13348-inmates-take-strike-.

70. *CBC News,* "Prisoners Go on Strike," October 2, 2013, cbc.ca/player/play/2409874501/.

71. Quoted in House, "Making Prison Work," 242.

72. Kelly Struthers Montford, "Land, Agriculture, and the Carceral: The Territorializing Function of Penitentiary Farms," *Radical Philosophy Review* 22, 1 (2019): 114.

73. Philip Goodman and Meghan Dawe, "Prisoners, Cows, and Abattoirs: The Closing of Canada's Prison Farms as a Political Penal Drama," *British Journal of Criminology* 56, 4 (July 2016): 793–812. Also see Meghan Dawe and Philip Goodman, "Conservative Politics, Sacred Cows, and Sacrificial Lambs: The (Mis)Use of Evidence in Canada's Political and Penal Fields," *Canadian Review of Sociology* 54, 2 (May 2017): 129–146.

74. Correctional Service of Canada, "Briefing Note to the Commissioner: Reopening of CORCAN Farm at Collins Bay Institution," December 16, 2016: 12. Access to Information and Privacy release.

75. Evolve our Prison Farms, "Evidence of the Scale of the Planned Goat Operation and Other Problems with the New Prison Farms in Kingston" October 2020, unpublished document.

76. Paul Manly, "Petition to Cancel the Prison Agribusiness," August 21, 2020, paulmanlymp.ca/post/petition-prison-farm. Emphasis added.

77. Evolve Our Prison Farms, "Legal Issues Arising from the Export of Prison-Sourced Infant Formula," (n.d.), evolveourprisonfarms.ca/exporting-prison-produced-goods/. Emphasis in original.

78. Correctional Service of Canada, email to Marie Pier Lecuyer from redacted regarding agreements between CSC and Feihe International or Canada Royal

Milk, August 6, 2019: 27, Access to Information and Privacy release.

79.   Isabelle Robitaille, "Prison Farm Has Many Positives," *Kingston Whig-Standard,* March 21, 2021, thewhig.com/opinion/letters-to-the-editor-prison-farm-has-many-positives-clinic-a-success.

80.   Helen Forsey, "csc Should Abandon its Industrial Goat Farm Fiasco," *The Hill Times,* April 5, 2021, evolveourprisonfarms.ca/wp-content/uploads/2021/04/040521_ht_1-Helen-Forsey.pdf.

81.   Calvin Neufeld, "Bloody Bad Business: Report on the Joyceville Institution Abattoir," Evolve Our Prison Farms, August 31, 2021, evolveourprisonfarms.ca/wp-content/uploads/2021/09/Bloody-Bad-Business-Joyceville-Abattoir-Report-Evolve-Our-Prison-Farms.pdf.

82.   Neufeld, "Bloody Bad Business," 5.

83.   Government of Canada, "Salaries and wages – Canadian Industry Statistics: Meat Product Manufacturing – 3116," July 27, 2021, ic.gc.ca/app/scr/app/cis/salaries-salaires/3116;jsessionid=0001SLQLMFqdyeGSIt8sWTa55KY:-C7AEJO.

84.   Correctional Service of Canada, "Appendix B: Offender Training Agreement Between corcan and the Abattoir Licensee," October, 2019: 17–18, Access to Information and Privacy release; Ontario, "Minimum Wage," March 25, 2021, ontario.ca/document/your-guide-employment-standards-act-0/minimum-wage.

85.   Correctional Service of Canada, "Offender Hours Worked," (n.d.), Access to Information and Privacy release.

86.   Neufeld, "Bloody Bad Business," 13.

87.   Glenburnie Grocery, "Glenburnie Grocery Brands," (2022), glenburniegrocery.ca/site/glenburnie-kingston-local-brands.

88.   Criminalization and Punishment Education Project, "Tracking Politics of Criminalization and Punishment in Canada," February 27, 2022, tpcp-canada.blogspot.com/2022/02/over-21600-covid-19-cases-linked-to.html.

89.   Rachel Ward, "Senator Calls for Inmate Release to Prevent Potential Prison covid-19 'Disaster,'" *cbc News,* March 25, 2020, cbc.ca/news/canada/calgary/senator-calls-release-inmates-covid-19-1.5509086.

90.   Terri Theodore, "Lawyers, Advocate Call for Inmate Release Before covid-19 Spreads," *National Post,* April 9, 2020, nationalpost.com/pmn/news-pmn/canada-news-pmn/lawyers-advocate-call-for-inmate-release-before-covid-19-spreads.

91.   Adelina Iftene, "covid-19, Human Rights and Public Health in Prisons: A Case Study of Nova Scotia's Experience During the First Wave of the of the Pandemic," *Dalhousie Law Journal* 44, 2 (2021): 5–6.

92.   Alex Cooke, "N.S. Prison Reform Groups Call for Inmate Releases as covid-19 Spreads," *Global News,* January 1, 2022, globalnews.ca/news/8483490/ns-prison-inmate-release-covid-19/.

93.   Jordan House and Asaf Rashid, "Failure to Protect Essential Prisoner Workers Undermines Public Safety," *Canadian Dimension,* December 28, 2020,

canadiandimension.com/articles/view/failure-to-protect-essential-prisoner-workers-undermines-public-safety.

94. Zi-Ann Lum, "Canadian Inmates Have Made 821,703 Face Masks During The Pandemic," *HuffPost,* December 12, 2020, huffingtonpost.ca/entry/canada-prison-labour-covid-face-masks_ca_5fdd1a5ac5b6e5158fa70360.

95. Ivan Zinger, "Officer of the Correctional Investigator COVID-19 Status Update," April 23, 2020: 4, oci-bec.gc.ca/cnt/rpt/pdf/oth-aut/oth-aut20200423-eng.pdf.

96. Jeremiah Rodriguez, "Inmates Fear 'Leaving in a Body Bag' as COVID-19 Outbreaks in Prisons Worsen," *CTV News,* January 4, 2021, ctvnews.ca/health/coronavirus/inmates-fear-leaving-in-a-body-bag-as-covid-19-outbreaks-in-prisons-worsen-1.5253369.

97. Zinger, "Officer of the Correctional Investigator," 4.

98. Justin Ling, personal communication, April 26, 2020.

99. Toronto Prisoners' Rights Project, "Joyceville Correctional Centre Labour Strike," March 19, 2021, facebook.com/TorontoPrisonersRightsProject/photos/289057185967528/.

100. Iftene,"COVID-19, Human Rights and Public Health in Prisons," 15.

101. Mark Melnychuk, "Offenders in Work Program Fear Rules Could Cost Them Jobs; Yorkton Facility Has Restricted Inmates From Leaving Site as Pandemic Precaution," *Leader Post,* October 24, 2020: A6.

CHAPTER 3: INJURY, ILLNESS AND DEATH

1. Anonymous Whistleblower, "What Will You Do?" *Journal of Prisoners on Prisons* 28, 2 (2020): 142–147; Justin Ling, "Houses of Hate: How Canada's Prison System Is Broken," *Maclean's,* February 28, 2021, macleans.ca/news/canada/houses-of-hate-how-canadas-prison-system-is-broken/; Jorge Barrera and Joseph Loiero, "This Man Is on His Deathbed Because of the Health Care He Received in Prison, Lawsuit Alleges," *CBC News,* March 5, 2021, cbc.ca/news/canada/prison-health-care-lawsuits-1.5939078; Claire Bodkin, Matthew Bonn and Sheila Wildeman, "Fuelling a Crisis: Lack of Treatment for Opioid Use in Canada's Prisons and Jails," *The Conversation,* March 4, 2020, theconversation.com/fuelling-a-crisis-lack-of-treatment-for-opioid-use-in-canadas-prisons-and-jails-130779.

2. Nick Purdon, "PTSD Taking its Toll on Canada's Prison Guards," *CBC News,* July 24, 2015, cbc.ca/news/canada/ptsd-taking-its-toll-on-canada-s-prison-guards-1.3166791; Cheryl Regehr et al., "Prevalence of PTSD, Depression and Anxiety Disorders in Correctional Officers: A Systematic Review," *Corrections,* 6, 3, 229–241.

3. See Sara Mojtehedzadeh, "'Do Not Enter': Why Are Migrant Worker Bunkhouses Not Part of Workplace Safety Inspections?" *Toronto Star,* September 18, 2021, thestar.com/news/gta/2021/09/18/do-not-enter-should-migrant-

worker-bunkhouses-be-part-of-workplace-safety-inspections.html;   ITF Seafarers, "'I Have Had to Swim to Shore Every Few Days to Get Food and Water' – Meet the Seafarer Trapped on Board the *MV Aman* for Four Years (and Counting)," March 19, 2021, itfseafarers.org/en/news/i-have-had-swim-shore-every-few-days-get-food-and-water-meet-seafarer-trapped-board-mv-aman.

4.   "Fetal Alcohol Spectrum Disorder and the Criminal Justice System: A Poor Fit," *John Howard Society of Ontario Factsheet* 26 (2010), johnhoward.on.ca/wp-content/uploads/2014/09/facts-26-fasd-and-the-criminal-justice-system-december-2010.pdf; Angela Colantonio et al., "Traumatic Brain Injury and Early Life Experiences Among Men and Women in a Prison Population," *Journal of Correctional Healthcare* 20, 4 (2014): 271–279.

5.   Fiona Kouyoumdjian et al., "Health Status of Prisoners in Canada: Narrative Review," *Canadian Family Physician* 62 (March 2016): 217.

6.   Kouyoumdjian et al., "Health Status of Prisoners in Canada," 217.

7.   Correctional Service of Canada, "National Inventory of Asbestos in Correctional Service of Canada Buildings," n.d., csc-scc.gc.ca/health-and-safety/001006-1002-en.shtml.

8.   To give just one example, a 2008 asbestos assessment of Dorchester Penitentiary in New Brunswick recommended that floor tiles containing asbestos be removed from the CORCAN metal shop office, among other parts of the facility. See Rene Morais, "Asbestos Assessment Dorchester Penitentiary Dorchester, NB," Correctional Services Canada, September 8, 2008, buyandsell.gc.ca/cds/public/2019/10/08/53fe5d54bf1246a87303df139a9e5fc2/asbestos_assessment_dorchester_penitentiary.pdf.

9.   Correctional Service of Canada, "National Inventory of Asbestos in Correctional Service of Canada Buildings."

10. Julie Ireton, "Contractor in Fight with Public Works After Asbestos Exposure," CBC News, April 25, 2013, cbc.ca/news/canada/ottawa/contractor-in-fight-with-public-works-after-asbestos-exposure-1.1336575.

11. CBC News, "Government Officials Should Be Charged in Sydney Jail Asbestos Case: Union," June 3, 2008, cbc.ca/news/canada/nova-scotia/government-officials-should-be-charged-in-sydney-jail-asbestos-case-union-1.747689.

12. Marsha McLeod, "'The Jail Is Just a Death Trap': Stories of Overcrowding, Understaffing and Violence in Thunder Bay," *Globe and Mail*, October 8, 2020, theglobeandmail.com/canada/article-the-jail-is-just-a-death-trap-stories-of-overcrowding/.

13. For example, see "Corrections-Van Crash Reignites Safety Issues," *Winnipeg Free Press*, November 8, 2014, winnipegfreepress.com/local/corrections-van-crash-reignites-safety-issues-282013231.html.

14. Correctional Service of Canada, "Response to the 47th Annual Report of the Correctional Investigator 2019–2020," August 20, 2020, csc-scc.gc.ca/publications/005007-2811-en.shtml.

15. Correctional Service of Canada, "Response to the 47th Annual Report."

16. *Occupational Health and Safety Act,* RSO 1990, c O.1; *Canada Health Act,* RSC 1985, c C-6.

17. Jorge Barrera and Joseph Loier, "This Man Is on His Deathbed." Access to health care has also been an ongoing priority for the Office of the Correctional Investigator. See Office of the Correctional Investigator, "Priority: Access to Physical and Mental Health Care," February, 14, 2016, oci-bec.gc.ca/cnt/priorites-priorites/health-sante-eng.aspx.

18. Adelina Iftene, Lynne Hanson and Allan Manso, "Tort Claims and Canadian Prisoners," *Queen's Law Journal* 39, 2 (2014): 1–28.

19. Office of the Correctional Investigator, *Office of the Correctional Investigator Annual Report 2019–2020,* oci-bec.gc.ca/cnt/rpt/annrpt/annrpt20192020-eng.aspx.

20. Correctional Service of Canada. Commissioner's Directives. "Guidelines 081-1 Offender Complaint and Grievance Process," June 28, 2019, csc-scc.gc.ca/politiques-et-lois/081-1-gl-en.shtml.

21. Minister of Human Resources Development Canada, "Guide to Accident Compensation for Federal Offenders," June 20, 2014, canada.ca/en/employment-social-development/services/health-safety/compensation/offenders.html.

22. See Andre Montoya-Barthelemy, "The Occupational Health of Prison Inmates: An Ignored Population and an Opportunity" *Journal of Occupational and Environmental Medicine* 61, 2 (February 2019): 74–76; Spencer Woodman, "California Blames Incarcerated Workers for Unsafe Conditions and Amputations," *The Intercept,* December 28, 2016, theintercept.com/2016/12/28/california-blames-incarcerated-workers-for-unsafe-conditions-and-amputations/.

23. *Globe,* "Prisoner Killed by Fall," October 9, 1914: 11.

24. *Globe and Mail,* "Discrepancies Report to House: Accident Fatal at Reformatory," March 11, 1932: 3.

25. O.C.J. Withrow, "Kingston Well Supplied on Stern Strenuous Side with Prison Stonepile," *Globe,* September 9, 1933: 1.

26. *Globe,* "Burwash Convicts Charge Brutality by Officer," January 31, 1933: 1.

27. Jordan House, "The 1934 British Columbia Penitentiary Strike and Prisoners' Wages in Canada," *Active History,* April 26, 2019, activehistory.ca/2019/04/the-1934-british-columbia-penitentiary-strike-and-prisoners-wages-in-canada/.

28. *Globe and Mail,* "Accident Kills Guelph Inmate," August 5, 1949: 8.

29. Office of the Correctional Investigator, *Office of the Correctional Investigator Annual Report 2019–2020.*

30. Office of the Correctional Investigator, *Office of the Correctional Investigator Annual Report 2002–2003,* oci-bec.gc.ca/cnt/rpt/pdf/annrpt/annrpt20022003-pdf/annrpt20022003-6-eng.pdf.

31. Office of the Correctional Investigator, *In the Dark: An Investigation of Death in Custody Information Sharing and Disclosure Practices in Federal Correc-*

tions — Final Report, August 2, 2016, oci-bec.gc.ca/cnt/rpt/oth-aut/oth-aut20160802-eng.aspx?pedisable=true.

32.   Independent Review of Ontario Corrections, "Corrections in Ontario: Directions for Reform," Queen's Printer, September 2017: 62, files.ontario.ca/solgen-corrections_in_ontario_directions_for_reform.pdf.

33.   CORCAN, *Occupational Development Programs: CORCAN Report on Performance, 1988/89* 12, ojp.gov/ncjrs/virtual-library/abstracts/occupational-development-programs-corcan-report-performance-198889.

34.   Iftene, Hanson and Manso, "Tort Claims": 28.

35.   *MacLean v. R.,* 1972 CanLII 124 (SCC), [1973] SCR 2.

36.   Bank of Canada, "Bank of Canada Inflation Calculator," n.d., bankofcanada.ca/rates/related/inflation-calculator/.

37.   *Pridy v. British Columbia,* 1994 CanLII 669 (BCSC)(*Pridy*).

38.   *Times-Colonist,* "Ex-Nanaimo Centre Inmate Seeks $185,000 Damages Following Tractor Accident," February 20, 1994: 1.

39.   *Pridy,* p. 10

40.   *Mcguire c. Canada,* 1997 CanLII 16898 (CF).

41.   *Sarvanis v. Canada,* [2002] 1 S.C.R. 921, 2002 SCC 28 (*Saarvanis*); Janice Tibbetts, "Inmate Can Sue Government after Fall at Federal Prison: Top Court Rejects Government's Claim of Double Dipping," *Ottawa Citizen,* March 22, 2002: A7.

42.   *Sarvanis v. Canada,* 1998 CanLII 8398 (FC) at para 3.

43.   *Sarvanis,* at para 38; "Injured Inmate Can Sue Ottawa, Supreme Court Rules," CBC *News,* March 21, 2002, cbc.ca/news/canada/injured-inmate-can-sue-ottawa-supreme-court-rules-1.345390.

44.   Iftene, Hanson and Manso, "Tort Claims": 660.

45.   Barnetson, *The Political Economy of Workplace Injury in Canada* (Edmonton: AU Press, 2010): 22.

46.   Barnetson, *The Political Economy,* 110.

47.   Barnetson, *The Political Economy,* 21.

48.   *Roasting v. Blood Band,* 1999 ABQB 126 (CanLII)

49.   Kainai Transition Centre Society, "Community Corrections," (2022), ktcs-bloodtribe.com/ktcs-programs/community-corrections/.

50.   *Roasting v. Blood Band,* 1999 ABQB 126 (CanLII)

51.   Barnetson, *The Political Economy,* 174–175.

52.   *Foulds v. British Columbia,* 2012 BCSC 941 (CanLII).

53.   *Foulds v. British Columbia,* 2012 BCSC 941 (CanLII).

54.   *Foulds,* at para 24.

55.   *Foulds,* at para 32.

56.   *Foulds,* at para 34.

57.   *Chilton v. Canada,* 2008 FC 1047.

58.   *Chilton v. Canada,* 2008 FC 1047, at para 14 (*Chilton*).

59.   *Chilton,* at para 16.

60.   Iftene, Hanson and Manso, "Tort Claims": 6.

61. *Chilton v. Canada,* 2008 FC 1047.

62. *Chilton v. Canada,* 2008 FC 1047.

63. *Chilton v. Canada,* 2008 FC 1047.

64. Stephanie Ross, Larry Savage, Errol Black and Jim Silver, *Building a Better World: An Introduction to the Labour Movement in Canada* (third edition) (Halifax and Winnipeg: Fernwood Publishing, 2015), 132.

65. Brooklyn Neustaeter, "Majority of Canadians' Work Refusal Claims Being Denied Amid COVID-19," *CTV News,* June 25, 2020, ctvnews.ca/health/coronavirus/majority-of-canadians-work-refusal-claims-being-denied-amid-covid-19-1.4999369.

66. Lynda Robson et al., "Updating a Study of the Union Effect on Safety in the ICI Construction Sector: A Report Prepared by the Institute for Work & Health for the Ontario Construction Secretariat," Institute for Work and Health (January 2021), iwh.on.ca/sites/iwh/files/iwh/reports/iwh_report_union_safety_effect_construction_update_2021.pdf.

67. See Ted McCoy, *Hard Time: Reforming the Penitentiary in Nineteenth-Century Canada* (Edmonton: AU Press, 2012), Chapter 5.

68. See Office of the Correctional Investigator, *Office of the Correctional Investigator Annual Report 2019–2020*; Office of the Correctional Investigator, *Aging and Dying in Prison: An Investigation into the Experiences of Older Individuals in Federal Custody* (February 28, 2019), oci-bec.gc.ca/cnt/rpt/oth-aut/oth-aut20190228-eng.aspx; Syrus Ware, Joan Ruzsa and Giselle Dias, "It Can't Be Fixed Because It's Not Broken: Racism and Disability in the Prison Industrial Complex," in *Disability Incarcerated: Imprisonment and Disability in the United States and Canada,* edited by Liat Ben-Moshe, Chris Chapman and Allison C. Carey (New York: Palgrave Macmillan, 2014): 163–184.

69. Alberta Civil Liberties Research Centre, "Keeping the Peace: Prisoners' Rights and Employment Programs," static1.squarespace.com/static/511bd4e0e4b0c ecdc77b114b/t/5d237a13e48a5a0001896e76/1562606102833/6+Keeping+the +Peace+Prisoners+and+Employement+Programs+2014.pdf, 36.

70. Alberta Civil Liberties Research Centre, "Keeping the Peace," 113.

71. Erin Hatton, *Coerced: Work Under Threat of Punishment* (Oakland: University of California, 2020): 158.

72. Hatton, *Coerced,* 158.

73. Jordan House and Asaf Rashid, "Failure to Protect Essential Prisoner Workers Undermines Public Safety," *Canadian Dimension,* December 28, 2020, canadiandimension.com/articles/view/failure-to-protect-essential-prisoner-workers-undermines-public-safety.

74. House and Rashid, "Failure to Protect Essential Prisoner Workers."

75. Bill Graveland, "COVID-19 Outbreaks Over in Federal Prisons, Staff Preparing for 'New Normal,'" *CP24,* August 8, 2020, cp24.com/news/covid-19-outbreaks-over-in-federal-prisons-staff-preparing-for-new-normal-1.5056494?cache=zyujtxhn.

76. Jordan House, "When Prisoners Had a Union: The Canadian Food and Allied

Workers Union Local 240," *Labour/Le Travail* 82 (Fall 2018): 26.

77. Quoted in House, "When Prisoners Had a Union," 35.

78. Toronto Prisoners' Rights Project, "Joyceville Correctional Centre Labour Strike," March 19, 2021, facebook.com/TorontoPrisonersRightsProject/photos/289057185967528.

79. Shauna Cunningham, "No More Active Cases of COVID-19 at Joyceville Institution after Major Outbreak," *Global News,* February 22, 2021, globalnews. ca/news/7614535/active-COVID-19-joyceville-institution-coronavirus-outbreak/; Ian MacAlpine, "Joyceville Inmate Committee Speaks Out on Current COVID-19 Conditions," *Whig-Standard,* December 22, 2020, thewhig.com/ news/joyceville-inmate-committee-speaks-out-on-current-covid-19-conditions.

80. Quoted in House and Rashid, "Failure to Protect Essential Prisoner Workers."

81. Eric Tucker, "Diverging Trends in Worker Health and Safety Protection and Participation in Canada, 1985–2000." *Relations industrielles / Industrial Relations* 58, 3 (2003): 395–426; Bob Barnetson, *The Political Economy of Workplace Injury,* 178.

CHAPTER 4: "SWEAT THE EVIL OUT"

1. Rainer Baehre, "Prison as Factory, Convict as Worker: A Study of the Mid-Victorian St John Penitentiary, 1841–1880," in *Essays in the History of Canadian Law: Crime and Criminal Justice in Canadian History,* edited by Susan Lewthwaite, Tina Loo and Jim Phillips (Toronto: University of Toronto Press, 1994), 441–442.

2. See Peter Oliver, *'Terror to Evil-Doers': Prisons and Punishment in Nineteenth-Century Ontario* (Toronto: Osgoode Society, 1998): 30; Douglas Hay, "Property, Authority, and the Criminal Law," in *Albion's Fatal Tree: Crime and Society in Eighteenth-Century England,* edited by Doulas Hay, Peter Linebaugh, John G. Rule, E.P. Thompson, and Cal Winslow (New York: Pantheon, 1975): 17–63.

3. Baehre, "Prison as Factory," 441.

4. Oliver, *'Terror to Evil-Doers,'* 97–99. Also see Rainer Baehre, "Origins of the Penitentiary System in Upper Canada," *Ontario History* 69 (September 1977), 186–187.

5. See Peter D'Agostino, "Craniums, Criminals, and the 'Cursed Race': Italian Anthropology in American Racial Thought, 1861–1924," *Comparative Studies in Society and History* 44, 2 (2002): 319–343.

6. See Baehre, "Prison as Factory"; Michel Foucault, *Discipline and Punish: The Birth of the Prison* (New York: Vintage Books, 1995); Michael Ignatieff, *A Just Measure of Pain: The Penitentiary in the Industrial Revolution 1750–1850* (New York: Pantheon, 1978); Dario Melossi and Massimo Pavarini, *The Prison and the Factory: Origins of the Penitentiary System* (40th Anniversary Edition) (London: Palgrave Macmillan UK, 2018); Ted McCoy, *Hard Time: Reforming*

the Penitentiary in Nineteenth-Century Canada (Edmonton: AU Press, 2012); Norval Morris and David J. Rothman (eds.), *The Oxford History of the Prison: The Practice of Punishment in Western Society* (New York and Oxford: Oxford University Press, 1995); Oliver, *'Terror to Evil-Doers'*; Bryan D. Palmer, "The New New Poor Law: A Chapter in the Current Class War Waged from Above," *Labour / Le Travail* 84 (2019); Gerog Rusche and Otto Kirchheimer, *Punishment and Social Structure* (New York: Russell & Russell, 1968).

7. Baehre, "Prison as Factory," 442. Also see Rainer Baehre, "Origins of the Penitentiary System," 191–194; David J. Rothman, "Perfecting the Prison: United States, 1789-1865," in *The Oxford History of the Prison: The Practice of Punishment in Western Society,* edited by Norval Morris and David J. Rothman (New York and Oxford: Oxford University Press, 1995), 111–129.

8. See Oliver, *'Terror to Evil-Doers,'* 111–114; McCoy, *Hard Time,* 56–57; Baehre, "Prison as Factory," 442.

9. Melossi and Pavarini, *The Prison and the Factory.*

10. Baehre, "Prison as Factory," 439.

11. Baehre, "Prison as Factory," 440. Emphasis added.

12. McCoy, *Hard Time,* 34.

13. See McCoy, *Hard Time,* 128–129; Jan Chaboyer and Errol Black, "Conspiracy in Winnipeg: How the 1919 General Strike Leaders Were Railroaded into Prison and What We Must Do Now to Make Amends," CCPA *Review Labour Notes* (March 2006), policyalternatives.ca/sites/default/files/uploads/publications/Manitoba_Pubs/2006/Conspiracy_in_Winnipeg.pdf.

14. James E. Muirhead and Robert Rhodes, "Literacy Level of Canadian Federal Offenders," *Journal of Correctional Education* 49, 2 (1998): 59.

15. Baehre, "Prison as Factory," 449. Emphasis added.

16. McCoy, *Hard Time,* 14; *Globe and Mail,* "Production Put First and Prisoners Last, Guelph Inquiry Told," February 22, 1937: 13.

17. Edwin C. Guillet, *Early Life in Upper Canada* (Toronto: University of Toronto Press, 1933): 95, 282.

18. *Globe,* "Pioneers Meted Out Odd Punishment," June 22, 1922: 16.

19. For example, see the *Globe and Mail,* "Conductor and Brakeman Sent Down to Hard Labor," February 9, 1914: 15.

20. *Globe,* "A Hard Labor," September 1, 1928: 1.

21. *Globe and Mail,* "Court Orders Hard Labor For Drunk Driver," August 31, 1955: 4; *Globe and Mail,* "Called Road Menace: Month at Hard Labor for Careless Driving," September 24, 1963: 4.

22. *Globe and Mail,* "Given Hard Labor," July 16, 1941: 5.

23. *Globe and Mail,* "Stabbed Wife, Gets 6 Months at Hard Labor," December 22, 1939: 9.

24. *Globe and Mail,* "Jail, Hard Labor for Manslaughter," November 4, 1947: 26.

25. *Globe and Mail,* "Steve Harkin Given 30 Days," February 6, 1942: 23.

26. *Globe,* "Nickle Asks Report on 4-Year Sentence for $4.50 Forgery," November 25, 1925: 9.

27.   *Globe and Mail,* "Teen-Age Girl Given Hard Labor," February 14, 1946: 23.

28.   *Globe,* "Trading with Enemy Is High Crime," November 2, 1914: 9.

29.   O.C.J. Withrow, "Kingston Well Supplied on Stern Strenuous Side with Prison Stonepile," *Globe,* September 9, 1933: 1.

30.   *Globe,* "Speaker Arrested at Mass Meeting," May 2, 1931: A2; *Globe,* "Communist Leaders Given Record Terms For Part In Riot," September 25, 1931: 1.

31.   *Globe,* "Ottawa Mayor Asks Hepburn To Stop Trek," July 13, 1935: 1.

32.   *Globe and Mail,* "Jail, Hard Labor for Union Leader in Textile Strike," July 9, 1947: 7.

33.   See Gail Hinge, "Consolidation of Indian Legislation, Vol: II: Indian Acts and Amendments, 1868–1975," (n.d.), publications.gc.ca/collections/collection_2017/aanc-inac/R5-158-2-1978-eng.pdf.

34.   *Globe and Mail,* "Hard Labor Proposed for Elusive Husbands," August 26, 1953: 9.

35.   *Globe and Mail,* "Hard Labor Proposed for Elusive Husbands," 9.

36.   *Globe and Mail,* "Fireworks Bylaws Muddled," May 20, 1963: 21.

37.   *Globe and Mail,* "Hard Labor Faces Drivers in Smithville," September 18, 1975: 8.

38.   *Foreign Enlistment Act,* RSC 1985, c F-28, lois-laws.justice.gc.ca/eng/acts/F-28/FullText.html

39.   For further analysis of discourses used to justify contemporary prison labour schemes, see Shanisse Kleuskens, "Legitimating the 'Fiasco': Canadian State Justifications of CORCAN Prison Labour," Master's thesis, University of Ottawa, 2015.

40.   Greg McElligott, "Invested in Prisons: Prison Expansion and Community Development in Canada," *Studies in Social Justice* 11, 1 (2017): 86–112.

41.   See Bronwyn Dobchuk-Land and James Wilt, "Prison Unionism" *Briarpatch,* July 2, 2020, briarpatchmagazine.com/articles/view/prison-unionism; Joshua Page, "Politically Realistic Unionism: The California Prison Officers Association and the Struggle Over the 'Public Good,'" *WorkingUSA* 15, 3 (2012): 377–396.

42.   United Nations Department of Economic and Social Affairs, *Prison Labor* (New York: United Nations Publications, 1955).

43.   See Matthew J. Mancini, *One Dies, Get Another: Convict Leasing in the American South, 1866–1928* (Columbia, SC: University of South Carolina Press, 1996); Alex Lichtenstein, *Twice the Work of Free Labor: The Political Economy of Convict Labor in the New South* (London and New York: Verso, 1996).

44.   United Nations Department of Economic and Social Affairs, *Prison Labor.*

45.   Baehre, "Prison as Factory," 449–451.

46.   Joseph Gondor Berkovits, "Prisoners for Profit: Convict Labour in the Ontario Central Prison. 1814–1915," in *Essays in the History of Canadian Law, Volume V: Crime and Criminal Justice,* edited by Jim Phillips, Tina Loo and Susan Lewthwaite (Toronto, Buffalo, and London: University of Toronto Press, 1994): 478–515.

47. Berkovits, "Prisoners for Profit," 483.

48. Berkovits, "Prisoners for Profit," 483.

49. Eugene Forsey, *Trade Unions in Canada, 1812–1902* (Toronto, Buffalo, London: University of Toronto Press, 1982): 116; 124.

50. Bryan D. Palmer, "Kingston Mechanics and the Rise of the Penitentiary, 1833–1836," *Histoire sociale/Social History* XIII: 25 (1980): 7–32. Prison labour was also a central concern of the first labour councils in Quebec. Forsey, *Trade Unions in Canada*, 399; 401.

51. H. Clare Pentland, *Labour and Capital in Canada 1650–1860* (Toronto: Lorimer, 1981), 21.

52. John Kidman, *The Canadian Prison: The Story of a Tragedy* (Toronto: Ryerson Press, 1947), 67; Forsey, *Trade Unions in Canada*, 137.

53. Quoted in Chris Clarkson and Melissa Munn, *Disruptive Prisoners: Resistance, Reform, and the New Deal* (Toronto, Buffalo, and London: Toronto University Press, 2021), 49.

54. Clarkson and Munn, *Disruptive Prisoners*, 55.

55. Correctional Service of Canada, "1940–1959: Times of Change" October 20, 2014, csc-scc.gc.ca/about-us/006-2003-eng.shtml. Also see C.W. Topping, *Canadian Penal Institutions* [revised edition] (Toronto: Ryerson Press, 1947 [1929]), 124–125.

56. Kidman, *The Canadian Prison*, 66.

57. John Edwards, "Industry in Canadian Federal Prisons: Glimpses into History," *Forum on Corrections Research* 8, 1 (January 1996): 6.

58. Kidman, *The Canadian Prison*, 66.

59. Quoted in Clarkson and Munn, *Disruptive Prisoners*, 133.

60. Clarkson and Munn, *Disruptive Prisoners*, 134.

61. Clarkson and Munn, *Disruptive Prisoners*, 134–135.

62. Correctional Service of Canada, "1940–1959: Times of Change," October 20, 2014, csc-scc.gc.ca/about-us/006-2003-eng.shtml. For a more detailed discussion of the politics at play in prison reform efforts in the lead up to the war, see Clarkson and Munn, *Disruptive Prisoners*, 135.

63. Scott Young, "Prison Training: What For?" *Globe and Mail*, July 13, 1966: 6.

64. Mark MacGuigan, *Report to Parliament by the Sub-Committee on the Penitentiary System in Canada* (Ottawa: Government of Canada, 1977): 5. Hereafter *MacGuigan Report*.

65. Jessica Evans, "Penal Nationalism in the Settler Colony: On the Construction and Maintenance of 'National Whiteness' in Settler Canada," *Punishment and Society* 23, 4 (2021): 13–14.

66. *MacGuigan Report*, 106.

67. *MacGuigan Report*, 107.

68. *MacGuigan Report*, 106.

69. *MacGuigan Report*, 106.

70. *MacGuigan Report*, 107.

71. *MacGuigan Report*, 107.

72. *MacGuigan Report,* 107.

73. *MacGuigan Report,* 111.

74. *MacGuigan Report,* 112.

75. *MacGuigan Report,* 107.

76. *MacGuigan Report,* 108.

77. *MacGuigan Report,* 108.

78. *MacGuigan Report,* 110.

79. *MacGuigan Report,* 109.

80. Solicitor General of Canada, *Solicitor General Annual Report 1981–1982* (1983): 67, publicsafety.gc.ca/lbrr/archives/sg-arsg-1981-1982-eng.pdf.

81. Correctional Service of Canada, "History of CORCAN and the Evolution of Prison Industries," January 15, 2013, csc-scc.gc.ca/corcan/002005-0004-eng.shtml.

82. Solicitor General of Canada, *Solicitor General Annual Report 1981–1982,* 67.

83. CORCAN, *CORCAN Annual Report, 1981–1982* (1982): 11, publicsafety.gc.ca/lbrr/archives/csc-arcorcan-1981-1982-eng.pdf.

84. Correctional Service of Canada, "Third Annual Report, 1982–83: Inspector General's Branch," (1983), publicsafety.gc.ca/lbrr/archives/csc-arigb1-1982-1983-eng.pdf.

85. Correctional Service of Canada, "Fourth Annual Report, 1983–84: Inspector General's Branch," (1984): 16, publicsafety.gc.ca/lbrr/archives/csc-arigb1-1983-1984-eng.pdf.

86. David Lancashire, "Springhill: Creating Life on the Street," *Globe and Mail,* May 18, 1981: 7.

87. *Globe and Mail,* "Jail Jobs Benefit All," April 7, 1981: 6.

88. Charles Rusnell, "Workshop Gives Convicts Fresh Start," *Ottawa Citizen,* January 6, 1986: C3.

89. Kathleen Kenna, "Prison Staff 'Use Convicts as Slave Labor': Beaver Creek Personnel Accused of Putting Inmates to Work at Home," *Toronto Star,* August 11, 1988: A1.

90. Kenna, "Prison Staff 'Use Convicts as Slave Labor,'" A1.

91. Adrienne Tanner, "Inmates Hired by Prison Staff," *Province,* April 15, 2001: A3.

92. *CORCAN Express,* "New Ventures: A CORCAN Business Initiative," 3, 5 (September 1994): 1.

93. *CORCAN Express,* "ISO Certification," 3, 2 (May 1994): 2; *CORCAN Express,* "CORCAN Research Projects," 3, 2 (May 1994): 2.

94. *CORCAN Express,* "CORCAN Community Programs in Quebec," 3, 5 (September 1994): 1–2.

95. Paul TL Urmson, "Contract Manufacturing: One Manager's Experience," *CORCAN Express* 3, 9 (Janury 1995): 2.

96. Brian MacLeod, "Prison Job Program Under Fire: Business Community Can't Compete with Cheap Labour," *Calgary Herald,* January 7, 2000: B1. Also see David O'Brien, "Federal Prisoners Competing Directly with Private Business,"

Montreal Gazette, April 14 1998: A12.

97. Mark Gollom, "Business a Steal for Prison Labourers," *Ottawa Citizen,* February 15, 1998: A6.

98. MacLeod, "Prison Job Program Under Fire," B1.

99. O'Brien, "Federal Prisoners Competing Directly with Private Business," A12.

CHAPTER 5: WHAT ARE THE ALTERNATIVES?

1. See Anthony Doob, "The Harper Revolution in Criminal Justice Policy… and What Comes Next," *Policy Options,* May 4, 2015, policyoptions.irpp.org/fr/magazines/entre-prosperite-et-turbulences/doob-webster/.

2. "Abolish Prison Labour in the USA," *Change.org* (2016), change.org/p/federal-bureau-of-prisons-abolish-prison-labour-in-the-usa.

3. Quoted in Jordan House, "Making Prison Work: Prison Labour and Resistance in Canada," PhD dissertation, York University (2020): 282.

4. Luc Gosselin, *Prisons in Canada* (Montréal: Black Rose Books, 1982): 180.

5. Gosselin, *Prisons in Canada,* 196.

6. Gosselin, *Prisons in Canada,* 196.

7. Gosselin, *Prisons in Canada,* 197.

8. Gosselin, *Prisons in Canada,* 198.

9. Stephen P. Garvey, "Freeing Prisoners' Labor," *Stanford Law Review* 50 (1997–1998): 339–398.

10. See Matthew J. Mancini, *One Dies, Get Another: Convict Leasing in the American South, 1866–1928* (Columbia, SC: University of South Carolina Press, 1996).

11. For an analysis on the links between racial slavery and the penitentiary system in the United States, see Angela Davis, *Are Prisons Obsolete?* (New York: Seven Stories Press, 2007).

12. Quoted in Samuel Melville, *Letters From Attica* (New York: William Morrow and Company, 1972): 178.

13. Norm, "Industry for Penitentiaries (Just a Passing Thought)," *The Outlook,* December 1978: 14. Gaucher/Munn Penal Press Collection, penalpress.com/wp-content/uploads/The_Outlook_Xmas1978.pdf.

14. See Jordan House, "When Prisoners Had a Union: The Canadian Food and Allied Workers Union Local 240." *Labour/Le Travail* 82, 36 (Fall, 2018).

15. See Jessica Gordon Nembhard, "How Prisoner Co-ops Reduce Recidivism: Lessons from Puerto Rico and Beyond," *Nonprofit Quarterly,* May 19, 2020, nonprofitquarterly.org/how-prisoner-co-ops-reduce-recidivism-lessons-from-puerto-rico-and-beyond/; John Howard Society of Canada, "Prisoner-Based Co-operatives: Working It Out in Canada," March 2013, docplayer.net/39319679-Prisoner-based-co-operatives-working-it-out-in-canada.html.

16. Meegan Moriarty, "From Bars to Freedom: Prisoner Co-ops Boost Employment, Self-esteem and Support Re-entry into Society," *Rural Cooperatives*

(January/February 2016), 4–18; 37.

17.   Greg McElligott, "Beyond Service, Beyond Coercion? Prisoner Co-ops and the Path to Democratic Administration," in *From the Streets to the State: Changing the World by Taking Power,* edited by Paul Christopher Gray (Albany, NY: State University of New York Press, 2018): 230.

18.   See Seth Adema, "'Our Destiny is Not Negotiable': Native Brotherhoods and Decolonization in Ontario's Federal Prisons, 1970–1982," *Left History* 16, 2 (Fall/Winter 2012): 35.

19.   Charles W. Hill, *Research Report to the Department of Justice and Solicitor General (Canada) Concerning the Native Brotherhood Organizations in Penal Institutions,* (n.d.): 30, publicsafety.gc.ca/lbrr/archives/e%2098.c87%20h5-eng.pdf.

20.   Hill, *Research Report to the Department of Justice and Solicitor General,* 29.

21.   Hill. *Research Report to the Department of Justice and Solicitor General,* 29.

22.   Hill, *Research Report to the Department of Justice and Solicitor General,* 30.

23.   Con-versely, "Native Brotherhood," June 1976: 12, Gaucher/Munn Penal Press Collection, penalpress.com/wp-content/uploads/Conversely_June1976.pdf.

24.   Jorge Barrera, "Federal Prison Corporation's Selling of Moccasins, Drums for Revenue 'Exploitative,' Says Cree- Metis Artist," *APTN,* November 16, 2016, aptnnews.ca/2016/11/16/federal-prison-corporations-selling-of-moccasins-drums-for-revenue-exploitative-says-cree-metis-artist/.

25.   *Off the Wall,* "Native Indian Fine Arts & Crafts," 1, 2 (June 12, 1981): 1, Gaucher/Munn Penal Press Collection, penalpress.com/wp-content/uploads/Off-TheWall_June1981_V1No2.pdf.

26.   W. Clifford, John Braithwaite and Jack Sandry (eds)., *Regional Developments in Corrections: Proceedings of the Second Asian and Pacific Conference of Correctional Administrators, Bangkok,* July 6–10, 1981 (Canberra: Australian Institute of Criminology, 1982): 214–218.

27.   Government of Canada, "Federal Corporation Information - 087118-4," February 2, 2022, ic.gc.ca/app/scr/cc/CorporationsCanada/fdrlCrpDtls.html?corpId=871184&V_TOKEN=null&crpNm=&crpNmbr=871184&bsNmbr=.

28.   Correctional Service of Canada, Commissioner's Directive 737, "Inmate-Operated Business Enterprises," January 24, 1997, qp.alberta.ca/1266.cfm?page=c29.cfm&leg_type=Acts&isbncln=9780779831326.

29.   InsideArt, "The Story," (2005), web.archive.org/web/20090623040331/http://www.insideart.ca/thestory.html.

30.   Stacey Corriveau, "A Passion for Renewal: Co-operation and Commerce Within Prison Walls," *Making Waves* 18, 2 (2007): 5–8, communityrenewal.ca/sites/all/files/resource/MW180205.pdf.

31.   Adam McDowell, "Brush Strokes With the Law," *National Post,* August 22, 2009, pressreader.com/canada/national-post-latest-edition/20090822/283240209027795.

32.   Corriveau, "A Passion for Renewal," 5–8.

33. Corriveau, "A Passion for Renewal," 7.
34. John Howard Society, "Prisoner-Based Co-operatives," 24.
35. Corriveau, "A Passion for Renewal," 7.
36. Corriveau, "A Passion for Renewal," 8; John Howard Society, "Prisoner-based Co-operatives," 24.
37. McElligott, "Beyond Service, Beyond Coercion?," 239.
38. McElligott, "Beyond Service, Beyond Coercion?," 243.
39. See Sam Gindin, "Chasing Utopia," *Jacobin,* March 10, 2016, jacobinmag.com/2016/03/workers-control-coops-wright-wolff-alperovitz; Sharryn Kasmir, "Cooperative Democracy or Cooperative Competitiveness: Rethinking Mondragon," in *The Socialist Register 2018: Rethinking Democracy,* edited by Leo Panitch and Greg Albo (London: Merlin, 2017): 202–223.
40. McElligott, "Beyond Service, Beyond Coercion?," 239.
41. McElligott, "Beyond Service, Beyond Coercion?," 238.
42. Donald Grant, "'For Once in My Life, I'm Really Enjoying Something': Prisoners Serve Their Time in the Toy Shop," *Globe and Mail,* November 7, 1983: A4.
43. Donald Grant, "'For Once in My Life, I'm Really Enjoying Something'," A4.
44. See House, "Making Prison Work"; Bradley B. Falkof, "Prisoner Representative Organizations, Prison Reform, and Jones v. North Carolina Prisoners' Labor Union: An Argument for Increased Court Intervention in Prison Administration," *The Journal of Criminal Law and Criminology* 70, 1 (1979): 42–56; Tom Murton, "Shared Decision Making as a Treatment Technique in Prison Management," *Offender Rehabilitation* 1, 1 (1976): 17–31; Steven C. Bennett, "The Privacy and Procedural Due Process Rights of Hunger Striking Prisoners," *New York University Law Review* 58, 5 (November 1983): 1157–1230; Hans Toch, "Democratizing Prisons" *The Prison Journal* 73, 1 (1994): 62–72; Peter Scharf, "Democracy and Prison Reform: A Theory of Democratic Participation in Prison," *The Prison Journal* 55, 2 (1975): 32.
45. House, "Making Prison Work," 156.
46. Eric Cummins, *The Rise and Fall of California's Radical Prison Movement* (Stanford, CA: Stanford University Press, 1994).
47. Donald Tibbs, *From Black Power to Prison Power: The Making of Jones v. North Carolina Prisoners' Labor Union* (New York: Palgrave Macmillan, 2012): 155; Amanda Bell Hughett, "Silencing the Cell Block: The Making of Modern Prison Policy in North Carolina and the Nation," PhD dissertation, Duke University (2017): 111.
48. See Mike Fitzgerald, *Prisoners in Revolt* (London: Penguin, 1977); House, "Making Prison Work."
49. See House, "Making Prison Work," 266.
50. Clarence Ronald Huff, "Unionization Behind the Walls: An Analytic Study of the Ohio's Prisoners' Labor Union Movement," PhD dissertation, Ohio State University (1974).
51. See House, "Making Prison Work."
52. See House, "Making Prison Work."

53. See Incarcerated Workers Organizing Committee, (n.d.), incarceratedwork-ers.org/; Dan Berger, *Captive Nation: Black Prison Organizing in the Civil Rights Era* (Chapel Hill: The University of North Carolina Press, 2014), 186.

54. See Berger, *Captive Nation,* 185–192. Also see House, "Making Prison Work," 66n136.

55. Virginia McArthur, "Inmate Grievance Mechanisms: A Survey of 209 American Prisons," *Federal Probation* 38, 4 (December 1974): 44.

56. John Irwin, *Prisons in Turmoil* (Boston and Toronto: Little, Brown and Company, 1980): 243–244.

57. Juanita Diaz-Cotto, *Gender, Ethnicity and the State: Latina and Latino Prison Politics* (Albany, NY: State University of New York Press, 1996): 162–164.

58. Hughett, "Silencing the Cell Block, 83.

59. See House, "Making Prison Work."

60. House, "Making Prison Work," 156.

CHAPTER 6: THE CASE FOR PRISONERS' LABOUR UNIONS

1. *Jolivet v. Treasury Board (Correctional Service of Canada)* 2013 PSLRAB 1 (*Jolivet 2013*) and *Canadian Prisoners' Labour Confederation v Correctional Service Canada,* 2015 CIRB 779 (CPLC 2015).

2. *MacGuigan Report,* 5.

3. Statistics Canada, "Unionization Rates Falling," May 17, 2018, www150.statcan.gc.ca/n1/pub/11-630-x/11-630-x2015005-eng.htm.

4. Linda Briskin, "From Person-Days Lost to Labour Militancy: A New Look at the Canadian Work Stoppage Data," *Relations industrielles / Industrial Relations* 62, 1 (2007): 31–65.

5. See Jordan House, "Making Prison Work: Prison Labour and Resistance in Canada," PhD dissertation, York University (2020), 144.

6. House, "Making Prison Work," 158–161.

7. Jordan House, "When Prisoners Had a Union: The Canadian Food and Allied Workers Union Local 240," *Labour/Le Travail* 82, 36 (Fall, 2018): 4.

8. House, "When Prisoners Had a Union," 16.

9. House, "When Prisoners Had a Union," 9.

10. House, "When Prisoners Had a Union," 19.

11. House, "When Prisoners Had a Union," 21.

12. House, "When Prisoners Had a Union," 25.

13. *Jolivet v. Treasury Board (Correctional Service of Canada)* 2013 PSLRAB 1 (*Jolivet 2013*), paras 1–2. An unfair labour practice complaint by an employee under the PSLRA is made under section 190(g)

14. *Jolivet 2013,* para 44.

15. *Jolivet 2013,* paras 35–37. The decision referred to is referenced: *Amalgamated Meat Cutters and Butcher Workmen of North America v. Guelph Beef Centre Inc.,* 1977 CanLII 489 (OLRB).

16. *Jolivet 2013,* at para 39.
17. *Jolivet v. Canada (Correctional Service)* 2014 FCA 1 (*Jolivet 2014*).
18. *Jolivet 2014,* para 10.
19. *Canada Labour Code,* RSC 1985, c L-2, s. 94(1).
20. *Canadian Prisoners' Labour Confederation v. Correctional Service Canada,* 2015 CIRB 779 (CPLC *2015*), at para 13.
21. CPLC *2015* at para 22 and 29.
22. CPLC *2015,* para 30.
23. *Guérin v. Canada (Attorney General),* 2018 FC 94 (*Guérin 2018*).
24. *Guérin 2018,* at para 109–111.
25. *Guérin 2018,* paras 113–119.
26. *Guérin 2018,* para 120.
27. *Guérin 2018,* para 126.
28. *Guérin 2018,* at para 130.
29. *Guérin 2018,* at para 130.
30. *Guérin v. Canada (Attorney General),* 2019 FCA 272 (*Guérin 2019*).
31. *Guérin 2019* at paras 53–57.
32. *Guérin 2019* at para 60.
33. Jessica Evans, "Capitalism, Prisons and COVID-19: On 'Surplus Labour,'" *Spring Magazine,* May 27, 2020, springmag.ca/capitalism-prisons-and-covid-19-on-surplus-labour.
34. Correctional Service of Canada, Commissioner's Directive 726, "Correctional Programs," November 8, 2021, csc-scc.gc.ca/politiques-et-lois/726-cd-en.shtml; *Corrections and Conditional Release Act,* SC 1992, c 20, s. 3.
35. Correctional Service of Canada. "CORCAN," (n.d.), csc-scc.gc.ca/corcan/index-eng.shtml.
36. *Canadian Union of Postal Workers v. Foodora Inc. d.b.a. Foodora,* 2020 CanLII 16750 (*Foodora 2020*).
37. Office of the Correctional Investigator, *Office of the Correctional Investigator Annual Report 2019–2020,* 78.
38. Correctional Service of Canada, Commissioner's Directive 735, "Employment and Employability Program," May 15, 2017, csc-scc.gc.ca/acts-and-regulations/735-cd-eng.shtml.
39. Office of the Correctional Investigator, *Office of the Correctional Investigator Annual Report 2019–2020.*
40. Office of the Correctional Investigator, *Office of the Correctional Investigator Annual Report 2014–2015.*
41. Ghassan Salah, letter to Paul Quick at the Queens University Prison Law clinic, February 23, 2021. Document provided to the authors. Emphasis in original.
42. Salah, letter to Paul Quick at the Queens University Prison Law clinic. Emphasis in original.
43. Irene Klassen, "Offender Employment and Employability: An Overview," *FORUM on Corrections Research* (2005), csc-scc.gc.ca/research/forum/Vol17No1/

v17n1h_e.pdf.

44.   Klassen, "Offender Employment and Employability."

45.   Amanda Nolan, "Research at a Glance," (January 2014), csc-scc.
      gc.ca/005/008/092/005008-0283-eng.pdf.

46.   Claire Brownell, "Prisoners Making $1.95 a Day Want a Raise. Taxpayers Want
      a Break," *Financial Post,* August 30, 2017, financialpost.com/news/court-chal-
      lenge-to-inmate-pay-places-prison-labour-program-in-the-crosshairs.

47.   Rick Sauvé, "Prison Labour Session," Canadian Association of Labour Law-
      yers, 2021 Conference, June 11, 2021.

48.   Correctional Service of Canada, "Correctional Service of Canada, Return-
      ing to the Workforce: Offenders Graduate from Training Program in Pacific
      Region" May 26 2016, lte-ene.ca/en/returning-workforce-offenders-graduate-
      training-program-pacific-region.

49.   Stefany Rodriguez, "The Positive Impacts of CORCAN Work Experiences on
      Reintegration," Correctional Service of Canada, July 3, 2019, lte-ene.ca/en/
      positive-impacts-corcan-work-experiences-reintegration.

50.   Ghassan Salah, letter to Paul Quick at the Queens University Prison Law clin-
      ic.

51.   International Labour Organization (ILO), *Forced Labour Convention, C29,*
      June 28, 1930, C29, article 2.

52.   *Amalgamated Meat Cutters and Butcher Workmen of North America v. Guelph
      Beef Centre Inc.,* 1977 CanLII 489 (OLRB).

53.   *Amalgamated Meat Cutters and Butcher Workmen of North America v. Guelph
      Beef Centre Inc.,* 1977 CanLII 489 (OLRB).

54.   *Fenton v. British Columbia* (1991), 56 B.C.L.R. (2d) 170 (B.C.C.A.)(*Fenton
      1991*), 35.

55.   *Fenton 1991,* 35.

56.   Megan Linton, "A Penny a Poppy," *Briarpatch,* November 4, 2021, briar-
      patchmagazine.com/articles/view/sheltered-workshops-poppies-disabled-
      workers.

57.   Linton, "A Penny a Poppy."

58.   *St. Paul's Hospital (Re) Between: St. Paul's Hospital (Hospital), and Professional
      Association of Residents and Interns (Applicant),* [1976] B.C.L.R.B.D. No. 43 at
      12.

59.   *University of Toronto (Governing Council),* [2012] O.L.R.D. No. 179 at para
      107.

60.   *International Brotherhood of Electrical Workers, Local 353 v. Hotwire Electric-
      All Inc.,* 2016 CanLII 14148 (OLRB), at para 93.

61.   *Canadian Union of Postal Workers v. Foodora Inc. d.b.a. Foodora,* 2020 CanLII
      16750, at para 147.

62.   *Foodora 2020,* at para 172.

63.   Correctional Service of Canada, "Audit of Employment and Employ-
      ability Programs for Offenders," December 16, 2013: 5, csc-scc.gc.ca/
      publications/005007-2527-eng.shtml.

64. Correctional Service of Canada, "History of CORCAN and the Evolution of Prison Industries," January 15, 2013, csc-scc.gc.ca/002/005/002005-0001-en.shtml.

65. *Rizzo & Rizzo Shoes Ltd. (Re)*, [1998] S.C.J. No. 2 at para 36 (*Rizzo 1998*).

66. Law Commission of Ontario, *Vulnerable Workers and Precarious Work: Final Report*, December 2012, lco-cdo.org/wp-content/uploads/2013/03/vulnerable-workers-final-report.pdf.

67. Justin Ling, "The CSC Is Censoring Whistleblower Complaints about COVID-19 in Federal Prisons," *National Post*, April 8, 2020, nationalpost.com/opinion/justin-ling-the-csc-is-censoring-whistleblower-complaints-about-covid-19-in-federal-prisons.

68. *Rizzo 1998*, at para 36.

69. *Mounted Police Association of Ontario v. Canada (Attorney General)*, 2015 SCC 1 at para 58 (*Mounted Police*).

70. *Jolivet 2013*.

71. *Canada (Attorney General) v. Public Service Alliance of Canada* [1991] S.C.J. No. 19 at para 26 (Econosult).

72. *Dunmore v. Ontario (Attorney General)*, 2001 SCC 94 at para 26 (*Dunmore*).

73. *Dunmore* at para 48.

74. *Ontario (Attorney General) v. Fraser*, [2011] 2 S.C.R. 3 at para 34.

75. *Machtinger v. HOJ Industries Ltd.*, [1992] 1 S.C.R. 986 at para 32.

76. *Federal Public Sector Labour Relations Act*, SC 2003, c 22, s. 2 (find the version prior to the change on CanLii (canlii.org/en/) by searching previous versions).

77. *Mounted Police* at para 142.

78. *Mounted Police* at para 152–158.

79. *Dunmore* at para 22.

80. *Health Services and Support - Facilities Subsector Bargaining Assn v British Columbia*, 2007 SCC 27 at para 34.

81. *Canada Labour Code*, RSC 1985, c L-2, s. 4.

82. *Dart Aerospace Ltd. v. Duval*, [2010] F.C.J. No. 919 at para 20.

83. Public Safety Canada, "Corrections and Criminal Justice," December 1, 2020, publicsafety.gc.ca/cnt/cntrng-crm/crrctns/index-en.aspx.

84. The Constitution Act, 1867 (UK), 30 & 31 Victoria, c 3, s. 91(28).

85. Saskatoon Editorial Staff, "Organizing a Prisoners' Trade Union," *Transition* 2, 4 (July/August 1974): 32.

86. Employment and Social Development Canada, "Hire a Temporary Worker Through the Seasonal Agricultural Worker Program: Overview," February 8, 2022, canada.ca/en/employment-social-development/services/foreign-workers/agricultural/seasonal-agricultural.html.

87. Employment and Social Development Canada, "Hire a Temporary Worker."

88. Migrant Workers Alliance for Change, "Unheeded Warnings: COVID-19 and Migrant Workers in Canada," (June 2020), migrantworkersalliance.org/wp-content/uploads/2020/06/Unheeded-Warnings-COVID19-and-Migrant-Workers.pdf.

89. See Brady Strachan, "Migrant Farm Workers Complain of Overcrowded Dorm Rooms and Agricultural Chemical Exposure on Kelowna Farm," CBC *News,* October 10, 2019, cbc.ca/news/canada/british-columbia/migrant-workers-kelowna-sawp-program-complaint-sandher-farm-1.5316512.

90. Tiffany Crawford, "B.C. Prisoners Trying to Form Labour Union," *National Post,* March 4, 2011, nationalpost.com/news/b-c-prisoners-trying-to-form-labour-union.

91. House, "Making Prison Work," 179.

92. Betty Noir, "Prison Protest in BC," *This Magazine,* September–October 1975: 3–6.

93. *Globe and Mail,* "Prisoners Want a Union to Fight for Release," February 3, 1983.

94. House, "Making Prison Work," 184–185.

95. House, "Making Prison Work," 168–171.

96. Saskatoon Editorial Staff, "Organizing a Prisoners' Trade Union," *Transition* 2, 4 (July/August 1974): 31.

97. "Pie in the Sky," *Transition* (July/August 1956): 5, *Gaucher/Munn Penal Press Collection,* penalpress.com/wp-content/uploads/BCPenTrans_JulAug_56. pdf; Chris Clarkson and Melissa Munn, *Disruptive Prisoners: Resistance, Reform, and the New Deal* (Toronto, Buffalo, and London: Toronto University Press, 2021): 142.

98. Sam Gindin, "Rethinking Unions, Registering Socialism," in *The Socialist Register 2013: A Question of Strategy,* edited byLeo Panitch and Vivek Chibber (London: Merlin, 2012): 32.

99. Gindin, "Rethinking Unions, Registering Socialism," 43; also see Bill Fletcher, Jr. and Fernando Gapasin, Solidarity Divided: The Crisis in Organized Labor and a New Path Toward Social Justice (Berkeley: University of California Press, 2008).

100. Correctional Service of Canada, "Public Perceptions of Corrections, 2010," July 2012, csc-scc.gc.ca/research/005008-rs12-07-eng.shtml.

101. Department of Justice, "Public Perception of Crime and Justice in Canada: A Review of Opinion Polls," January 7, 2015, justice.gc.ca/eng/rp-pr/csj-sjc/crime/rr01_1/p4_1.html.

102. House, "Making Prison Work," 235.

103. Angus Reid Institute, "Defend or Defund? One-in-Four Support Cutting Local Police Budgets; Most Back Social Welfare over Hiring More Cops," October 26, 2020, angusreid.org/wp-content/uploads/2020/10/2020.10.24_Policing2.pdf.

104. See Prisoners United, "Prisoners United," (n.d.), prisonersunited.org/.

105. Abolition Coalition, "Choosing Real Safety: A Historic Declaration to Divest from Policing and Prisons and Build Safer Communities for All," January 21, 2021, wgsi.utoronto.ca/choosing-real-safety-a-historic-declaration-to-divest-from-policing-and-prisons-and-build-safer-communities-for-all/.

106. Ruth Wilson Gilmore and James Kilgore, "Some Reflections on Prison Labor,"

The Brooklyn Rail, June 2019, brooklynrail.org/2019/06/field-notes/Some-Reflections-on-Prison-Labor.

107. House, "Making Prison Work," 182.

108. *Globe and Mail,* "Prisoners Want a Union to Fight for Release," February 3, 1983.

CONCLUSION: AND JUSTICE FOR ALL?

1. Correctional Service of Canada, "Correctional Service of Canada News Release — Inmate Protest at Collins Bay Institution" (June 28, 2011), Access to Information and Privacy release.

2. Correctional Service of Canada, "From Julie Blasko to Inmate Population: Memorandum: Offender Work Refusal" (June 29, 2011), Access to Information and Privacy release; Correctional Service of Canada, "From Julie Blasko to 440-CBI-All Staff: Inmate Work Stoppage" (July 4, 2011), Access to Information and Privacy release.

3. Correctional Service of Canada, "From Julie Blasko to Inmate Population."

4. Correctional Service of Canada, "From Wayne Buller (ONT) to 440-CBI-All Staff: Offender Work Refusal" (June 27, 2011), Access to Information and Privacy release.

5. Office of the Correctional Investigator, *Office of the Correctional Investigator Annual Report 2017–2018,* June 29, 2018, oci-bec.gc.ca/cnt/rpt/annrpt/annrpt20172018-eng.aspx.

6. Government of Canada, "Salaries and Wages — Canadian Industry Statistics — Furniture and Related Product Manufacturing," February 2, 2022, ic.gc.ca/app/scr/app/cis/salaries-salaires/337;jsessionid=0001NgtB1qI4VsxSN1D H_otmPd:-C7AEJO.

7. Robert Devet, "Interview: El Jones on Supporting the Burnside Jail Protest," *Nova Scotia Advocate,* August 22, 2018, nsadvocate.org/2018/08/22/interview-el-jones-on-supporting-the-burnside-jail-protest/.

8. For example, see Silver Donald Cameron, *The Education of Everett Richardson: The Nova Scotia Fishermen's Strike: 1970–71* (Toronto: McClelland and Stewart, 1977).

9. Prisoners United, "Prisoners Union of Canada," (n.d.), prisonersunited.org/prisonersunionofcanada.

REFERENCES

PERSONAL COMMUNICATION

Gregory McMaster, personal communication, February 29, 2020.
Justin Ling, personal communication, April 26, 2020.
Rick Sauvé, personal communication, August 10, 2021.

LEGISLATION, REGULATIONS AND INTERNATIONAL LAW

Canada Health Act, RSC 1985, c C-6.
Canada Labour Code, RSC 1985, c L-2
Constitution Act, 1867 (UK), 30 & 31 Victoria, c 3
Convention Against Torture and Other Cruel, Inhuman or Degrading Treatment or Punishment, United Nations, Treaty Series, vol. 1465, 85.
Correctional Services Act, SNS 2005, c 37
Corrections Act, RSA 2000, c C-29.
Corrections and Conditional Release Act, SC 1992, c 20.
Federal Public Sector Labour Relations Act, SC 2003, c 22.
Foreign Enlistment Act, RSC 1985
General Regulation, NB Reg 84-257
International Labour Organization, "C029 - Forced Labour Convention, 1930 (No. 29)," <ilo.org/dyn/normlex/en/f?p=NORMLEXPUB:12100:0::NO::P12100_ILO_CODE:C029>.
Occupational Health and Safety Act, RSO 1990, c O.1.
Prisons and Reformatories Act, RSC 1985, c P-20.
United Nations General Assembly, *United Nations Standard Minimum Rules for the Treatment of Prisoners (the Nelson Mandela Rules), resolution / adopted by the General Assembly,* 8 January 2016, A/RES/70/175, <refworld.org/docid/5698a3a44.html>
United States Constitution. Amendment XIII, Section I. <senate.gov/civics/constitution_item/constitution.htm>

CASES

Amalgamated Meat Cutters and Butcher Workmen of North America v. Guelph Beef Centre Inc., 1977 CanLII 489 (OLRB).

Canada (Attorney General) v. Public Service Alliance of Canada [1991] S.C.J. No. 19.

Canadian Civil Liberties Association v. Canada, 2019 ONCA 243 (CanLII).

Canadian Prisoners' Labour Confederation v Correctional Service Canada, 2015 CIRB 779.

Canadian Union of Postal Workers v. Foodora Inc. d.b.a. Foodora, 2020 CanLII 16750.

Chilton v. Canada, 2008 FC 1047.

Dart Aerospace Ltd. v. Duval, [2010] F.C.J. No. 919.

Dunmore v. Ontario (Attorney General), 2001 SCC 94.

Ewert v. Canada, 2018 SCC 30 (CanLII), [2018] 2 SCR 165.

Fenton v. British Columbia (1991), 56 B.C.L.R. (2d) 170 (B.C.C.A.).

Foulds v. British Columbia, 2012 BCSC 941 (CanLII).

Gosselin v. Québec (Attorney General), 2002 SCC 84 (CanLII), [2002] 4 SCR 429.

Guérin v. Canada (Attorney General), 2018 FC 94.

Guérin v. Canada (Attorney General), 2019 FCA 272.

Health Services and Support - Facilities Subsector Bargaining Assn. v. British Columbia, 2007 SCC 27, [2007] 2 SCR 391.

International Brotherhood of Electrical Workers, Local 353 v. Hotwire Electric-All Inc., 2016 CanLII 14148 (ON LRB).

Jolivet v. Canada (Correctional Service) 2014 FCA 1.

Jolivet v. Treasury Board (Correctional Service of Canada) 2013 PSLRAB 1.

Lauzon v. Canada (Attorney General), 2014 ONSC 2811 (CanLII).

Machtinger v. HOJ Industries Ltd., [1992] 1 S.C.R. 986.

MacLean v. R., 1972 CanLII 124 (SCC), [1973] SCR 2.

Martineau v. Matsqui Institution, 1979 CanLII 184 (SCC), [1980] 1 SCR 602

Mcguire c. Canada, 1997 CanLII 16898 (CF).

Mounted Police Association of Ontario v. Canada (Attorney General), 2015 SCC 1.

Ontario (Attorney General) v. Fraser, [2011] 2 S.C.R. 3.

Pridy v. British Columbia, 1994 CanLII 669 (BC SC).

R. v. Capay, 2019 ONSC 535 (CanLII).

R. v. Oakes, 1986 CanLII 46 (SCC), [1986] 1 SCR 103.

Reference Re Public Service Employee Relations Act (Alta.), 1987 CanLII 88 (SCC), [1987] 1 SCR 313.

Rizzo & Rizzo Shoes Ltd. (Re), [1998] S.C.J. No. 2.

Roasting v. Blood Band, 1999 ABQB 126 (CanLII).

Sarvanis v. Canada, 1998 CanLII 8398 (FC).

Sarvanis v. Canada, [2002] 1 S.C.R. 921, 2002 SCC 28

Sauvé v. Canada (Chief Electoral Officer), 2002 SCC 68 (CanLII).

Solosky v. The Queen, [1980] 1 SCR 821, 1979 CanLII 9 (SCC).

St. Paul's Hospital (Re) Between: St. Paul's Hospital (Hospital), and Professional Association of Residents and Interns (Applicant), [1976] B.C.L.R.B.D. No. 43 at 12.

University of Toronto (Governing Council), [2012] O.L.R.D. No. 179.

BOOKS, ARTICLES, NEWSPAPERS, AND PERIODICALS

"Abolish Prison Labour in the USA." 2016. *Change.org*. <change.org/p/federal-bureau-of-prisons-abolish-prison-labour-in-the-usa>.

Abolition Coalition. 2021. "Choosing Real Safety: A Historic Declaration to Divest from Policing and Prisons and Build Safer Communities for All." January 21. <wgsi.utoronto.ca/choosing-real-safety-a-historic-declaration-to-divest-from-policing-and-prisons-and-build-safer-communities-for-all/>.

Adams, M.J. 2021. "Chip Away at It." *Briarpatch,* July 5. <briarpatchmagazine.com/articles/view/chip-away-at-it>.

Adema, Seth. 2012. "'Our Destiny Is Not Negotiable': Native Brotherhoods and Decolonization in Ontario's Federal Prisons, 1970–1982." *Left History* 16, 2 (Fall/Winter).

___. 2016. "More than Stone and Iron: Indigenous History and Incarceration in Canada, 1834–1996." PhD dissertation, Wilfrid Laurier University.

Ajadi, Tari, Harry Critchley, El Jones, and Julia Rodgers. n.d. "Defunding the Police: Defining the way forward for the HRM," Halifax Board of Police Commissioner's Subcommittee to Define Defunding. <halifax.ca/sites/default/files/documents/city-hall/boards-committees-commissions/220117bopc1021.pdf>.

Alberta Civil Liberties Research Centre. 2014. "Keeping the Peace: Prisoners' Rights and Employment Programs." <static1.squarespace.com/static/511bd4e0e4b0cecdc77b114b/t/5d237a13e48a5a0001896e76/1562606102833/6+Keeping+the+Peace+Prisoners+and+Employement+Programs+2014.pdf>.

Amnesty International. 2021. "Op-ed: Canada Should Get on the Path to Abolishing Immigration Detention." June 18. <amnesty.org/en/latest/news/2021/06/canada-path-abolishing-immigration-detention/>.

Andrew-Gee, Eric. 2015. *The Toronto Star* "Prisoners Lose Appeal in Upside-Down Maple Leaf T-Shirt Lawsuit." May 15. <thestar.com/news/gta/2015/05/15/prisoners-lose-appeal-in-upside-down-maple-leaf-t-shirt-lawsuit.html>.

Angus Reid Institute. 2020. "Defend or Defund? One-in-four Support Cutting Local Police Budgets; Most Back Social Welfare Over Hiring More Cops." October 26. <angusreid.org/wp-content/uploads/2020/10/2020.10.24_Policing2.pdf>.

Annable, Kristin. 2018. "Manitoba Government Ends Employment Training Program for Provincial Inmates." *CBC News,* May 1. <cbc.ca/news/canada/manitoba/jail-mancor-closes-employment-1.4642073>.

Anonymous Whistleblower. 2020. "What Will You Do?" *Journal of Prisoners on Prisons* 28, 2.

Associated Press. 2018. "Man Says He Wanted 'Three Hots and a Cot,' So He Set Fire." July 31. <wowt.com/content/news/Man-says-he-wanted-three-hots-and-a-cot-so-he-set-fire-489627041.html>.

Baber, Steve Everett. 2020. "Responses to Mass-Incarceration by Faith Communities." PhD dissertation, Seattle University. <scholarworks.seattleu.edu/cgi/viewcontent.cgi?article=1006&context=dmin-projects>.

Baehre, Rainer. 1977. "Origins of the Penitentiary System in Upper Canada." *On-*

tario History, 69 (September).

____. 1994. "Prison as Factory, Convict as Worker: A Study of the Mid-Victorian St John Penitentiary, 1841–1880." In *Essays in the History of Canadian Law: Crime and Criminal Justice in Canadian History,* edited by Susan Lewthwaite, Tina Loo and J. Phillips. Toronto: University of Toronto Press.

Bandele, Asha. 2016. "Jay Z: 'The War on Drugs Is an Epic Fail.'" *New York Times,* September 15. <nytimes.com/2016/09/15/opinion/jay-z-the-war-on-drugs-is-an-epic-fail.html>.

Bank of Canada. n.d. "Inflation Calculator." <bankofcanada.ca/rates/related/inflation-calculator/>.

Barnetson, Bob. 2010. *The Political Economy of Workplace Injury in Canada.* Edmonton: AU Press.

Barrera, Jorge. 2016. "Federal Prison Corporation's Selling of Moccasins, Drums for Revenue 'Exploitative,' Says Cree-Metis Artist." APTN, November 16. <aptnnews.ca/2016/11/16/federal-prison-corporations-selling-of-moccasins-drums-for-revenue-exploitative-says-cree-metis-artist/>.

Barrera, Jorge, and Joseph Loier. 2021. "This Man Is on His Deathbed Because of the Health Care He Received in Prison, Lawsuit Alleges." CBC *News,* March 5. <cbc.ca/news/canada/prison-health-care-lawsuits-1.5939078>.

Barrett, Meredith Robeson, Kim Allenby, and Kelly Taylor. 2010. "Twenty Years Later: Revisiting the Task Force on Federally Sentenced Women." *Correctional Service of Canada,* July. <csc-scc.gc.ca/research/005008-0222-01-eng.shtml>.

Battacharya, Tithi. 2017. "How Not to Skip Class: Social Reproduction of Labour and the Global Working Class." In *Social Reproduction Theory: Remapping Class, Recentring Oppression,* edited by Tithi Battacharya. London: Pluto Press.

Bauer, Shane. 2014. "How Conservatives Learned to Love Prison Reform." *Mother Jones,* March/April. <motherjones.com/politics/2014/02/conservatives-prison-reform-right-on-crime>.

Belmonte, Adriana. 2020. "NBA Teams Become Latest Voices on Prison Reform." *Yahoo! Finance,* February 29. <finance.yahoo.com/news/nba-teams-prison-reform-155959725.html>.

Bennett, Steven C. 1983. "The Privacy and Procedural Due Process Rights of Hunger Striking Prisoners." *New York University Law Review* 58, 5. (November).

Berger, Dan. 2014. *Captive Nation: Black Prison Organizing in the Civil Rights Era.* Chapel Hill: The University of North Carolina Press.

Berger, Dan and Toussaint Loiser. 2018. *Rethinking the American Prison Movement.* New York and London: Routledge.

Berkovits, Joseph Gondor. 1994. "Prisoners for Profit: Convict Labour in the Ontario Central Prison. 1814–1915." In *Essays in the History of Canadian Law, Volume V: Crime and Criminal Justice,* edited by Jim Phillips, Tina Loo, and Susan Lewthwaite. Toronto, Buffalo, and London: University of Toronto Press.

Bittle, Steven, Dean Curran, and Laureen Snider. 2018. "Crimes of the Powerful: The Canadian Context." *Critical Criminology* 26.

Black Lives Matter Canada. 2022. "Defund the Police." <defundthepolice.org/can-

ada/>.

Bodkin, Claire, Matthew Bonn, and Sheila Wildeman. 2020. "Fuelling a Crisis: Lack of Treatment for Opioid Use in Canada's Prisons and Jails." *The Conversation*, March 4. <theconversation.com/fuelling-a-crisis-lack-of-treatment-for-opioid-use-in-canadas-prisons-and-jails-130779>.

Bodkin, Claire, Lucie Pivnick, Susan J. Bondy, et al. 2019. "History of Childhood Abuse in Populations Incarcerated in Canada: A Systematic Review and Meta-Analysis." *American Journal of Public Health* 109, 3.

Borgia, Stéphanie. 2019. "Fonds de soutien à la réinsertion sociale des établissements de détention: Rapport d'activités 2019." <cdn-contenu.quebec.ca/cdn-contenu/adm/min/securite-publique/publications-adm/publications-secteurs/services-correctionnels/reinsertion-sociale/rapport_activites_FCSRS_2019.pdf?1624456703>.

Bourbeau, Emmanuelle, and Andrew Fields. 2017. "Annual Review of the Labour Market, 2016." *Statistics Canada*, April 28. <www150.statcan.gc.ca/n1/pub/75-004-m/75-004-m2017001-eng.htm>.

Briskin, Linda. 2007. "From Person-Days Lost to Labour Militancy: A New Look at the Canadian Work Stoppage Data." *Relations industrielles / Industrial Relations* 62, 1.

Brownell, Claire. 2017. "Prisoners Making $1.95 a Day Want a Raise. Taxpayers Want a Break." *Financial Post*, August 30. <financialpost.com/news/court-challenge-to-inmate-pay-places-prison-labour-program-in-the-crosshairs>.

Cain, Patrick. 2018. "Canada's Last Military Prison Costs $2M a Year. About Half the Time, It Has No Prisoners." *Global News*, May 23. <globalnews.ca/news/4097208/military-prison-edmonton-empty/>.

Cameron, Silver Donald. 1977. *The Education of Everett Richardson: The Nova Scotia Fishermen's Strike: 1970–71*. Toronto: McClelland and Stewart.

Canadian Bar Association. 2013. "Reaching Equal Justice: An Invitation to Envision and Act." November. <cba.org/CBA-Equal-Justice/Equal-Justice-Initiative/Reports>.

Canadian Civil Liberties Association and Education Trust. 2014. "Set Up to Fail: Bail and the Revolving Door of Pre-trial Detention." July. <ccla.org/wp-content/uploads/2021/07/Set-up-to-fail-FINAL.pdf>.

Canadian Press. 2017. "B.C. Thanks Inmates Who Helped During the Province's Worst-Ever Wildfire Season." *Toronto Star*, October 3. <thestar.com/news/canada/2017/10/03/bc-thanks-inmates-who-helped-battle-the-provinces-worst-ever-wildfire-season.html>.

Cardinal, Cory Charles. 2021. "Prisons Are Built on Our Backs." *Briarpatch Magazine*, September 2. <briarpatchmagazine.com/articles/view/prisons-are-built-on-our-backs>.

Carrigan, D. Owen. 1991. *Crime and Punishment in Canada: A History*. Toronto: McClelland & Stewart Inc.

CBC News. 2002. "Injured Inmate Can Sue Ottawa, Supreme Court Rules." March 21. <cbc.ca/news/canada/injured-inmate-can-sue-ottawa-supreme-court-

rules-1.345390>.

___. 2008. "Government Officials Should be Charged in Sydney Jail Asbestos Case: Union." June 3. <cbc.ca/news/canada/nova-scotia/government-officials-should-be-charged-in-sydney-jail-asbestos-case-union-1.747689>.

___. 2013. "Prisoners Go on Strike." October 2. <cbc.ca/player/play/2409874501>.

___. 2016. "'At Some Point, They Have To Arrest Me': Homeless Man Wants to Go to Jail to Stay Warm." December 24. <cbc.ca/news/canada/manitoba/homeless-man-jail-winter-1.3912199>.

Cell Count. 2014. "Re: Inmate Pay Cut." 73 (Spring) <prisonfreepress.org/Cell_Count/Cell_Count_-_Issue_73.pdf>.

Chaboyer, Jan, and Errol Black. 2006. "Conspiracy in Winnipeg: How the 1919 General Strike Leaders Were Railroaded into Prison and What We Must Do Now to Make Amends." CCPA *Review Labour Notes* (March). <policyalternatives. ca/sites/default/files/uploads/publications/Manitoba_Pubs/2006/Conspiracy_in_Winnipeg.pdf>.

Choudry, Aziz, and Adiran Smith (eds.). 2016. *Unfree Labour? Struggles of Migrant and Immigrant Workers in Canada.* Oakland: PM Press.

Clarke, John. 2019. "A Tale of Two Austerities." *Canadian Dimension,* January 24. <https://canadiandimension.com/articles/view/a-tale-of-two-austerities>.

Clarkson, Chris, and Melissa Munn. 2021. *Disruptive Prisoners: Resistance, Reform, and the New Deal.* Toronto, Buffalo, and London: Toronto University Press.

Clifford, W., John Braithwaite, and Jack Sandry (eds). 1982. *Regional Developments in Corrections: Proceedings of the Second Asian and Pacific Conference of Correctional Administrators, Bangkok, July 6–10, 1981.* Canberra: Australian Institute of Criminology.

Cohen, Tobi. 2012. "Prisoner Purchases Offer Peek at Life Inside the Penitentiary; Inmates Buy Shoes, Games, Body Wash." *Windsor Star,* September 15.

Colantonio, Angela, et al. 2014. "Traumatic Brain Injury and Early Life Experiences Among Men and Women in a Prison Population." *Journal of Correctional Healthcare* 20, 4.

Comack, Elizabeth, Cara Fabre, and Shanise Burgher. 2015. "The Impact of the Harper Government's 'Tough on Crime' Strategy: Hearing from Front-line Workers." *Canadian Centre for Policy Alternatives.* <policyalternatives. ca/sites/default/files/uploads/publications/Manitoba%20Office/2015/09/ Tough%20on%20Crime%20WEB.pdf>.

Con-versely. 1976. "Native Brotherhood." June. Gaucher/Munn Penal Press Collection. <penalpress.com/wp-content/uploads/Conversely_June1976.pdf>.

Cooke, Alex. 2022. "N.S. Prison Reform Groups Call for Inmate Releases as COVID-19 Spreads." *Global News.* January 1. <https://globalnews.ca/news/8483490/ns-prison-inmate-release-covid-19/>.

Cooper, Sam. 2013. "Rising Threat of Violence: Guards; Prisons: Cuts to Inmate Wages, Benefits Lead to Compounding Dangers in Already-Volatile Situations." *The Province,* October 3.

CORCAN. 1982. CORCAN *Annual Report, 1981–1982* <publicsafety.gc.ca/lbrr/ar-

chives/csc-arcorcan-1981-1982-eng.pdf>.

___. 1989. *Occupational Development Programs:* CORCAN *Report on Performance, 1988/89.* <ojp.gov/ncjrs/virtual-library/abstracts/occupational-development-programs-corcan-report-performance-198889>.

CORCAN *Express.* 1994. "CORCAN Community Programs in Quebec," 3: 5 (September): 1–2.

___. 1994. "CORCAN Research Projects," 3, 2 (May).

___. 1994. "ISO Certification," 3, 2 (May).

___. 1994. "New Ventures: A CORCAN Business Initiative," 3, 5 (September).

Cordoso, Tom. 2020. "Bias Behind Bars: A Globe Investigation Finds a Prison System Stacked Against Black and Indigenous Inmates." *Globe and Mail,* October 24. <theglobeandmail.com/canada/article-investigation-racial-bias-in-canadian-prison-risk-assessments/>.

Correctional Service of Canada. n.d. "CORCAN," <csc-scc.gc.ca/corcan/index-eng.shtml>.

___. n.d. "Offender Hours Worked." Access to Information and Privacy release.

___. 1983. "Third Annual Report, 1982–83: Inspector General's Branch." <public-safety.gc.ca/lbrr/archives/csc-arigb1-1982-1983-eng.pdf>.

___. 1984."Fourth Annual Report, 1983–84: Inspector General's Branch." <public-safety.gc.ca/lbrr/archives/csc-arigb1-1983-1984-eng.pdf>.

___. 1997. "Commissioner's Directive 737. Inmate-Operated Business Enterprises." January 24. <qp.alberta.ca/1266.cfm?page=c29.cfm&leg_type=Acts&isbncln=9780779831326>.

___. 2011. "Correctional Service of Canada News Release — Inmate Protest at Collins Bay Institution." June 28. Access to Information and Privacy release.

___. 2011. "From Julie Blasko to 440-CBI-All Staff: Inmate Work Stoppage." July 4. Access to Information and Privacy release.

___. 2011. "From Julie Blasko to Inmate Population: Memorandum: Offender Work Refusal." June 29. Access to Information and Privacy release.

___. 2011. "From Wayne Buller (ONT) to 440-CBI-All Staff: Offender Work Refusal." June 27. Access to Information and Privacy release.

___. 2012. "Public Perceptions of Corrections, 2010." July. <csc-scc.gc.ca/research/005008-rs12-07-eng.shtml>.

___. 2013. "Audit of Employment and Employability Programs for Offenders." December 13. <csc-scc.gc.ca/publications/005007-2527-eng.shtml>.

___. 2013. "History of CORCAN and the Evolution of Prison Industries." January 15. <csc-scc.gc.ca/corcan/002005-0004-eng.shtml>.

___. 2014. "1940–1959: Times of Change." October 20. <csc-scc.gc.ca/about-us/006-2003-eng.shtml>.

___. 2016. "Briefing Note to the Commissioner: Re-opening of CORCAN Farm at Collins Bay Institution." December 16. Access to Information and Privacy release.

___. 2016. "Correctional Service of Canada, Returning to the Workforce: Offenders Graduate from Training Program in Pacific Region." May 26. <lte-ene.ca/en/

returning-workforce-offenders-graduate-training-program-pacific-region>.

___. 2017. "Commissioner's Directive 735: Employment and Employability Program." May 15. <csc-scc.gc.ca/acts-and-regulations/735-cd-eng.shtml>.

___. 2018. "CORCAN — Employment and Employability." July 9. <csc-scc.gc.ca/publications/005007-3016-en.shtml>.

___. 2018. "CORCAN: Overview." November 13. <csc-scc.gc.ca/corcan/002005-0001-eng.shtml>.

___. 2019. "Appendix B: Offender Training Agreement Between CORCAN and the Abattoir Licensee." October. Access to Information and Privacy release.

___. 2019. "Commissioner's Directives. Guidelines 081-1 Offender Complaint and Grievance Process." June 28. <csc-scc.gc.ca/politiques-et-lois/081-1-gl-en.shtml>.

___. 2019. Email to Marie Pier Lecuyer from redacted regarding agreements between CSC and Feihe International or Canada Royal Milk. August 6. Access to Information and Privacy release.

___. 2020. "Response to the 47th Annual Report of the Correctional Investigator 2019–2020." August 20. <csc-scc.gc.ca/publications/005007-2811-en.shtml>.

___. 2021. Commissioner's Directive 726, "Correctional Programs." November 8. <csc-scc.gc.ca/politiques-et-lois/726-cd-en.shtml>.

___. 2022. "National Inventory of Asbestos in Correctional Service of Canada Buildings." July 27. <csc-scc.gc.ca/health-and-safety/001006-1002-en.shtml>.

Corriveau, Stacey. 2007. "A Passion for Renewal: Co-operation and Commerce within Prison Walls," *Making Waves* 18, 2. <communityrenewal.ca/sites/all/files/resource/MW180205.pdf>.

Cox, Damien. 1989. "Inmates at Four Penitentiaries Stop Work to Protest Pay Rates." *Toronto Star,* January 24.

Coyle, Emilie, and Jackie Omstead. 2022. "The Use of Solitary Confinement Continues in Canada," *Policy Options,* January 18. <policyoptions.irpp.org/magazines/january-2022/the-use-of-solitary-confinement-continues-in-canada/>.

Crawford, Tiffany. 2011. "B.C. Prisoners Trying to Form Labour Union." *National Post,* March 4. <nationalpost.com/news/b-c-prisoners-trying-to-form-labour-union>.

Crete, Jean-Philippe. 2013. "A Disciplined Healing: The New Language of Indigenous Imprisonment in Canada." MA thesis, Carleton University.

___. 2017. "Punitive Healing and Penal Relics: Indigenous Prison Labour and the (Re)production of Cultural Artefacts," In *The Palgrave Handbook of Prison Tourism,* edited by Jacqueline Z. Wilson, Sarah Hodgkinson, Justin Piché, and Kevin Walby.London: Palgrave MacMillan.

Criminalization and Punishment Education Project. 2022. "Tracking Politics of Criminalization and Punishment in Canada." February 27. <tpcp-canada.blogspot.com/2022/02/over-21600-covid-19-cases-linked-to.html>.

CTV News. 2015. "First Look at Where Ontario Inmates Make Blankets, Licence Plates." March 17. <london.ctvnews.ca/first-look-at-where-ontario-inmates-make-blankets-licence-plates-1.2284452>.

____. 2017. "Some Working Inmates at Regina Correctional Centre Strike Over Wage Cut." May 4. <regina.ctvnews.ca/some-working-inmates-at-regina-correctional-centre-strike-over-wage-cut-1.3399137>.

Culhane, Claire. 1986. "To the Guys at Kent." *Kent Times,* August 10. Gaucher/ Munn Penal Press Collection. <penalpress.com/wp-content/uploads/Kent-Times_V1_I1_Aug1986.pdf>.

Cummins, Eric. 1994. *The Rise and Fall of California's Radical Prison Movement.* Stanford: Stanford University Press.

Cunningham, Shauna. 2021. "No More Active Cases of COVID-19 at Joyceville Institution After Major Outbreak." *Global News,* February 22. <globalnews.ca/news/7614535/active-covid-19-joyceville-institution-coronavirus-outbreak/>.

D'Agostino, Peter. 2002. "Craniums, Criminals, and the 'Cursed Race': Italian Anthropology in American Racial Thought, 1861–1924." *Comparative Studies in Society and History* 44, 2.

D'Arcy, Steve. 2016. "The Political Vocabulary of the Post-New Left: How Activists Articulate Their Politics and Why It Matters." In *A World to Win: Contemporary Social Movements & Counter Hegemony,* edited by William K. Carroll and Kanchan Sarker. Winnipeg: ARP Press.

Davis, Angela. 2007. *Are Prisons Obsolete?* New York: Seven Stories Press.

Dawe, Meghan, and Philip Goodman. 2017. "Conservative Politics, Sacred Cows, and Sacrificial Lambs: The (Mis)Use of Evidence in Canada's Political and Penal Fields." *Canadian Review of Sociology* 54, 2 (May).

Debs, Eugene V. 1973. *Walls and Bars.* Chicago: Charles H. Kerr & Company.

DeGurse, Carl. 2019. "All Should Be Welcome in Storm Cleanup." *Winnipeg Free Press,* October 26.

Department of Justice Canada. 2015. "Public Perception of Crime and Justice in Canada: A Review of Opinion Polls." January 7. <justice.gc.ca/eng/rp-pr/csj-sjc/crime/rr01_1/p4_1.html>.

____. 2021. "State of the Criminal Justice System: Focus on Women." <justice.gc.ca/eng/cj-jp/state-etat/2021rpt-rap2021/pdf/SOCJS_2020_en.pdf>.

Devet, Robert. 2018. "Interview: El Jones on Supporting the Burnside Jail Protest." *The Nova Scotia Advocate,* August 22. <nsadvocate.org/2018/08/22/interview-el-jones-on-supporting-the-burnside-jail-protest>.

Devoy, Desmond. 2017. "Forget 'Club Fed': Inside Canada's Aging, Segregated Prisons." *Perth Courier,* February 20. <insideottawavalley.com/news-story/7146391-forget-club-fed-inside-canada-s-aging-segregated-prisons/>

Diaz-Cotto, Juanita. 1996. *Gender, Ethnicity and the State: Latina and Latin Prison Politics.* Albany: State University of New York Press.

DiManno, Rosie. 2019. "Why Toronto South Detention Centre is known as Guantanamo South, a $1-billion Hellhole, and the Plea Factory." *Toronto Star,* December 14. <thestar.com/opinion/star-columnists/2019/12/13/toronto-south-detention-centre-a-giant-black-hole-for-those-who-disappear-there-head-of-criminal-lawyers-body.html>.

Do, Deniz, René Houle and Martin Turcotte. 2020. "Canada's Black Population: Education, Labour and Resilience." *Statistics Canada,* February 25. <www150.statcan.gc.ca/n1/pub/89-657-x/89-657-x2020002-eng.htm>.

Dobchuk-Land, Bronwyn, and James Wilt. 2020. "Prison Unionism." *Briarpatch,* July 2. <briarpatchmagazine.com/articles/view/prison-unionism>.

Doob, Antony. 2015. "The Harper Revolution in Criminal Justice Policy... and What Comes Next." *Policy Options,* May 4. <policyoptions.irpp.org/fr/magazines/entre-prosperite-et-turbulences/doob-webster/>

Drumheller Mail. "Inmates Take Strike Action." October 9 <https://www.drumhellermail.com/news/13348-inmates-take-strike->.

Duggan, Kyle. 2017. "The Proposed Budget 2017 Lines Canadians Couldn't Stomach." *iPolitics,* July 20. <ipolitics.ca/2017/07/20/the-proposed-budget-2017-lines-canadians-couldnt-stomach/>.

Edwards, John. 1996. "Industry in Canadian Federal Prisons: Glimpses into History." *Forum on Corrections Research* 8, 1 (January).

Employment and Social Development Canada. 2022. "Hire a Temporary Worker Through the Seasonal Agricultural Worker Program: Overview." February 8. <canada.ca/en/employment-social-development/services/foreign-workers/agricultural/seasonal-agricultural.html>.

Evans, Bryan. 2012. "The New Democratic Party in the Era of Neoliberalism." In *Rethinking the Politics of Labour in Canada,* edited by Stephanie Ross and Larry Savage. Halifax and Winnipeg: Fernwood Publishing.

___. 2013. "When Your Boss Is the State: The Paradoxes of Public Sector Work." In *Public Sector Unions in the Age of Austerity,* edited by Stephanie Ross and Larry Savage.Halifax and Winnipeg: Fernwood Publishing.

Evans, Jessica. 2020. "Capitalism, Prisons and COVID-19: On 'Surplus Labour.'" *Spring Magazine,* May 27. <springmag.ca/capitalism-prisons-and-covid-19-on-surplus-labour>.

___. 2021. "Penal Nationalism in the Settler Colony: On the Construction and Maintenance of 'National Whiteness' in Settler Canada," *Punishment and Society* 23, 4.

Evolve Our Prison Farms. n.d. "Legal Issues Arising from the Export of Prison-Sourced Infant Formula." <evolveourprisonfarms.ca/exporting-prison-produced-goods/>.

___. 2020. "Evidence of the Scale of the Planned Goat Operation and Other Problems with the New Prison Farms in Kingston." October. Unpublished document.

Falkof, Bradley B. 1979. "Prisoner Representative Organizations, Prison Reform, and Jones v. North Carolina Prisoners' Labor Union: An Argument for Increased Court Intervention in Prison Administration." *The Journal of Criminal Law and Criminology* 70, 1.

Fitzgerald, Mike. 1977. *Prisoners in Revolt.* London: Penguin.

Fletcher, Bill Jr. and Fernando Gapasin. 2008. *Solidarity Divided: The Crisis in Organized Labor and a New Path Toward Social Justice.* Berkeley: University of

California Press.

Forsey, Eugene. 1982. *Trade Unions in Canada, 1812–1902*. Toronto, Buffalo, London: University of Toronto Press.

Forsey, Helen. 2021. "CSC Should Abandon Its Industrial Goat Farm Fiasco." *The Hill Times,* April 5. <evolveourprisonfarms.ca/wp-content/uploads/2021/04/040521_ht_1-Helen-Forsey.pdf>.

Foucault, Michel. 1995. *Discipline and Punish: The Birth of the Prison*. New York: Vintage Books.

Fox, Barry M. 1972. "First Amendment Rights of Prisoners." *Criminal Law Criminology and Police Science* 63, 2.

Fraser, D.C. 2017. "Protest Underway at Regina Jail Over Recent Cuts to Inmates' Pay." *Leader Post,* May 3.

Fudge, Judy, Elene Lam, Sandra Ka Hon Chu, and Vincent Wong. 2021. "Caught in the Carceral Web: Anti-Trafficking Laws and Policies and Their Impact on Migrant Sex Workers." <gflc.ca/wp-content/uploads/2020/10/MSW-Report-Final-Sept-26.pdf>.

Fudge, Judy, and Eric Tucker. 2001. *Labour Before the Law: The Regulation of Workers' Collective Action in Canada, 1900–1948*. Oxford and New York: Oxford University Press.

Fuller, Thomas. 2020. "Coronavirus Limits California's Efforts to Fight Fires With Prison Labor." *New York Times,* August 22. <nytimes.com/2020/08/22/us/california-wildfires-prisoners.html>.

Garvey, Stephen P. 1997-1988. "Freeing Prisoners' Labor." *Stanford Law Review* 50.

Gendreau Paul, Claire Goggin, and Francis T. Cullen. 1999. "The Effects of Prison Sentences on Recidivism," Public Works and Government Services Canada Cat. No.: J42-87/1999E. <publicsafety.gc.ca/cnt/rsrcs/pblctns/ffcts-prsn-sntncs-rcdvsm/ffcts-prsn-sntncs-rcdvsm-eng.pdf>.

Gibson, Victoria, and Nadine Yousif. 2021. "Nearly One in Four People Sent to Toronto's Detention Centres in 2020 Were Homeless — The Worst Rate Seen in Years." *Toronto Star,* May 7. <thestar.com/news/gta/2021/05/07/nearly-one-in-four-people-sent-to-torontos-detention-centres-in-2020-were-homeless-the-worst-rate-seen-in-years.html?utm_source=Twitter&utm_medium=SocialMedia&utm_campaign=GTA&utm_content=homeless-detention>.

Gilmore, Ruth Wilson, and James Kilgore. 2019. "Some Reflections on Prison Labor." *The Brooklyn Rail.* June 6. <brooklynrail.org/2019/06/field-notes/Some-Reflections-on-Prison-Labor>.

Gindin, Sam. 2012. "Rethinking Unions, Registering Socialism." In *The Socialist Register 2013: A Question of Strategy,* edited by Leo Panitch and Viviek Chibber. London: Merlin.

___. 2016. "Chasing Utopia." *Jacobin,* March 10. <jacobinmag.com/2016/03/workers-control-coops-wright-wolff-alperovitz>.

Glasbeek, Harry. 2018. *Capitalism: A Crime Story*. Toronto: Between the Lines.

Glenburnie Grocery. 2022. "Glenburnie Grocery Brands." <glenburniegrocery.ca/

site/glenburnie-kingston-local-brands>.

Global Detention Project. 2018. "Immigration Detention in Canada: Important Reforms, Ongoing Concerns." June. <globaldetentionproject.org/immigration-detention-in-canada-important-reforms-ongoing-concerns>.

Globe. 1914. "Prisoner Killed by Fall." October 9.

___. 1914. "Trading with Enemy Is High Crime." November 2.

___. 1922. "Pioneers Meted Out Odd Punishment." June 22.

___. 1925. "Nickle Asks Report on 4-Year Sentence for $4.50 Forger." November 25.

___. 1928. "A Hard Labor." September 1.

___. 1931. "Communist Leaders Given Record Terms For Part In Riot." September 25.

___. 1931. "Speaker Arrested at Mass Meeting." May 2.

___. 1933. "Burwash Convicts Charge Brutality by Officer." January 31.

___. 1935. "Ottawa Mayor Asks Hepburn to Stop Trek." July 13.

Globe and Mail. 1914. "Conductor and Brakeman Sent Down to Hard Labor." February 9.

___. 1932. "Discrepancies Report to House: Accident Fatal at Reformatory." March 11.

___. 1937. "Production Put First and Prisoners Last, Guelph Inquiry Told." February 22.

___. 1939. "Stabbed Wife, Gets 6 Months at Hard Labor." December 22.

___. 1941. "Given Hard Labor." July 16.

___. 1942. "Steve Harkin Given 30 Days." February 6.

___. 1946. "Teen-Age Girl Given Hard Labor." February 14.

___. 1947. "Jail, Hard Labor for Manslaughter." November 4.

___. 1947. "Jail, Hard Labor For Union Leader In Textile Strike." July 9.

___. 1953. "Hard Labor Proposed for Elusive Husbands." August 26.

___. 1955. "Court Orders Hard Labor For Drunk Driver." August 31.

___. 1963. "Called Road Menace: Month at Hard Labor for Careless Driving." September 24.

___. 1963. "Fireworks Bylaws Muddled." May 20.

___. 1975. "Hard Labor Faces Drivers in Smithville." September 18.

___. 1978. "Inmates Will Be Foresters in Hallow." August 14.

___. 1981. "Jail Jobs Benefit All." April 7.

___. 1983. "Prisoners Want a Union to Fight for Release." February 3.

___. 1949. "Accident Kills Guelph Inmate." August 5.

Go, Johann J. 2020. "Structure, Choice, and Responsibility." *Ethics & Behavior* 30, 3.

Gollom, Mark. 1998. "Business a Steal for Prison Labourers." *Ottawa Citizen,* February 15.

Goodman, Philip. 2012. "Hero and Inmate: Work, Prisons, and Punishment in California's Fire Camps." *WorkingUSA* 15, 3.

Goodman, Philip, and Meghan Dawe. 2016. "Prisoners, Cows, and Abattoirs: The Closing of Canada's Prison Farms as a Political Penal Drama." *British Journal of Criminology* 56, 4 (July).

Gordon, Todd. 2019. "Capitalism, Neoliberalism, and Unfree Labour." *Critical Sociology* 45, 6.

Gorz, Andre. 1968. "Reform and Revolution." In *Socialist Register 1968,* edited by Ralph Milliband and John Saville. London: Merlin Press.

Gosselin, Luc. 1982. *Prisons in Canada.* Montréal: Black Rose Books.

Government of Canada. 2020. *Public Accounts of Canada 2020 Volume III: Additional Information and Analyses.* <publications.gc.ca/collections/collection_2020/spac-pspc/P51-1-2020-3-eng.pdf>.

___. 2021. "Federal Corporation Information - 087118-4." February 2. <ic.gc.ca/app/scr/cc/CorporationsCanada/fdrlCrpDtls.html?corpId=871184&V_TOKEN=null&crpNm=&crpNmbr=871184&bsNmbr=>.

___. 2021. "Salaries and wages — Canadian Industry Statistics — Meat product manufacturing — 3116." July 27. <ic.gc.ca/app/scr/app/cis/salaries-salaires/3116;jsessionid=0001SLQLMFqdyeGSIt8sWTa55KY:-C7AEJO>.

___. 2022. "Salaries and wages — Canadian Industry Statistics — Furniture and Related Product Manufacturing." February 2. <ic.gc.ca/app/scr/app/cis/salaries-salaires/337;jsessionid=0001NgtB1qI4VsxSN1D-H_otmPd:-C7AEJO>.

Grant, Donald. 1983. "'For Once in My Life, I'm Really Enjoying Something': Prisoners Serve Their Time in the Toy Shop." *Globe and Mail,* November 7.

Graveland, Bill. 2020. "COVID-19 Outbreaks Over in Federal Prisons, Staff Preparing for 'New Normal.'" *CP24,* August 8. <cp24.com/news/covid-19-outbreaks-over-in-federal-prisons-staff-preparing-for-new-normal-1.5056494?cache=zyujtxhn>.

Gray, Malcolm. 1981. "Arsonists and Inmates." *Maclean's,* November 30. <archive.macleans.ca/article/1981/11/30/arsonists-and-inmates>.

___. 1981. "Meltdown in the Gilded Cage." *Maclean's,* June 15. <archive.macleans.ca/article/1981/6/15/meltdown-in-the-gilded-cage>.

Guilett, Edwin C. 1933. *Early Life in Upper Canada.* Toronto: University of Toronto Press.

Hamilton, Charles. 2013. "Inmates Hard at Work in Urban Camp." *StarPhoenix,* February 4.

Hannah-Moffat, Kelly. 2005. "Criminogenic Needs and the Transformative Risk Subject: Hybridizations of Risk/Need in Penality." *Punishment & Society* 7, 1 (January).

Hannah-Moffat, Kelly, and Margaret Shaw (eds.). 2000. *An Ideal Prison: Critical Essays on Women's Imprisonment in Canada.* Halifax: Fernwood Publishing.

Harris, Kathleen. 2018. "Canada's Prison System Overhauls Transgender Inmate Policy." *CBC News,* January 31. <cbc.ca/news/politics/transgender-inmates-csc-policy-1.4512510>.

Hatton, Erin. 2020. *Coerced: Work Under Threat of Punishment.* Oakland: University of California.

Hay, Douglas. 1975. "Property, Authority, and the Criminal Law." In *Albion's Fatal Tree: Crime and Society in Eighteenth-Century England,* edited by Douglas Hay, Peter Linebaugh, John G. Rule, E.P. Thompson, and Cal Winslow. New

York: Pantheon.

Heffernan, Seamus. 2020. "We Are Feeding Our Prisoners Gruel and Using Hunger as Punishment." *The Line,* November 19. <theline.substack.com/p/seamus-heffernan-we-are-feeding-our>.

Hill, Charles W. 1975. *Research Report to the Department of Justice and Solicitor General (Canada) Concerning the Native Brotherhood Organizations in Penal Institutions.* <publicsafety.gc.ca/lbrr/archives/e%2098.c87%20h5-eng.pdf>

Hinge, Gail. n.d. "Consolidation of Indian Legislation, Vol: II: Indian Acts and Amendments, 1868–1975." <publications.gc.ca/collections/collection_2017/aanc-inac/R5-158-2-1978-eng.pdf>.

House, Jordan. 2018. "When Prisoners Had a Union: The Canadian Food and Allied Workers Union Local 240." *Labour/Le Travail* 82, 36 (Fall).

___. 2019. "The 1934 British Columbia Penitentiary Strike and Prisoners' Wages in Canada." *Active History,* April 26. <activehistory.ca/2019/04/the-1934-british-columbia-penitentiary-strike-and-prisoners-wages-in-canada/>.

___. 2020. "Making Prisons Work: Prison Labour and Resistance in Canada." PhD dissertation, York University.

House, Jordan, and Asaf Rashid. 2020. "Failure to Protect Essential Prisoner Workers Undermines Public Safety." *Canadian Dimension,* December 28. <canadiandimension.com/articles/view/failure-to-protect-essential-prisoner-workers-undermines-public-safety>.

Hoye, Bryce. 2020. "Manitoba Looks to Private Sector to Help Reduce Youth Recidivism Through Social Impact Bond." CBC *News,* July 8. <cbc.ca/news/canada/manitoba/manitoba-youth-recidivism-social-impact-bond-1.5642957>.

Huff, Clarence Ronald. 1974. "Unionization Behind the Walls: An Analytic Study of the Ohio's Prisoners' Labor Union Movement." PhD dissertation, Ohio State University.

Hughett, Amanda Bell. 2017. "Silencing the Cell Block: The Making of Modern Prison Policy in North Carolina and the Nation." PhD dissertation, Duke University.

___. 2019. "A 'Safe Outlet' for Prisoner Discontent: How Prison Grievance Procedures Helped Stymie Prison Organizing During the 1970s." *Law & Social Inquiry* 44, 4.

Huncar, Andrea. 2021. "How Systemic Racism Is Factoring into Sentences for Black Albertans." CBC *News,* March 24. <cbc.ca/news/canada/edmonton/black-indigenous-offenders-gladue-enhanced-pre-sentence-reports-1.5951638>.

Iftene, Adelina. 2021. "COVID-19, Human Rights and Public Health in Prisons: A Case Study of Nova Scotia's Experience During the First Wave of the of the Pandemic." *Dalhousie Law Journal* 44, 2.

Iftene, Adelina, Lynne Hanson and Allan Manso. 2014. "Tort Claims and Canadian Prisoners." *Queen's Law Journal* 39, 2.

Ignatieff, Michael. 1978. *A Just Measure of Pain: The Penitentiary in the Industrial Revolution 1750–1850.* New York: Pantheon.

Incarcerated Workers Organizing Committee. n.d. <incarceratedworkers.org/>.

INCITE! Women of Color Against Violence and Critical Resistance. 2008. "The Critical Resistance INCITE! Statement on Gender Violence and the Prison Industrial Complex," in *Abolition Now! Ten Years of Strategy and Struggle Against the Prison Industrial Complex,* edited by the CR10 Publications Collective. Oakland and Edinburgh: AK Press.

Independent Review of Ontario Corrections. 2017. *Corrections in Ontario: Directions for Reform.* September. <files.ontario.ca/solgen-corrections_in_ontario_directions_for_reform.pdf>.

Indigenous Corporate Training, Inc. 2016. "10 Quotes John A. Macdonald Made about First Nations." June 28. <ictinc.ca/blog/10-quotes-john-a.-macdonald-made-about-first-nations>.

InsideArt. 2005. "The Story." <web.archive.org/web/20090623040331/http://www.insideart.ca/thestory.html>.

iPolitics. 2013. "Verbatim: Stephen Harper's Speech to the Calgary Convention." November 1. <ipolitics.ca/2013/11/01/verbatim-stephen-harpers-speech-to-the-calgary-convention/>.

Ireton, Julie. 2013. "Contractor in Fight with Public Works After Asbestos Exposure." *CBC News,* April 25. <cbc.ca/news/canada/ottawa/contractor-in-fight-with-public-works-after-asbestos-exposure-1.1336575>.

Irwin, John. 1980. *Prisons in Turmoil.* Boston and Toronto: Little, Brown and Company.

ITF Seafarers. 2021. "'I Have Had to Swim to Shore Every Few Days to Get Food and Water' — Meet the Seafarer Trapped on Board the *MV Aman* for Four Years (and Counting)." March 19. <itfseafarers.org/en/news/i-have-had-swim-shore-every-few-days-get-food-and-water-meet-seafarer-trapped-board-mv-aman>.

Jackson, Michael. 1974. "Justice Behind the Walls: A Study of the Disciplinary Process in a Canadian Penitentiary." *Osgoode Hall Law Journal* 12, 1.

___. 2002. *Justice Behind the Walls: Human Rights in Canadian Prisons.* Vancouver: Douglas & McIntyre.

John Howard Society of Canada. 2013. "Prisoner-Based Co-operatives: Working It Out in Canada." March. <docplayer.net/39319679-Prisoner-based-co-operatives-working-it-out-in-canada.html>.

___. 2018. "Financial Facts on Canadian Prisons." August 18 <johnhoward.ca/blog/financial-facts-canadian-prisons/>.

John Howard Society of Ontario. 2009. "Crime and Unemployment: What's the Link?" *FactSheet* 24. <johnhoward.on.ca/wp-content/uploads/2014/09/facts-24-crime-and-unemployment-whats-the-link-march-2009.pdf>.

___. 2010. "Fetal Alcohol Spectrum Disorder and the Criminal Justice System: A Poor Fit." *Factsheet* 26. <johnhoward.on.ca/wp-content/uploads/2014/09/facts-26-fasd-and-the-criminal-justice-system-december-2010.pdf>.

John Howard Society of Toronto. 2010. "Homeless and Jailed: Jailed and Homeless." August. <johnhoward.ca/wp-content/uploads/2016/12/Amber-Kellen-Homeless-and-Jailed-Jailed-and-Homeless.pdf>.

Kainai Transition Centre Society. 2022. "Community Corrections." <ktcsbloodtribe.com/ktcs-programs/community-corrections/>.

Kasmir, Sharryn. 2017. "Cooperative Democracy or Cooperative Competitiveness: Rethinking Mondragon." In *The Socialist Register 2018: Rethinking Democracy,* edited by Leo Panitch and Greg Albo. London: Merlin.

Kenna, Kathleen. 1988. "Prison Staff 'Use Convicts as Slave Labor': Beaver Creek Personnel Accused of Putting Inmates to Work at Home." *Toronto Star,* August 11.

Kidman, John. 1947. *The Canadian Prison: The Story of a Tragedy.* Toronto: Ryerson Press.

King, Adam D.K. 2021. "How the Right to Strike Is Being Eroded in Canada," *Passage,* June 30. <readpassage.com/p/how-the-right-to-strike-is-being-eroded-in-canada/>.

___. 2021. "Uber's Flexible Work+ Proposal Is a Ploy to Undermine Workers' Rights and Protections." *Passage,* March 16. <readpassage.com/p/ubers-new-flexible-work-plan-is-bad-for-workers>.

Kingston Whig-Standard. 2003. "Inmates Lose Jobs after TV Show Move." February 22.

Klassen, Irene. 2005. "Offender Employment and Employability: An Overview," FORUM *on Corrections Research.* <csc-scc.gc.ca/research/forum/Vol17No1/v17n1h_e.pdf>.

Kleuskens, Shanisse. 2015. "Legitimating the 'Fiasco': Canadian State Justifications of CORCAN Prison Labour." Master's thesis, University of Ottawa.

Klippenstein, Ken. 2021. "Documents Show Amazon Is Aware Drivers Pee in Bottles and Even Defecate En Route, Despite Company Denial." *The Intercept,* March 25. <theintercept.com/2021/03/25/amazon-drivers-pee-bottles-union/>.

Kouyoumdjian, Fiona, et al. 2016. "Health Status of Prisoners in Canada: Narrative Review." *Canadian Family Physician* 62 (March).

Kubinec, Vera-Lynn. 2021. "'A Dungeon Inside a Prison': Lawsuit Seeks Compensation for Manitoba Inmates Held in Solitary Confinement." CBC *News,* June. <cbc.ca/news/canada/manitoba/solitary-confinement-lawsuit-class-action-1.6047810>.

Lancashire, David. 1981. "Springhill: Creating Life on the Street." *Globe and Mail,* May 18.

Law Commission of Ontario. 2012. "Vulnerable Workers and Precarious Work: Final Report." December. <lco-cdo.org/wp-content/uploads/2013/03/vulnerable-workers-final-report.pdf>.

Lewis, Nathaniel. 2018. "Locking Up the Lower Class." *Jacobin.* January 10. <jacobinmag.com/2018/01/mass-incarceration-race-class-peoples-policy-project>.

Lichtenstein, Alex. 1996. *Twice the Work of Free Labor: The Political Economy of Convict Labor in the New South.* London and New York: Verso.

Ling, Justin. 2020. "The CSC Is Censoring Whistleblower Complaints about CO-VID-19 in Federal Prisons." *National Post,* April 8. <nationalpost.com/opin-

ion/justin-ling-the-csc-is-censoring-whistleblower-complaints-about-covid-19-in-federal-prisons>.

___. 2021. "Houses of Hate: How Canada's Prison System Is Broken." *Maclean's*, February 28. <macleans.ca/news/canada/houses-of-hate-how-canadas-prison-system-is-broken>.

Linton, Megan. 2021. "A Penny a Poppy," *Briarpatch*. November 4. <briarpatchmag-azine.com/articles/view/sheltered-workshops-poppies-disabled-workers>.

Lopez, German. 2018. "America's Prisoners Are Going on Strike in at Least 17 States." *Vox*, August 22. <vox.com/2018/8/17/17664048/national-prison-strike-2018>.

Lum, Zi-Ann. 2020. "Canadian Inmates Have Made 821,703 Face Masks During the Pandemic." *HuffPost*, December 12. <huffingtonpost.ca/entry/canada-prison-labour-covid-face-masks_ca_5fdd1a5ac5b6e5158fa70360>.

MacAlpine, Ian. 2020. "Joyceville Inmate Committee Speaks Out on Current COVID-19 Conditions." *Whig-Standard*, Dec 22. <thewhig.com/news/joyce-ville-inmate-committee-speaks-out-on-current-covid-19-conditions>.

Macdonald, Nancy. 2016. "Canada's Prisons Are the 'New Residential Schools.'" *Maclean's*, February 18. <macleans.ca/news/canada/canadas-prisons-are-the-new-residential-schools>.

MacGuigan, Mark. 1977. *Report to Parliament by the Sub-committee on the Penitentiary System in Canada*. Ottawa: Government of Canada.

MacLeod, Brian. 2000. "Prison Job Program Under Fire: Business Community Can't Compete with Cheap Labour." *Calgary Herald*, January 7.

Makin, Kirk. 1981. "Federal Prisoners' Pay Tripled to Meet Minimum Rate." *Globe and Mail*, April 22.

___. 1989. "Low Pay Leads to Thievery in Penitentiaries." *Globe and Mail*, April 17: A4.

Mallea, Paula. 2011. *Fearmonger: Stephen Harper's Tough-on-Crime Agenda*. Toronto: Lorimer.

___. 2017. *Beyond Incarceration: Safety and True Criminal Justice*. Toronto: Dundurn Press.

Mancini, Matthew J. 1996. *One Dies, Get Another: Convict Leasing in the American South, 1866–1928*. Columbia: University of South Carolina Press.

Manly, Paul. 2020. "Petition to Cancel the Prison Agribusiness." August 21. <paul-manlymp.ca/post/petition-prison-farm>.

Marin, Andre. 2013. "The Code: Investigation into the Ministry of Community Safety and Correctional Services' Response to Allegations of Excessive Use of Force Against Inmates." Ombudsman Ontario. <ombudsman.on.ca/Files/sitemedia/Documents/Investigations/SORT%20Investigations/The-Code-EN.pdf>.

Martin, Ashley. 2016. "Inmate Kitchen Training to Return; In the Beginning, It Will Only Be Offered at Yorkton Facility." *StarPhoenix*, January 15.

Marx, Karl. 1978. "Wage Labour and Capital." In *The Marx-Engels Reader* (second edition), edited by Robert C. Tucker. New York: Norton.

Mason, Robert. 2020. "Wrongful Convictions in Canada." *Parliamentary Information Service Publication No. 2020-77-E,* September 23. <lop.parl.ca/sites/PublicWebsite/default/en_CA/ResearchPublications/202077E>.

Mathiesen, Thomas. 2015. *The Politics of Abolition Revisited.* Abingdon, Oxon and New York: Routledge.

McArthur, Virginia. 1974. "Inmate Grievance Mechanisms: A Survey of 209 American Prisons." *Federal Probation* 38, 4 (December).

McCoy, Ted. 2012. *Hard Time: Reforming the Penitentiary in Nineteenth-Century Canada.* Edmonton: AU Press.

___. 2019. *Four Unruly Women: Stories of Incarceration and Resistance from Canada's Most Notorious Prison.* Vancouver and Toronto: UBC Press.

McDowell, Adam 2009. "Brush Strokes With the Law." *National Post,* August 22. <pressreader.com/canada/national-post-latest-edition/20090822/283240209027795>.

McElligott, Greg. 2017. "Invested in Prisons: Prison Expansion and Community Development in Canada." *Studies in Social Justice* 11, 1.

___. 2018. "Beyond Service, Beyond Coercion? Prisoner Co-ops and the Path to Democratic Administration," In *From the Streets to the State: Changing the World by Taking Power,* edited by Paul Christopher Gray. Albany: State University of New York Press.

McLeod, Marsha. 2020. "'The Jail Is Just a Death Trap': Stories of Overcrowding, Understaffing and Violence in Thunder Bay." *Globe and Mail,* October 8. <theglobeandmail.com/canada/article-the-jail-is-just-a-death-trap-stories-of-overcrowding/>.

___. 2021. "Broken Telephone: How Ontario's Prison-Phone System Leaves Inmates Disconnected." TVO, February 11. <tvo.org/article/broken-telephone-how-ontarios-prison-phone-system-leaves-inmates disconnected>.

Melnychuk, Mark. 2020. "Offenders in Work Program Fear Rules Could Cost Them Jobs; Yorkton Facility Has Restricted Inmates from Leaving Site as Pandemic Precaution." *Leader Post,* October 24.

Melossi, Dario, and Massimo Pavarini. 2018. *The Prison and the Factory: Origins of the Penitentiary System* (40th Anniversary Edition). London: Palgrave Macmillan UK.

Melville, Samuel. 1972. *Letters From Attica.* New York: William Morrow and Company.

Mental Health Commission of Canada. 2020. "Mental Health and the Criminal Justice System: 'What We Heard.'" <mentalhealthcommission.ca/wp-content/uploads/drupal/2020-08/mental_health_and_the_law_evidence_summary_report_eng.pdf>.

Migrant Workers Alliance for Change. 2020. "Unheeded Warnings: COVID-19 and Migrant Workers in Canada." June. <migrantworkersalliance.org/wp-content/uploads/2020/06/Unheeded-Warnings-COVID19-and-Migrant-Workers.pdf>.

Minister of Human Resources Development Canada. 2014. "Guide to Accident

Compensation for Federal Offenders." June 20. <canada.ca/en/employment-social-development/services/health-safety/compensation/offenders.html>.

Ministère de la Sécurité publique. n.d. "Fonds central de soutien à la réinsertion sociale." <solutionmaindoeuvre.ca/>.

Ministry of the Attorney General. 2021. "Inmate Information Guide for Adult Correctional Facilities." September 13. <ontario.ca/page/inmate-information-guide-adult-correctional-facilities>.

Mojtehedzadeh, Sara. 2021. "'Do Not Enter': Why Are Migrant Worker Bunkhouses Not Part of Workplace Safety Inspections?" *Toronto Star,* September 18. <thestar.com/news/gta/2021/09/18/do-not-enter-should-migrant-worker-bunk-houses-be-part-of-workplace-safety-inspections.html>.

Montford, Kelly Struthers. 2019. "Land, Agriculture, and the Carceral: The Territorializing Function of Penitentiary Farms." *Radical Philosophy Review* 22, 1.

Montoya-Barthelemy, Andre. 2019. "The Occupational Health of Prison Inmates: An Ignored Population and an Opportunity." *Journal of Occupational and Environmental Medicine* 61, 2 (February).

Morais, Rene. 2008. "Asbestos Assessment Dorchester Penitentiary Dorchester, NB." Correctional Services Canada, September 8. <buyandsell.gc.ca/cds/pu blic/2019/10/08/53fe5d54bf1246a87303df139a9e5fc2/asbestos_assessment_dorchester_penitentiary.pdf>.

Moriarty, Meegan. 2016. "From Bars to Freedom: Prisoner Co-ops Boost Employment, Self-esteem and Support Re-entry into Society." *Rural Cooperatives* (January/February).

Morris, Norval, and David J. Rothman (eds.). 1995. *The Oxford History of the Prison: The Practice of Punishment in Western Society.* New York and Oxford: Oxford University Press.

Morris, Ruth. 1995. *Penal Abolition: The Practical Choice.* Toronto: Canadian Scholars' Press.

Mourão, Aline Nogueira Menezes. 2018. "Understanding the Effects of Carceral Employment Programs in Canada: Exploring the Perspectives of Former Federal Prisoners." Master's thesis, University of Ottawa.

Muirhead, James E., and Robert Rhodes. 1998. "Literacy Level of Canadian Federal Offenders." *Journal of Correctional Education* 49, 2.

Murray, Karen Bridget. 2017. "The Violence Within: Canadian Modern Statehood and the Pan-Territorial Residential School System Ideal." *Canadian Journal of Political Science / Revue canadienne de science politique* 50, 3.

Murton, Tom. 1976. "Shared Decision Making as a Treatment Technique in Prison Management." *Offender Rehabilitation* 1, 1.

Neil, Brennan. 2018. "'The Prices Are Outrageous': Concerns Raised Over Monopoly on Ordered Goods in Federal Prisons." December 19. <cbc.ca/news/canada/montreal/federal-prison-prices-catalogue-1.4950577>.

Nembhard, Jessica Gordon. 2020. "How Prisoner Co-ops Reduce Recidivism: Lessons from Puerto Rico and Beyond." *Nonprofit Quarterly,* May 19. <nonprofit-quarterly.org/how-prisoner-co-ops-reduce-recidivism-lessons-from-puerto-

rico-and-beyond/>.

Neufeld, Calvin. 2021. *Bloody Bad Business: Report on the Joyceville Institution Abattoir, Evolve Our Prison Farms.* Evolve Our Prison Farms. <evolveourprisonfarms.ca/wp-content/uploads/2021/09/Bloody-Bad-Business-Joyceville-Abattoir-Report-Evolve-Our-Prison-Farms.pdf>.

Neufeld, Roger. 1998. "Cabals, Quarrels, Strikes, and Impudence: Kingston Penitentiary, 1890–1914." *Histoire Sociale / Social History* 31, 61.

Neustaeter, Brooklyn. 2020. "Majority of Canadians' Work Refusal Claims Being Denied Amid COVID-19." *CTV News,* June 25. <ctvnews.ca/health/coronavirus/majority-of-canadians-work-refusal-claims-being-denied-amid-covid-19-1.4999369>.

Noël, Brigitte. 2017. "Les Prisons Québécoises Sont Surpeuplées, Délabrées et Débilitantes," *Vice News,* February 22. <vice.com/fr/article/78mnda/les-prisons-quebecoises-sont-surpeuplees-delabrees-et-debilitantes>.

Noir, Betty. 1975. "Prison Protest in BC." *This Magazine,* September-October.

Norm. 1978. "Industry for Penitentiaries (Just a Passing Thought)." *The Outlook.* December: 14. Gaucher/Munn Penal Press Collection. <penalpress.com/wp-content/uploads/The_Outlook_Xmas1978.pdf>.

Nova Scotia Justice Correctional Services. n.d. "Fine Option Program." <novascotia.ca/just/Corrections/_docs/FineOptionsProgram.pdf>.

O'Brien, David. 1998. "Federal Prisoners Competing Directly with Private Business." *Montreal Gazette,* April 14.

Obama, Barack. 2017. "The President's Role in Advancing Criminal Justice Reform." *Harvard Law Review* 130, 3.

Off the Wall. 1981. "Native Indian Fine Arts & Crafts." 1, 2 (June 12). Gaucher/Munn Penal Press Collection. <penalpress.com/wp-content/uploads/OffTheWall_June1981_V1No2.pdf>.

Office of the Auditor General of Ontario. 2019. *Annual Report 2019, Volume 3.* (Fall). <auditor.on.ca/en/content/annualreports/arreports/en19/2019AR_v3_en_web.pdf>.

Office of the Correctional Investigator. 2014. *Office of the Correctional Investigator Annual Report 2013–2014.* June 27. <oci-bec.gc.ca/cnt/rpt/annrpt/ann-rpt20132014-eng.aspx?pedisable=true>.

___. 2016. *In the Dark: An Investigation of Death in Custody Information Sharing and Disclosure Practices in Federal Corrections — Final Report.* August 2. <oci-bec.gc.ca/cnt/rpt/oth-aut/oth-aut20160802-eng.aspx?pedisable=true>.

___. 2016. "Federally Sentenced Women." March 14. <oci-bec.gc.ca/cnt/priorities-priorites/women-femmes-eng.aspx>.

___. 2016. "Priority: Access to Physical and Mental Health Care." February, 14. <oci-bec.gc.ca/cnt/priorities-priorites/health-sante-eng.aspx>.

___. 2019. *Aging and Dying in Prison: An Investigation into the Experiences of Older Individuals in Federal Custody.* February 28. <oci-bec.gc.ca/cnt/rpt/oth-aut/oth-aut20190228-eng.aspx>.

___. 2020. "Indigenous People in Federal Custody Surpasses 30% Correctional Investigator Issues Statement and Challenge." January 21. <oci-bec.gc.ca/cnt/comm/press/press20200121-eng.aspx>

___. 2003. *Office of the Correctional Investigator Annual Report 2002–2003.* <oci-bec.gc.ca/cnt/rpt/pdf/annrpt/annrpt20022003-pdf/annrpt20022003-6-eng.pdf>.

___. 2015. *Office of the Correctional Investigator Annual Report 2014–2015.* <oci-bec.gc.ca/cnt/rpt/annrpt/annrpt20142015-eng.aspx#s3>.

___. 2017. *Office of the Correctional Investigator Annual Report 2016–2017.* <oci-bec.gc.ca/cnt/rpt/pdf/annrpt/annrpt20162017-eng.pdf>.

___. 2018. *Office of the Correctional Investigator Annual Report 2017–2018.* <oci-bec.gc.ca/cnt/rpt/annrpt/annrpt20172018-eng.aspx>.

___. 2020. *Office of the Correctional Investigator Annual Report 2019–2020.* <oci-bec.gc.ca/cnt/rpt/annrpt/annrpt20192020-eng.aspx#fn65-rf>.

Oliver, Peter. 1998. *"Terror to Evil-Doers": Prisons and Punishment in Nineteenth-Century Ontario.* Toronto: Osgoode Society.

Ontario. 2021. "Minimum Wage." March 25. <ontario.ca/document/your-guide-employment-standards-act-0/minimum-wage>.

Ontario, Ministry of the Solicitor General. 2019. "Rehabilitation Programs and Services for Offenders." September 14. <ontario.ca/page/rehabilitation-programs-and-services-offenders>.

Owusu-Bempah, Akwasi, Maria Jung, Firdaous Sbaï, Andrew S. Wilton, and Fiona Kouyoumdjian. 2021. "Race and Incarceration: The Representation and Characteristics of Black People in Provincial Correctional Facilities in Ontario, Canada." *Race and Justice* (April).

Page, Joshua. 2012. "Politically Realistic Unionism: The California Prison Officers Association and the Struggle Over the Public 'Good.'" *WorkingUSA* 15, 3.

Palmer, Bryan D. 1980. "Kingston Mechanics and the Rise of the Penitentiary, 1833–1836." *Histoire sociale/Social History* XIII: 25.

___. 2019. "The New New Poor Law: A Chapter in the Current Class War Waged from Above." *Labour / Le Travail* 84.

Patrick, Jeremy. 2006. "Creating a Federal Inmate Grievance Tribunal." *Canadian Journal of Criminology and Criminal Justice* 48, 2.

Paynter, Martha, and Emilie Coyle. 2021. "In Canada's Federal Women's Prisons, Reproductive Rights Are Under Threat." *Briarpatch Magazine,* February 8. <briarpatchmagazine.com/articles/view/in-canadas-federal-womens-prisons-reproductive-rights-are-under-threat>.

Pellerin, Brigitte. 2021. "Reviewing Wrongful Convictions." *CBA/ABC National,* October 6. <nationalmagazine.ca/en-ca/articles/cba-influence/submissions/2021/reviewing-wrongful-convictions>.

Pentland, H. Clare. 1981. *Labour and Capital in Canada 1650–1860.* Toronto: Lorimer.

Peritz, Ingrid. 1988. "Mexicans, Convicts Work Quebec Farms; They Like it, But at $4.95 an Hour They're Exploited Critics Complain." *Gazette,* June 4.

Piché, Justin. 2012. "Accessing the State of Imprisonment in Canada: Information

Barriers and Negotiation Strategies." In *Brokering Access: Power, Politics, and Freedom of Information in Canada,* edited by Mike Larsen and Kevin Walby. Vancouver and Toronto: UBC Press.

Poirier, Simmone. 2008. "Decades of Darkness — Moving Towards the Light: A Review of the Prison System in Newfoundland and Labrador." October. <gov.nl.ca/jps/files/publications-ac-report.pdf>.

Powell, Betsy. 2019. "Citing 'Unconscionable' Conditions at Toronto South Jail, Judge Imposes 7-Year Sentence but Says Man Should Face No Further Prison Time." *Toronto Star,* June 11. <thestar.com/news/gta/2019/06/11/citing-un-conscionable-conditions-at-toronto-south-jail-judge-imposes-7-year-sentence-but-says-man-should-face-no-further-prison-time.html>.

Prime Minister of Canada. 2017. "Statement by the Prime Minister of Canada on the 35th anniversary of the Canadian Charter of Rights and Freedoms." April 17. <pm.gc.ca/en/news/statements/2017/04/17/statement-prime-minister-canada-35th-anniversary-canadian-charter-rights>.

Primetime. 1981. "Inside View." August. Gaucher/Munn Penal Press Collection. <penalpress.com/wp-content/uploads/Primetime_Aug1981.pdf>.

Prince Edward Island, Community and Correctional Services. 2016. "Adult Custody Information Handbook."<princeedwardisland.ca/sites/default/files/publications/adult_custody_information_handbook_2016.pdf>.

Prisoners' Legal Services. 2018. "Writing an Effective Grievance." December. <prisonjustice.org/wp-content/uploads/2019/01/Federal-Grievance-2018.pdf>.

Prisoners United. n.d. "Prisoners United." <prisonersunited.org/>.

___. n.d. "Prisoners Union of Canada."<prisonersunited.org/prisonersunionofcanada>.

Province. 2013. "Federal Policy on Crime Just Plain Nasty: Retired Official." October 4.

Public Prosecution Service of Canada. 2018. "Innocence at Stake: The Need for Continued Vigilance to Prevent Wrongful Convictions in Canada." September. <ppsc-sppc.gc.ca/eng/pub/is-ip/index.html>.

Public Safety Canada. 2020. "Corrections and Criminal Justice." December 1. <publicsafety.gc.ca/cnt/cntrng-crm/crrctns/index-en.aspx>.

Purdon, Nick. 2015. "PTSD Taking Its Toll on Canada's Prison Guards." *CBC News,* July 24. <cbc.ca/news/canada/ptsd-taking-its-toll-on-canada-s-prison-guards-1.3166791>.

Rankin, Jim, Patty Winsa, Andrew Bailey, and Hidy Ng. 2014. "Carding Drops but Proportion of Blacks Stopped by Toronto Police Rises." *Toronto Star,* July 26. <thestar.com/news/insight/2014/07/26/carding_drops_but_proportion_of_blacks_stopped_by_toronto_police_rises.html>.

Regehr, Cheryl, et al. 2021. "Prevalence of PTSD, Depression and Anxiety Disorders in Correctional Officers: A Systematic Review." *Corrections* 6, 3.

Reich, Adam D., and Seth J. Prins. 2020. "The Disciplining Effect of Mass Incarceration on Labor Organization." *American Journal of Sociology* 125, 5 (March).

Reiman, Jeffrey, and Paul Leighton. 2016. *The Rich Get Richer and the Poor Get Pris-*

on (11th Edition). New York and London: Routledge.

Ricciardelli, Rose, and Adrienne M.F. Peters. 2017. *After Prison: Navigating Employment and Reintegration.* Waterloo: Wilfrid Laurier University Press.

Robin, Raizel. 2017. "The $1-Billion Hellhole." *Toronto Life,* February 15. <torontolife.com/city/inside-toronto-south-detention-centre-torontos-1-billion-hellhole/>.

Robitaille, Isabelle. 2021. "Prison Farm Has Many Positives." *Whig-Standard,* March 21. <thewhig.com/opinion/letters-to-the-editor-prison-farm-has-many-positives-clinic-a-success>.

Robson, Lynda, et al. 2021. "Updating a Study of the Union Effect on Safety in the ICI Construction Sector: A Report Prepared by the Institute for Work & Health for the Ontario Construction Secretariat." *Institute for Work and Health* (January). <iwh.on.ca/sites/iwh/files/iwh/reports/iwh_report_union_safety_effect_construction_update_2021.pdf>.

Rodriguez, Jeremiah. 2021. "Inmates Fear 'Leaving in a Body Bag' as COVID-19 Outbreaks in Prisons Worsen." *CTV News,* January 4. <ctvnews.ca/health/coronavirus/inmates-fear-leaving-in-a-body-bag-as-covid-19-outbreaks-in-prisons-worsen-1.5253369>.

Rodriguez, Stefany. 2019. "The Positive Impacts of CORCAN Work Experiences on Reintegration." Correctional Service of Canada, July 3. <lte-ene.ca/en/positive-impacts-corcan-work-experiences-reintegration>.

Rohner, Thomas. 2018. "Inmates of Iqaluit Jail Subjected to 'Shocking' Lengths of Solitary Confinement." *Vice News,* July 12. <vice.com/en/article/zm5vb5/inmates-in-notorious-iqaluit-jail-subjected-to-shocking-lengths-of-solitary-confinement>.

Rolston, Simon. 2021. "The Hidden Lives and Uncertain Future of Trans Prisoners." *Xtra,* October 6. <xtramagazine.com/power/trans-prisoners-canada-legal-fights-209961>.

Ross, Stephanie, Larry Savage, Errol Black, and Jim Silver. 2015. *Building a Better World: An Introduction to the Labour Movement in Canada* (third edition). Halifax and Winnipeg: Fernwood Publishing.

Rothman, David J. 1995. "Perfecting the Prison: United States, 1789–1865." In *The Oxford History of the Prison: The Practice of Punishment in Western Society,* edited by Norval Morris and David J. Rothman. New York and Oxford: Oxford University Press.

Rusche, Gerog, and Otto Kirchheimer. 1968. *Punishment and Social Structure.* New York: Russell & Russell.

Rusnell, Charles. 1986. "Workshop Gives Convicts Fresh Start." *Ottawa Citizen,* January 6.

Salah, Ghassan. 2021. Letter to Paul Quick at the Queens University Prison Law Clinic. February 23. Document provided to the authors.

Saskatoon Editorial Staff. 1974. "Organizing a Prisoners' Trade Union." *Transition* 2, 4 (July/August).

Satzewich, Vic. 1991. *Racism and the Incorporation of Foreign Labour: Farm Labour*

Migration to Canada Since 1945. London and New York: Routledge.

Sauvé, Rick. 2021. "Prison Labour Session." Canadian Association of Labour Lawyers, 2021 Conference. June 11.

Savage, Larry, and Charles W. Smith. 2017. *Unions in Court: Organized Labour and the Charter of Rights and Freedoms.* Vancouver: UBC Press.

Scharf, Peter. 1975. "Democracy and Prison Reform: A Theory of Democratic Participation in Prison." *Prison Journal* 55, 2.

Schroeder, Andreas. 1976. *Shaking It Rough: A Prison Memoir.* Toronto and New York: Doubleday.

Scott, Neil. 2004. "Training Programs Loss Protested." *Leader Post,* April 2.

Sieh, Edward W. 1989. "Less Eligibility: The Upper Limits of Penal Policy." *Criminal Justice Policy Review* 3, 2.

Smith, Christopher E. 1993. "Black Muslims and the Development of Prisoners' Rights." *Journal of Black Studies* 24, 2.

Solicitor General of Canada. 1983. *Solicitor General Annual Report 1981–1982.* <publicsafety.gc.ca/lbrr/archives/sg-arsg-1981-1982-eng.pdf>.

Spratt, Michael. 2020. "'Bell Let's Talk' Campaign and the Reality of Ontario's Jails." January 24. <michaelspratt.com/opinion/bell-lets-talk-campaign-and-the-reality-of-ontarios-jails/>.

Sprott, Jane B., and Anthony N. Doob. 2021. "Solitary Confinement, Torture, and Canada's Structured Intervention Units." February 23. <johnhoward.ca/drs-doob-sprott-report/>.

Standing Senate Committee on Human Rights. 2021. *Human Rights of Federally-Sentenced Persons.* June. <https://sencanada.ca/content/sen/committee/432/RIDR/reports/2021-06-16_FederallySentenced_e.pdf>.

Stark Raven Radio. 2013. "Prisoner Strikes." [Audio podcast episode]. October 7. <vcn.bc.ca/august10/audio/Oct7.mp3>.

Statistics Canada. 2018. "Unionization Rates Falling." May 17. <www150.statcan.gc.ca/n1/pub/11-630-x/11-630-x2015005-eng.htm>.

___. 2019. "Canada's Black Population: Growing in Number and Diversity." February 6. <www150.statcan.gc.ca/n1/pub/11-627-m/11-627-m2019006-eng.htm>.

___. 2020. "Adult and Youth Correctional Statistics in Canada, 2018/2019." December 21. <www150.statcan.gc.ca/n1/pub/85-002-x/2020001/article/00016-eng.htm>.

Stefanovich, Olivia. 2021. "'We're in Trouble': Advocates Urge Ottawa to Help Close the Access-to-Justice Gap." *CBC News,* April 18. <cbc.ca/news/politics/access-to-justice-federal-budget-2021-requests-1.5989872>.

Strachan, Brady. 2019. "Migrant Farm Workers Complain of Overcrowded Dorm Rooms and Agricultural Chemical Exposure on Kelowna Farm." *CBC News,* October 10. <cbc.ca/news/canada/british-columbia/migrant-workers-kelowna-sawp-program-complaint-sandher-farm-1.5316512>.

Sykes, Greshem M. 1958. *The Society of Captives: A Study of the Maximum Security Prison.* Princeton: Princeton University Press.

Taekema, Dan. 2016. "Inmates Protest Against More Lockdowns at Toronto South Detention Centre." *Toronto Star,* June 10. <thestar.com/news/gta/2016/06/10/inmates-protest-against-more-lockdowns-at-toronto-south-detention-centre.html>.

Tanner, Adrienne. 2011. "Inmates Hired by Prison Staff." *The Province,* April 15.

Theodore, Terri. 2020. "Lawyers, Advocate Call for Inmate Release Before COVID-19 Spreads." *National Post,* April 9. <nationalpost.com/pmn/news-pmn/canada-news-pmn/lawyers-advocate-call-for-inmate-release-before-covid-19-spreads>.

Thibault, Eric. 2014. "Federal Inmate Cost Soars to $117Gs Each Per Year." *Toronto Sun,* March 19. <torontosun.com/2014/03/18/federal-inmate-cost-soars-to-177gs-each-per-year>.

Thomas, Mark P., and Steven Tufts. 2019. "Blue Solidarity: Police Unions, Race and Authoritarian Populism in North America." *Work, Employment, and Society,* 34, 1.

Tibbetts, Janice. 2002. "Inmate Can Sue Government after Fall at Federal Prison: Top Court Rejects Government's Claim of Double Dipping." *Ottawa Citizen,* March 22.

Tibbs, Donald. 2012. *From Black Power to Prison Power: The Making of Jones v. North Carolina Prisoners' Labor Union.* New York: Palgrave Macmillan.

Times-Colonist. 1994. "Ex-Nanaimo Centre Inmate Seeks $185,000 Damages Following Tractor Accident." February 20, 1.

Toch, Hans. 1994. "Democratizing Prisons." *Prison Journal* 73.

Topping, C.W. 1947 [1929]. *Canadian Penal Institutions* [Revised Edition]. Toronto: Ryerson Press.

Toronto Prisoners' Rights Project. 2021. "Joyceville Correctional Centre Labour Strike." March 19. <facebook.com/TorontoPrisonersRightsProject/photos/289057185967528>.

Toronto Star. 1989. "Inmates Dine on Burgers and Fries." January 21.

Transition. 1956. "Pie in the Sky." July/August. Gaucher/Munn Penal Press Collection. <penalpress.com/wp-content/uploads/BCPenTrans_JulAug_56.pdf>.

Tucker, Eric. 2003. "Diverging Trends in Worker Health and Safety Protection and Participation in Canada, 1985–2000." *Relations industrielles / Industrial Relations* 58, 3.

United Nations Department of Economic and Social Affairs. 1955. *Prison Labor.* New York: United Nations Publications.

Urmson, Paul TL. 1995. "Contract Manufacturing: One Manager's Experience." CORCAN *Express* 3, 9 (January).

Ward, Rachel. 2020. "Senator Calls for Inmate Release to Prevent Potential Prison COVID-19 'Disaster.'" *CBC News,* March 25. <cbc.ca/news/canada/calgary/senator-calls-release-inmates-covid-19-1.5509086>.

Ware, Syrus, Joan Ruzsa, and Giselle Dias. 2014. "It Can't Be Fixed Because It's Not Broken: Racism and Disability in the Prison Industrial Complex." In *Disability Incarcerated: Imprisonment and Disability in the United States and Canada,* edited by Liat Ben-Moshe, Chris Chapman, and Allison C. Carey. New York: Palgrave Macmillan.

Warren, R.M. 1920. "A Defence of Burwash." *Globe,* September 21.

Webster, Cheryl Marie, and Anthony N. Doob. 2012. "Searching for Sasquatch: Deterrence of Crime Through Sentence Severity." In *Oxford Handbook on Sentencing and Corrections,* edited by Joan Petersilia and Kevin Reitz. New York: Oxford University Press.

Wemmers, Jo-Anne. 2002. "Restorative Justice For Victims of Crime: A Victim-Oriented Approach to Restorative Justice." *International Review of Victimology* 9.

Winnipeg Free Press. 2014. "Corrections-Van Crash Reignites Safety Issues." November 8. <winnipegfreepress.com/local/corrections-van-crash-reignites-safety-issues-282013231.html>.

Withrow, O.C.J. 1933. "Kingston Well Supplied on Stern Strenuous Side with Prison Stonepile." *Globe,* September 9.

Woodman, Spencer. 2016. "California Blames Incarcerated Workers for Unsafe Conditions and Amputations," *The Intercept,* December 28. <theintercept.com/2016/12/28/california-blames-incarcerated-workers-for-unsafe-conditions-and-amputations/>.

Young, James [pseud.]. 2017. "Work after Prison: One Man's Transition." In *After Prison: Navigating Employment and Reintegration,* edited by Rose Ricciardelli and Adrienne M.F. Peters. Waterloo: Wilfrid Laurier University Press.

Young, Scott. 1966. "Prison Training: What For?" *Globe and Mail,* July 13.

Zakreski, Dan. 2001. "Down on Her Luck." *StarPhoenix,* June 16.

Zerr, Arielle. 2013. "Inmates Help Clean Up Saskatoon." *StarPhoenix,* September 11.

Zinger, Ivan. 2020. "Officer of the Correctional Investigator COVID-19 Status Update." April 23. <oci-bec.gc.ca/cnt/rpt/pdf/oth-aut/oth-aut20200423-eng.pdf>.

INDEX

affermage, *see* convict leasing
ageing in prison, 84
agriculture, 63, 100
    See also prison farms
Alberta, 44, 48, 49, 60, 79, 80, 120
asbestos, 23, 72-73, 87, 88, 167, 190n8
Attica prison rebellion, 115, 124, 129
Auburn System, 91
    See also penitentiary system

Beaver Creek Institution, 106-107, 165
Black people
    discrimination against, 30, 140
    overincarceration of, 10, 32-33, 37-38, 128, 148, 156
    participation in prisoners' unions by, 125
    police killings of, 156
    prison unemployment and, 34, 56-57, 165
    Security Threat Group classification of, 33
    See also racism
Black women, 32-33
    See also women
Blood (Káínawa) Tribe, 79-80
Bloody Code, 90
British Columbia, 48-49, 63, 73, 75, 78, 81-82, 112, 117, 126, 132, 144, 161, 165
    British Columbia Labour Relations Board, 145
    prison strikes in, 60
    provincial prison industries in, 49
    Supreme Court of, 78, 81
British Columbia Penitentiary, 54, 75, 85, 101, 161

British North America, 90, 92

California, 52, 125, 126
Canada
    anti-human trafficking policies in, 29
    as class-based society, 37-39
    bias towards workers in, 95
    business community, 1-2, 38, 99, 105, 108-109
    capitalism in, 1, 6, 36, 92, 135-136
    colonialism, 6, 58, 92, 156
    cost of corrections in, 28, 96, 101, 147, 157
    cost of living in, 22
    defund prisons and police movement in, 157-159
    export processing zones in, 116
    fine option programs in, 44
    forms of coerced labour in, 2, 4, 6, 39-42, 81, 102-103, 106, 117, 128-129, 141-142, 165
    human rights in, 10, 13-20, 21, 24, 26, 100, 160, 169
    immigration detention system, 45, 157
    incarceration of legally innocent people, 15, 20-21, 23, 43
    incarceration of women in, 10, 30-36, 50, 87, 94, 123, 139-140
    income taxes in, 112
    "industrial pluralist" model of labour relations in, 5
    Industrial Revolution in, 1, 26, 92, 98
    international law and, 14-16, 19-20, 24, 63-66, 100, 136, 165-167

labour movement in, 4-8, 11, 17, 26, 98-99, 124, 126, 128-131, 143, 152, 154-156, 159, 164, 167, 169

marginalized populations in, 10-11, 15, 21, 37, 39, 66, 69-70, 71-72, 74-75, 128-129, 135, 143, 147-148, 151, 154-156, 163, 168-170

military prisoners in, 44

policing in, 15, 20, 28, 33, 37, 156

poor quality of prison food in, 24-25, 62

prison-produced goods and services in, 2-3, 10, 34, 35, 43, 45, 47, 49-53, 67-69, 80, 82, 87, 92, 100, 105-109, 116-117, 119-124, 142, 145, 164, 166, 167

prisoners' unions in, 10, 11-12, 124-127, 129-136, 149-151, 152, 154-155, 169-170

racial character of incarceration in, 4, 10, 21, 30-35, 37-38, 40-41, 56-57, 128, 140-142, 148, 156, 165

rates of incarceration, 50

recidivism in, 30, 34, 46, 93, 102, 116, 121, 130, 140, 163, 165

rehabilitation programming as employment, 143-149

youth corrections in, 31, 44, 50

See also COVID-19; health and safety; prison farms; prison industries

Canada Car Company, 98

Canada Labour Code, 133-135, 151

Canada Pension Plan, 78-79

Canada Royal Milk, *see* Feihe International

Canadian Charter of Rights and Freedoms, 13-14, 15, 16, 18, 136, 148-151, 167

Canadian Civil Liberties Association, 21

Canadian Food and Allied Workers Union, 11-12, 116, 126, 130-131, 155, 168

Canadian Industrial Relations Board, 133

Canadian Labour Congress, 154-155, 159

Canadian Labour Union, 99

Canadian Penitentiary Service, *see*

Correctional Service of Canada

Canadian Prisoners' Labour Confederation, 30, 125, 127, 132-136, 149, 153-154, 159, 168

Canadian Trades and Labour Congress, 99

Capay, Adam, 15, 73

capital punishment, 26, 90

capitalism, 1, 6, 7, 36, 135

captive workers, 72, 129

See also coerced labour

Cardinal, Cory Charles, 57-58

censorship 5, 8-9, 154

Central Prison (Toronto), 98-99

chain gangs, 40, 97, 110, 123

See also convict leasing

Chilton, Muri Peace, 83-84

class, 36-39

class bias in the criminal justice system, 15-16, 20, 36-39

difficulties determining the class status of prisoners, 37, 38

logic of, 37

need for a class-based labour movement, 11, 71, 155-156, 169

relationship between class and crime, 38-39, 91

relationship between class and prison, 6, 39

relationship between class and race, 20, 38-39,

See also lumpenproletariat; middle class; ruling class; working class

climate change, 51-52, 63, 123

coerced labour, 2, 39-42, 84, 128-129, 141-142

codetermination, 113

collective bargaining

by prisoners' unions, 126, 131, 167

prisoners' rights to, 4-5, 128, 131, 149-151

reforms achieved through, 83

workers' rights to, 38, 145, 148-151

workplace health and safety and, 77

Collins Bay institution, 55, 61-64, 101, 161-162

Collins, Peter, 156

colonialism, 5, 6, 58, 92, 156

communicable disease, 22, 67-69, 71, 72,

85, 87, 167
See also COVID-19
communism, 16, 95
Conservative Party of Canada, 27, 58, 61
convict leasing, 89, 97, 106, 107, 114,
    164, 165
Co-operative Commonwealth
    Federation, 95
co-ops, 11, 116-124, 160, 164-165,
CORCAN
    2013 national strike and, 61
    asbestos in CORCAN facilities, 73
    correctional training fees, 48, 65-66
    failure to meet needs of prisoners,
        108, 138-140, 163
    fur and shearling program, 32, 118
    gendered character of, 35
    health and safety issues and, 76-77,
        82-85
    hiring processes at, 53,
    incentive pay, 27, 55, 59-61, 65, 68,
        135, 145
    origins of, 46-48, 105-109
    participation in as employment, 2,
        151
    private partnerships, 48, 62-66, 124-
        125, 166
    prisoner union efforts at, 133-141
    production of personal protective
        equipment, 67-68
    rehabilitation and, 108-109, 136-142,
        146-147
    revenue generating mandate of, 45,
        47, 108-109, 147, 166
    See also pay; prison industries;
        Wallace Beef
correctional officers, *see* guards
Corrections and Conditional Release
    Act, 18, 59, 83, 132, 134-137, 151
Corrections and Conditional Release
    Regulations, 136
Correctional Service of Canada
    2013 strike and, 58-61
    asbestos control, 73
    calculation of recidivism by, 163
    censorship by, 18
    Commissioner's Directive on
        prisoner-operated businesses, 120-
        121

cultural biases in risk assessment
    tools in, 32
deaths in custody, 67, 75, 76, 87
definition of accident, 76
emphasis on soft skills, 141
escort vehicles, 73
failure to meet needs of disabled
    prisoners, 84
failure to support prisoners upon
    release, 139-140
"hire a prisoner" program, 106-107
injury reporting system, 75-77
lack of transparency in, 9
"modernization" of food prepara-
    tion, 24, 62
prison labour as subsidy to, 147, 159
private partnerships, 2, 64
refusal to recognize the Canadian
    Prisoners' Labour Confederation,
    132, 154
study of federally incarcerated
    women's history of abuse, 35,
work programming participants as
    employees, 133-138, 141, 151
    See also CORCAN; COVID-19; reha-
        bilitation
corvée labour, 40
COVID-19, 8, 10, 37, 42, 52, 58, 66, 67-69,
    70, 71, 85, 86-87, 157, 164, 167,
    181n120
crime, 15, 21, 33, 88, 91-92, 94-95, 102,
    122, 157
    crime and socio-economic class, 38-
        39
    crime as response to social and
        economic exclusion, 38, 59-60, 92,
        169
    crime rates, 1, 3, 39, 91, 122
    crimes of the powerful, 21, 39
    prisons as response to crime, 1, 5,
        22, 31, 36, 92
    prisons as "schools of crime", 26
    tough-on-crime approaches, 29, 58,
        96, 110, 160
    youth crime, 44
    See also wrongful convictions; vic-
        tims
criminal class, *see* lumpenproletariat
criminal law, 14, 20, 29-30, 36, 90, 94-95

Criminalization and Punishment Education Project, 67
criminogenic risk, 21, 32, 37, 95
Culhane, Claire, 6

deaths in custody, 67, 74, 75-77, 85, 114, 163
decarceration, 4, 7, 67, 158-159
disability, 78-79, 84
discipline, *see* punishment; work discipline
diseases, *see* communicable diseases
Don Jail, 23
Dorchester Penitentiary, 101, 190n8
duty of care, 67, 74, 81-82

education, 7, 37, 39, 46, 93, 95, 101, 113, 137-138, 144, 145-146, 156, 163, 170
    See also vocational training
Employment and Employability Programs, 138-142, 166
Evolve Our Prison Farms, 63-64

factory system, 92
Federal Court of Appeal, 133-135
Feihe International, 63-65
firefighting, 49, 51-52, 142
food, 16, 22, 24-25, 41, 47, 49, 55, 56, 59, 62, 86, 109, 112, 163
    food delivery workers, 137, 146, 168
    food services, 24-25, 47, 49, 50, 60, 62, 96, 103, 130, 140, 142
Foulds, Anton, 81
France, Anatole, 36
"free" labour, 2, 4-5, 20-21, 25, 39-42, 63-65, 95, 112, 114, 142, 164, 166-169
    competition with incarcerated labour, 11, 97, 108-109, 114, 164
freedom of association, 16, 125, 131, 148-149, 150-151

gangs, *see* Security Threat Groups
gender nonconforming people, 10, 35-36
gig economy, 128-143, 164, 137, 146
Green Party of Canada, 63
grievance procedures, 18-19, 25, 55, 83, 107, 131, 167
guards, 7, 24, 48, 60, 68, 71, 73, 80, 88, 100, 121-122, 129, 130, 152, 157, 165
guard unions, 50, 60, 73, 122, 124, 126, 130, 152, 169
Guelph Correctional Centre, 5, 11, 53, 75, 86, 99, 116, 126, 128, 130-131, 143, 168
Guelph Reformatory, *see* Guelph Correctional Centre

habits of industry, *see* work discipline
hard labour, 89, 94-96, 110
harm reduction, 169
Harper, Stephen, 25, 27, 58, 60, 61
health and safety, 71-88
    inspections, 113
    joint health and safety committees, 77
    key rights related to, 83-84
    laws, 4, 10, 20, 52, 70, 88, 124, 163, 166-167, 170
    statistics, 76-77
    unionization's impact on, 88
    work refusals, 83, 87
homelessness, 21, 37, 72
human rights, 10, 13-26, 28, 42, 100, 160, 169
    See also Standing Senate Committee on Human Rights
    See also Canadian Charter of Rights and Freedoms
    See also international law
human trafficking, 29, 40

immigration, 1, 148
    immigration detention, 45, 157
    See also migrant workers
Incarcerated Workers Organizing Committee, 125
Indian day schools, 92
    See also residential schools
Indigenous Peoples, 4, 15, 21, 32, 79-81
    culturally specific correctional programming for Indigenous prisoners, 32, 117-118, 164
    Indigenous overincarceration, 4, 10, 31, 34, 37, 38, 128, 156
    unequal treatment of Indigenous prisoners, 30, 32-34, 35, 56, 140,

148, 156, 165
 See also colonialism
Indigenous women, 31, 34-35
 See also women
Industrial Workers of the World, 125
industrialization, 1, 6, 26, 92, 98-100, 103
institutional maintenance work, 45-49,
 51, 55, 103-104, 147, 151
 as preferable to prison industry
  work, 47, 61
 as subsidy for prison systems, 2, 11,
  45, 51, 89, 115
 tension between meeting institutional and prison industry labour
  needs, 101-102
International Labour Organization (ILO),
 19, 63-64, 66
international law, 14-16, 19, 63, 100, 136
International Organization for Standards
 (ISO), 108
Inuit people, 32

jailhouse lawyers, 82
Jolivet, David, 132-135, 149
Joyceville Institution, 2, 18, 55, 62, 63,
 64-65, 68, 86-87
just transition, 8

Kainai Community Correctional Centre,
 79-80
 See also Blood (Káínawa) Tribe
Kent Institution, 73, 132
Kilgore, James, 158
Kingston Penitentiary, 31, 75, 98

Law Commission of Ontario, 147
League of Nations, 99
legal exclusion
 and employee status 142-143
 citizenship and, 112-113
 from health and safety protections,
  74-75, 83-84, 86, 88, 170
 from labour protections, 4, 26, 41,
  70-72, 79, 88, 124, 149-151, 170
 of RCMP from collective bargaining
  rights, 150
 undermining of rights of all workers, 10, 26
 vulnerability caused by 74-75

workers compensation, 79, 163
less eligibility, 25, 112
lifers, 47, 138, 169
Lombroso, Cesare, 91
lumpenproletariat, 38

MacLean, Thomas Francis, 77-78
Mandela Rules, 15, 19-20, 165
Manitoba, 44, 48, 50-51, 60, 77
Marx, Karl, 38, 41
Marxism, 38
McDonald's, 39, 55, 111
McGuire, Patrick, 78-79, 83
mental health, 10, 26, 37, 44, 109, 128,
 148, 151, 168
Métis people, 32
 See also colonialism; Indigenous
  people
Métis rebellion, 92
 See also colonialism; Indigenous
  people
middle class, 38
migrant workers, 29, 38, 71, 143, 152,
 164
 See also Seasonal Agricultural
  Workers Program; temporary
  foreign workers
military prison, 44
military service, 40

Nanaimo Regional Correctional Centre,
 78, 81-82
Native Brotherhood, 117-119
Native Extraordinary Line of Furniture,
 117-119, 164
 See also co-ops; Indigenous people
New Brunswick, 48, 60, 91, 93, 101, 126
New Democratic Party, 38
Newfoundland and Labrador, 48, 51
normalization of prison labour, 4, 10, 68,
 71, 79, 84, 86, 103, 112-115
 See also legal exclusions
Northwest Territories, 48
Nova Scotia, 48, 67, 69, 73
Nunavut, 48

occupational health and safety, *see* health
 and safety
Offender Accountability Initiative, 27-28,

58-61

Office of the Correctional Investigator, 18, 25, 27, 33, 35, 46, 56, 68, 75-76, 140

Ontario

Black overincarceration in provincial facilities, 32-33

exclusion of inmates from the definition of workers in Occupational Health and Safety Act, 74

conditions in provincial correctional facilities, 15, 24-25, 73, 75

lack of transparency around deaths in custody, 76

minimum wage in, 66

prison-made licence plates, 43, 52,

prisons located in, 11, 60, 62, 82, 101, 138, 161, 165

prisoners' unions in, 5, 126-127, 130-131

prison strikes in, 55, 60, 126, 161

provincial canteen spending rules, 57

provincial prison phone systems, 8

provincial prison labour, 43, 48-49, 52, 55, 60, 62, 75, 86, 98-99, 116, 123, 130-131

provincial prison industries, 45, 52, 62, 75, 86, 98-99, 116, 123, 130-131

sentences to hard labour in, 86, 95-96

Superior Court of, 18

Ontario Federation of Labour, 130

Ontario Labour Relations Act, 146, 149

Ontario Labour Relations Board, 131, 145-146

Outside Managed Industrial Programs (OMIP), 130

over-policing, 20, 33, 37, 156

parole, 4, 28, 29, 30, 33-34, 40, 42, 57, 59, 104, 139-140, 142, 159, 177n62

pay

as stipends rather than wages for work, 53-54, 56-57, 135-136, 144-145

canteen credits in lieu of, 45, 52, 57, 142

decreases to prison pay, 27-28, 60, 103, 135, 138, 154, 163, 169

decent pay, 34, 115, 157, 170

deductions made on prison pay, 25, 49, 55-56, 104, 130, 136-138, 153, 167

establishment of remuneration for prison labour, 54-55

impact of low pay on public safety, 27

incentive pay, 27, 54-55, 57, 59-61, 65, 68-69, 103-104, 142

increases to prison pay, 54-55, 68, 105, 107, 113, 158-159

lack of, 40, 111

low pay, 2-3, 22, 27, 55, 57, 69, 108-109, 111, 113, 115, 136-139, 142

"pandemic pay", 68-69

pay differentials between incarcerated and non-incarcerated workers, 98-99, 109, 112, 131, 167-168

pay rates and scales, 34, 49, 53-54, 56, 65-66, 98, 105, 113, 136-137, 141-142, 145, 154, 167

penitentiary system, 2, 6, 54, 89, 102, 129

origins of, 90-94

Pennsylvania system, 91

penology, 93-94, 100

personal protective equipment (PPE), 3, 67-69

piece-price prison labour schemes, 97

police, 6, 15, 18, 28, 33, 150, 156, 157

police unions, 8, 169

See also RCMP

political coalitions, 5, 6, 7, 17, 62, 82

Post-Doctoral Fellows, 145-146

See also students

poverty, 10, 15, 20, 21, 36-38, 72, 92, 128, 136, 148, 163, 169

precarity, 11, 26, 143, 147-148, 168

Pridy, Milton Holmes, 77-79

Prince Edward Island, 48, 186n37

prison abolitionism, 5-7, 13, 30, 110, 111, 158

prison farms, 10, 58, 61-64, 75, 76, 166, 169,

prison industrial complex, 96

prison industries, 19, 40, 43, 45-52, 147, 151, 163

as "businesslike", 19, 47, 53
as subsidy for prison systems, 1-2,
    11, 24, 45, 49, 53, 64-66, 89, 93,
    115, 130, 166
dairy operations, 61-66, 165
dual mandates of, 19, 49, 53, 89,
    108-109, 165-166
federal, *see* CORCAN
in Alberta, 49
in British Columbia, 49, 52
in Manitoba, 51-52
in the Maritimes, 51
in Ontario, 25, 43, 45, 48-49, 52, 69,
    75, 86, 98-99, 116, 123, 127-131
in Quebec, 49-50, 57
in Saskatchewan, 50
in the Territories, 51
incentives for participation in, 27,
    54-57, 59-61, 67, 103-104, 115
private management of, 2, 63-66,
    110, 114-116, 128, 130-131, 164,
    166-167
role in preparing prisoners for
    release, 46, 57
self-managed, 124, 164
state-use production, 2, 10
tension between meeting institu-
    tional and prison industry labour
    needs, 101-102
See also CORCAN; Feihe
    International; Outside Managed
    Industrial Programs (OMIP); state-
    use prison labour scheme; Trilcor;
    pay; prison farms; Wallace Beef
Prisoners Justice Day, 18
Prisoners' Union Committee, 126
Prisoners Union of Canada, 170
prisoners' unions
    and prison abolition, 5, 7
    as means to address workplace
        health and safety issues, 84, 86, 88
    as means to empower marginalized
        populations, 128-129, 143
    as strategic reform, 7, 10, 39, 61, 71,
        77, 84, 88, 107, 110-111, 113, 124,
        162-163, 165, 167-170
    Black leadership of, 125
    financing of, 154-155
    gains won by, 5, 86, 130-131, 168,

in the United States, 5, 125-126
obstacles faced by, 2-3, 11-12, 135-
    149, 153-157, 160
political unions versus labour un-
    ions, 125
relationships with trade unions, 125,
    155-157
revolutionary, 125
successful certification of, 5-6,
    11-12, 86, 126-128, 130-131, 133,
    149-151, 155, 168
See also Canadian Food and Allied
    Workers Union; Canadian
    Prisoners' Labour Confederation;
    Prisoners' Union Committee;
    Prisoners Union of Canada
private prisons, 96
See also prison industrial complex
privatization, 11, 113-116, 127
protest, 9, 19, 30, 50, 52, 54, 55, 62, 102,
    112, 126
See also resistance
psychiatric institutions, 44, 144
public account prison labour schemes,
    97
public health, 14, 86
See also COVID-19; communicable dis-
    eases; health and safety
Public Sector Labour Relations Act, 132,
    150
public sector unionism, 124, 130, 159
Public Service Labour Relations Board,
    132-133, 149
punishment
    as counter-productive, 27, 163
    as justice, 29
    as response to criminal behaviour,
        26, 89-91
    corporal punishment, 26, 40, 90
    cruel and unusual, 14-15
    hard labour as, 94-96
    political economy of, 96
    prison labour as, 1, 2, 89-90, 94-96,
        100, 170
    secondary punishments, 91-91
    transportation, 90
    work performance and, 40, 46, 48-
        49, 103, 115, 142, 144, 149
    See also capital punishment; penol-

ogy; work discipline
purchasing power, 55-57, 59
    See also pay

Quebec, 49, 57, 60, 75, 85, 90, 95, 101,
    112, 120

racism, 21, 30-34, 37, 40-41, 56, 111, 114,
    151, 156, 163
    anti-Black racism, 40
    racial disparities, 3, 20, 33, 37, 43,
        136, 140, 148
    racial theories of crime, 91
recidivism, 30, 34, 46, 93, 116, 121, 130,
    140, 158, 163, 165
reform
    criminal justice reform, 60, 90
    guards as barrier to, 122
    moral reform,
    personal reformation, 3, 26, 96, 103
    police reform, 28
    prison reform, 28, 54-57, 82-83, 100-
        105, 124, 129
    reform versus revolution, 6
    reformism, 6, 110, 111-113
    sentencing reforms, 4, 159
    social reform, 90-93
    strategic reforms, 4-5, 7, 113, 162,
        168
    See also non-reformist reform; reha
        bilitation
rehabilitation
    as individual responsibility, 102
    barrier to prisoners' rights, 3-4, 12,
        14, 136-149, 154, 165-170
    criticism of, 1-4, 28, 45-46, 56-57,
        98, 107, 112, 131-149, 163-164,
        165-170
    lack of definition, 136
    Native Extraordinary Line of
        Furniture and, 118-119
    public support for, 156
    prison labour as, 2-4, 47-48, 51, 89-
        90, 93, 100-101, 102-105, 108-109,
        131-149, 159, 165-170
    undermining employment status,
        44-46, 56, 72, 128, 131-142
religion, 31, 44, 90, 91-93
remand, 21, 23, 43

residential schools, 31, 92, 179n78
riots, 24, 34, 54, 55, 85, 102, 124, 126, 129
Roasting, Phillip, 79-80
Royal Canadian Mounted Police (RCMP),
    150
    See also police
ruling class, 36-37, 93

Salah, Ghassan, 138-139, 141, 166, 169,
    170
Sarvanis, Ioannis, 77-79, 83
Saskatchewan, 24, 48, 50, 52, 57, 60, 69,
    74, 101, 107, 152
Saskatchewan Government and General
    Employees Union, 50
Sauvé, Rick, 33, 140
Seasonal Agricultural Workers Program,
    40, 152-153
    See also migrant workers
Security Threat Groups, 33-34
sex work, 29, 143
slavery, 3, 40-41, 95, 111, 114, 125,
    199n11
social determinants of health, 72
social reintegration support fund (FSRS),
    49
social reproduction feminism, 182n118
solitary confinement, 4, 7, 15, 22, 31, 24,
    27, 30, 49, 56, 91, 169
Standing Senate Committee on Human
    Rights, 37, 56
state-use prison labour schemes, 2, 43,
    65, 96, 97, 99, 160
Stony Mountain Institution, 77, 159
strikes
    by guards, 73, 126
    health and safety work refusal, 67,
        73, 87
    hunger strike, 52, 86,
    prison strikes, 10, 41, 54-55, 56-61,
        68, 86-87, 102, 112-113, 115, 126,
        129, 138, 156, 161-162
    prisoners as scab labour, 131
    right to strike, 17, 167
    Winnipeg General Strike, 92
structural reform, *see* non-reformist
    reform
students, 126, 145-146
    See also Post-Doctoral Fellows

Supreme Court of Canada, 14, 16, 18, 32, 78, 79, 128, 147, 148, 149-150, 151

taxes, 22, 28, 40, 50, 57, 65, 107, 109, 112, 114, 116, 121, 182n118
temporary foreign workers, 40, 50, 152-153
See also migrant workers; Seasonal Agricultural Workers Program
Thatcher, Collin, 107
Toronto South Detention Centre, 23-24
torture, 4, 15, 24
See also solitary confinement
trade unions
  as sectional organizations, 7, 156, 169
  basic aims of, 7
  "bread and butter" trade unionism, 125
  decline of, 8, 129
  former prisoners less likely to join, 39
  inclusion of prisoners, 125
  need to organize vulnerable workers, 143, 156
  opposition to prisoner labour by, 5, 98-99
  protections for, 167
  role in ensuring safe workplaces, 84
  support for prisoners' struggles, 10, 11, 125-126, 154-156
  trade unions and gig workers, 146
  union density, 129
  wage demands, 158-159
  See also dues; guards; labour movement; public sector unionism; prisoners' unions; strikes; working class
trans people, 10, 35-36
Transport Canada, 74
transportation, 59, 73-74, 87, 90, 111
Trilcor, 45, 49, 69
  See also prison industry
Trudeau, Justin, 13, 38

underemployment, 34, 56, 111
  See also unemployment
unemployment, 10, 21, 35, 37, 56, 72, 95, 111, 114, 135-136, 161, 162,

182n120
  See also underemployment
union dues, 154-155, 169
Union of Canadian Correctional Officers, 60
  See also guards
unions, see trade unions; prisoners' unions
United Nations, 15
United States, 3, 5, 16, 17, 19, 30, 39, 40-41, 45, 75, 84, 124, 158
  Black over-incarceration in, 3, 32
  emergence of the penitentiary system in, 91
  prison labour in, 3, 41, 58, 84-85, 97, 105, 111, 114-115, 125-126, 129
Upper Canada, 31, 90, 94

victims, 29-30, 34-35, 84
violence, 22, 24, 33-35, 54, 55, 60, 71, 72, 75, 85, 87, 94, 102, 124, 126, 129
  use of force by guards, 30, 32, 75, 169
  See also torture
vocational training
  CORCAN vocational programming, 47, 73, 147, 166
  Correctional Service of Canada commitment to, 138
  development of modern, 99-104
  difficulty of obtaining data related to injuries sustained during, 75
  failure to meet job market demands, 139
  impact on likelihood of reoffending, 46
  Mandela Rules on, 19, 166
  prisoner agitation around lack of, 112-113, 115, 170
  social reintegration support fund cost offsetting of, 49

wages, *see* pay
Wallace Beef, 2, 65-66, 166
Warkworth Institution, 55, 60, 82, 116
Winnipeg General Strike, 92
Women, 10, 31-36, 87, 94, 123, 126, 140
  women of colour, 35
  women's prisons, 31, 33, 34, 50, 87,

123
    See also Black women; Indigenous
        women
work discipline, 31-32, 92-93, 101, 103,
        135, 141, 144
workers' compensation, 74, 79-80, 115
working class
    capitalist control and disciplining of,
        135-136
    dependence on employers, 41
    disparities within, 38
    interests versus sectional trade
        unionism, 7, 11, 155-156
    lack of political representation for,
        38
    over-policing of working class peo-
        ple, 20, 37
    prisoners as part of, 39, 71, 125, 155,
        158, 168-169
    wage militancy and, 159
workplace injuries, *see* occupational
        health and safety
wrongful convictions, 15, 20-21

youth, 31, 44, 50
Yukon, 48